Chambers Guide to
The Castles of Scotland

Chambers Guide to
The Castles of Scotland

Susan Ross

Chambers

© Susan Ross 1973

© Revised edition, Susan Ross 1987

First published by George Philip and Son Limited 1973

This edition published by W & R Chambers Ltd Edinburgh 1987

British Library Cataloguing in Publication Data
Ross, Susan 1941
    Chambers guide to the castles of Scotland.
    —2nd ed.
    1. Castles—Scotland—Guide-books
    I. Title II. Ross, Susan, 1941–. Castles of Scotland
    914.11'04858   DA875
    ISBN 0–550–20492–X

To Richard who undertook most of the research

Cover photograph of Culzean Castle courtesy of the
National Trust for Scotland.

Text illustrations by Hazel McGlashan

Frontispiece: detail from Castle Fraser

Endpiece: detail from Caerlaverock Castle

Typeset by Buccleuch Printers, Hawick

Printed and bound in Great Britain by
Butler & Tanner Ltd, Frome and London

Introduction

The rugged scenery of the northern reaches of Scotland, the proximity to a rapacious and warring neighbour to the south—a vulnerability, in fact, to invasion—have always made the land look to its defences; and the proliferation of fortified dwellings and castles bears ample witness to the turbulence of the country's past.

The earliest fortified strongholds known in Scotland are the brochs—remarkable circular stone-built towers of 40 feet or more with walls as thick as 20 feet at the base. There are some five hundred of these towers, all dating from within the hundred years of the first century AD and, despite their scattered sites, all bearing clearly similar features. Brochs were more or less impregnable. Built behind ramparts and ditches, with no openings save one long, narrow passage for access, they were further protected by guard chambers and possibly a heavy stone slab door. Internally they enclosed a circular central courtyard; the base of the wall was solid, but the higher walls were hollow, with a tiered system of galleries paved and roofed with flagstones, with access by a stone staircase. From the top of the wall, a lookout would have an uninterrupted view in every direction.

Little is known about broch culture. Domestic relics—bone tools, cooking pots, scrapers and shovels—have been found in plenty of the brochs, but no weapons of war have been unearthed. They are clearly defensive structures, built to withstand scaling equipment, battering rams and fire, but they are not offensive. They always lie near the coast and close to arable land. Brochs proliferate north of the Great Glen—in other words, in the area outside the reach of Roman domination. Were they built to guard against Roman sea raiders in search of slaves? Whatever their purpose—and to this day it remains shrouded in mystery—the brochs are a remarkable and unique architectural phenomenon.

The timber-built motte construction of the Normans bore little resemblance to the stone broch. These wooden towers were fortified with the assistance of large earth mounds and ditches with timber fences or palisades. A further enclosure, the bailey, also protected by a ditch and bank, extended the fortification. Whereas the broch was found exclusively in the Highlands and Islands, the motte and bailey castle was largely restricted to the south of Scotland, the Borders from north of the Solway and inland to Nithsdale, Eskdale, Liddesdale and Annandale, although the motte can be found as far north as Aberdeenshire. Essentially ephemeral, nowadays only the foundations of the early motte and bailey castles remain as evidence of their existence.

While the broch was clearly a defensive structure, the motte was the result of the gradual imposition of a Norman style of land tenure. The feudal system, introduced in the north of England and the Border lands as early as the beginning of the 11th century, gained impetus under David I. Under this system, obligations were placed on the new feudal lords to build fortifications and provide guards. These castles were the mark of an alien power; and because they held garrisons and were military in intention rather than being fortified domestic dwellings, they could not reflect pomp or wealth. Architecturally they had no future, although elements of the construction—the tower and the palisade—became translated into the stone-built keep and the curtain walls of the great medieval castles.

It is clear from the ecclesiastical buildings of 12th-century Scotland—such great cathedrals and abbeys as Dunfermline, Kelso, St Andrews and Jedburgh—that Scotland was well up to date with the most advanced of European architectural trends of the time. It was not until the Wars of Independence at the end of the 13th century that Scotland started to become isolated from mainstream Europe. Yet in temporal architecture, there is very little evidence in Scotland of the massive Norman keeps so typical south of the Border. In the northern and western parts of the country, it was not the Norman but the Norse influence that was paramount, and castle-building was not common in Norway until at least the end of the 13th century. There is some evidence in Scotland of Norse castles, but the earliest existing structure is Castle Sween in Argyll, which has 11th-century architectural features.

Castles, being largely defensive structures, adapted to meet the exigencies of changing methods of warfare. In Scotland, the terrain itself often formed part of a defence—remoteness, the sea, rocky ground, these all provided natural protection against the unwieldy engines of war and the mines and fires employed as assault against defences in other situations. On the west coast of Scotland, a series of curtain wall strongholds, perched on rocky precipices, display all these characteristics. The ruins at Kisimul, Mingary, Tioram and Dunstaffnage all testify to the strategic importance of their locations, underlining the need in the early 13th century to challenge the power of Norway. It is probable that these castles were instrumental in achieving the end of Viking domination.

These castles have curtain walls which follow the line of the rocky prominence which forms their defence. Elsewhere, on the mainland, there are more castles from around this period which display similar characteristics, but with a more regular plan. Kinclaven, Hume and Kincardine are among such strongholds. In other places, the curtain wall pattern was modified by the addition of projecting defensive towers which increased the possible line of fire. Later, the most important architectural change—pioneered by English military architects—was the modification of the vulnerable gateway, securing it and embellishing it at one and the same time. This development in England of the architectural prominence of the gate tower, oddly, was to lay the foundation for the later development of the distinctively Scottish style of fortified building.

While the defensive capabilities of the castles of this period were of paramount importance, provision for domestic arrangements was both necessary and provided an outlet for the display of wealth and rank. The donjon, or keep, was an imposing tower usually placed at some distance from the main entrance, and provided apartments for the lord and his retinue which were consistent with his station. As the gatehouse assumed greater importance, the donjon too moved forward, so that all the strength of the castle became concentrated at one point. Such a development is seen, for example, at Doune, a late 14th-century castle which was conceived as a courtyard dwelling where the strength and wealth were all concentrated in the keep at the front of the castle, and where the curtain wall had become of secondary importance. Perhaps the most outstanding example of the style is seen at Tantallon, built probably around 1350. Tantallon's curtain wall stands across the corner of a cliff, two towers guard each end of the wall, and its huge central gatehouse keep stands a massive 80 feet high and 42 feet square containing four storeys of living accommodation.

More modest than the great castles was another group of defensible dwellings, the hall-house. Great halls were often incorporated into the castle structure, but few free-standing Scottish halls—akin to the English fortified manor—have survived. Craigie Castle is a rare example, Morton another and Rait near Nairn provides a third. The hall-house lost favour to the tower house, though many of its features were later to be incorporated into grander buildings.

In Scotland, where civil war ravaged the country after war with its southern neighbour ended, the fortified dwelling remained a necessary feature of life; and it was the central keep-gatehouse which was developed and which gave the country its own very distinctive style of architecture. The main walls of the tower houses of the late middle ages were left plain, while the defensive arrangements remained at the top of the structure, manifested in towers and corbelling which combined an acknowledge-ment of the need for security with aesthetic considerations, simplicity with architectural detail. In the early 14th century, such tower houses would rely on outer ditches and ramparts, as well as on the sheer thickness of their own walls, to resist attack. Windows were few—and the structure, in ways, was reminiscent of the ancient broch.

The early tower houses, of which Drum is a fine example, as well as being plain and featureless, reflected the impoverishment of the gentry; they had little decoration, few windows and only a few rooms placed one on top of another. These were not royal or baronial castles. By this period the local laird had found it necessary to provide himself with a dwelling secure from local skirmishing at least, and although Robert the Bruce had decisively defeated Edward II at Bannockburn in 1314, these were uneasy years. The building of large castles which could be taken by the English and used for their own ends was not encouraged—indeed, many existing castles were spoiled for just this reason.

However, by the second half of the 14th century the ambitions of the architect had grown, and it was not uncommon for a small wing to be added to the tower to provide additional accommodation, and for the vast thickness of the walls to be used to provide extra chambers. The vertical structure remained though and was to be ingrained in the Scottish attitude to castle building for over three hundred years.

The 15th century saw a proliferation of more ambitious castle building during the reigns of the first five Jameses. There was, for example, much building at Edinburgh and Stirling, and the palaces of Linlithgow and Falkland date from this period. The tower house, however, remained predominant. Expansion, in many instances, came through adding a range of buildings to the tower round a central courtyard; such additions were often ostentatious in their decorative detailing, reflecting an increase in the power of the barons and in the means with which to display it. From the solid, plain towers of the early 14th century, castles by the mid 15th displayed attention to features of detail—fireplaces, doorways and aumbries borrowed detailing from contemporary ecclesiastical architecture, reflected particularly in a penchant for heraldic devices. Painting came into fashion, and the heraldry would be emblazoned, while vaults and walls were also painted and sculptured. Windows were enlarged, more chambers were built and accommodation generally improved.

While the 15th century saw vigorous building, the early part of the 16th was a sad one; in the wake of Flodden, her greatest men slaughtered, Scotland saw little in the way of new building. The 'long pause', this period has been called—although it did witness an impressive body of work in the royal houses, influenced by the European Renaissance. At Stirling Castle, for example, sculptured statues and detailing on columns as well as the famous 'Stirling Heads'—fifty-six large oak carved portraits set into the ceiling of the King's presence chamber—all date from this period. The influence here must be ascribed to Scotland's long connections with France. It is probable that French masons were sent over to accomplish much of the work—although the Stirling Heads are thought to have been the work of local craftsmen.

The post-Reformation period, bolstered by new wealth from the dissolution of the monasteries and a distribution of church lands and properties, saw a new and vigorous phase of building. In Scotland it faithfully followed the much-loved tower house pattern, though imbued now with less regard for security and much more with romance. Many new, exuberant, towers were erected during this period, Menzies, Megginch and Fyvie among them; in the early 17th century, the impetus continued, culminating in towers of great poetry such as Crathes and Craigievar. These new towers displayed little attention to any requirement for defence, and dedicated themselves to the need for grander and more ample accommodation. This was achieved not by a radical departure from the tower principle, but simply by the effective grouping together of a series of towers, usually in the distinctive Z- or L-plans. Architects, freed from the restrictions imposed by the need for strength, elaborated on the earlier functional features through a great emphasis on secondary features which had, however, lost their original meaning. Round corbelled turrets and pedimented dormers reflect the imagination of the mason or patron and his personal tastes.

To leave the story of the Scottish castle at the early 17th century would be to ignore the many triumphs of later years, when early impoverishment had passed and buildings began to spread outwards rather than merely upwards. Glamis, dating from the late 17th century, bears many features of indigenous architecture, as does Drumlanrig, so expensive to build that its owner, the Duke of Queensberry, was said to have occupied it for only one day, while his wife was driven to write to a kinswoman, imploring her to buy her a dress. Later buildings such as Floors Castle, designed in 1718 by Vanbrugh but reworked in 1838–49 by Playfair, show many extraneous influences; while Inveraray, built originally around 1520, has been so remodelled and refurbished that it now shows a curious blend of the neo-Gothic and neo-Scottish baronial styles. Culzean in Ayrshire, built by Robert Adam in the 1780s, displays all the features of the classical Georgian style.

In the architecture of Scotland's castles, the turbulent history of the land may be traced; from Roman or Norse invader to English enemy, through the years of poverty to periods of increased wealth. The need for restraint and for defence is well displayed. Strongholds of stone, windowless and severe, were replaced by soaring romantic towers, then by spreading buildings of ever greater lavishness which absorbed, nevertheless, features of the indigenous style. In a land which had great need to defend itself, such buildings are many, and their features diverse. In tribute to the solidity of their building, many survive in a remarkable state of preservation, and will amply repay exploration.

Glossary of terms

The following is a glossary of some of the terms connected with the structure of castles which occur in the text:

ashlar square-cut smooth stone blocks

aumbry wall cupboard

bailey defended courtyard or ward of a castle

balustrade ornamental parapet of posts and railings

barbican fortified outwork defending gate of a castle or town

barmkin Scottish term for defended courtyard of a castle, often rather smaller than conventional ward or bailey; possibly a corruption of 'barbican'. Also, the wall enclosing such an area

bartizan overhanging corner turret

cap house small room at the top of a stair or wing

castellation battlements, implying use as decorative feature

chamfer bevelled face formed by cutting off corner of stone or timber structure

constable title of governor of castle; also warden, captain, castellan

corbel projecting stone (or timber) feature on a wall to support an overhanging parapet, platform or turret

crenellation fortification—a 'licence to crenellate' was official permission to raise a fortified building or fortify an existing structure. The 'crenel' was the gap or embrasure in the battlements along a wall

curtain wall wall enclosing a bailey, courtyard, or ward

donjon keep or great tower, the main citadel of a castle of the 11th and 12th centuries

entresol low storey between two main storeys of a building

fortalice old Scots term for a medium-sized fortified building

garderobe latrine

hall-house building with the rooms on the level end to end instead of above one another as in a tower house

jamb the straight side of a doorway, arch or window

keep see **donjon**

keep-gatehouse gateway that functioned as the lord's residence and the main stronghold

L-plan distinctive Scottish form of the tower house in which a wing was added at right angles to the main tower block thereby affording greater protection by covering fire

loggia open gallery of arches

machicolation openings in the floor of a projecting parapet or platform along a wall or above an archway, through which defenders could drop or shoot missiles vertically on attackers below

motte artificial (or improved natural) mound on which a castle was built. 'Motte and bailey' implies crude 11th-century defence comprising simple timber palisade on top of earth mound, with or without buildings inside

murder holes openings in the roofs of passageways, especially entrances, through which attackers could be ambushed

newel the central post around which a spiral staircase revolves

parapet protective wall on outer side of wall walk

pend vaulted passage

pit prison underground cell, with access through hatch in ceiling only

portcullis heavy wooden, iron, or combination grille protecting an entrance, either in isolation or combined with a conventional door; raised and lowered by winches in gatehouse

postern small door or gate, usually some distance from main entrance of castle or ward. Often obscure or actually hidden, they enabled defenders to slip in and out of a castle, without being vulnerable to major attacks

quoin dressed corner stone

solar private living quarters of lord, usually adjacent to great hall

tower house plain, featureless, secure building, with little decoration, few windows, and a few rooms placed one above the other

yett Scottish variation on portcullis—gate made of intersecting iron bars penetrating each other vertically and horizontally. This formidable defence was ultimately banned

Z-plan distinctive Scottish form of the tower house whereby two corner towers were added to the main tower block thereby affording greater protection by covering fire

A note on selection

The castles in this book are described alphabetically under their most common names. They are located by their nearest town or village, their district and region. To enable easy location on a map, straightline distances and approximate directions from the nearest town are quoted. It should be emphasised that the directions given should be correlated by potential visitors with a good local road map; the directions quoted are not claimed to be sufficient in every case, especially where surviving ruins may be fragmentary and isolated.

Conditions of access to castles are as at the time of going to press. Every effort has been made to validate this information. Some castles are not normally open to the public, but permission to view is often given on written application to the administrator of the site concerned. Many castles consider special conditions for visits by large parties. The publishers wish to emphasise *that where a site is on private land, whether or not the building is still in occupation, there is no public right of way.* If there is any doubt as to the public right of access to any particular site, *it is essential to make careful local inquiries.*

The criteria by which entries could be selected for a book on castles are several. The publishers have chosen not to attempt to define the term 'castle' according to any technical criterion, such as the relative military and/or residential importance of the original site; in many cases such judgements must necessarily be based on obscure or speculative data. All sites known by documentary evidence or common usage as '_____ Castle' or 'Castle _____' have been included.

A Brief Chronology of Scottish Military History

AD 81–84: *Agricola subdues Caledonian tribes at Mons Graupius*

Julius Agricola pushes the Roman domain northwards into Scotland and builds a line of forts and camps between the Firths of Clyde and Forth, preventing southward incursion by Pictish and Caledonian tribes. Caledonians defeated at Battle of Mons Graupius. A major fortress is established at Inchtuthil.

96–100: *First Roman withdrawal from Scotland*

Under pressure of relentless attacks most of the Roman forts in Scotland are abandoned.

117–122: *Hadrian's Wall is built in aftermath of major rising*

A major revolt breaks out in north Britain. The Emperor Hadrian visits Britain and orders many reforms, including the construction of a defensive wall from the Solway to the Tyne, to contain the northern tribes. Aulus Platorius Nepos commences the construction of the wall.

139–142: *Antonine Wall is commenced by Lollius Urbicus during reign of Antoninus Pius*

Governor Lollius Urbicus advances into Scotland and begins the construction of the less-formidable Antonine Wall on the Forth–Clyde line, following the disposition of the old Agricolan forts. During the following half-century there are numerous revolts in the north, and the Antonine Wall is overrun or abandoned on three occasions. In 197 Hadrian's Wall is overrun, and the tribes reach and sack York.

205–211: *Rebuilding of Hadrian's Wall and re-conquest of southern Scotland*

Major re-conquest of southern Scotland under the command of Severus, Geta and Caracalla. Caledonian tribes defeated. For a period southern Scotland is administered as a Roman protectorate, but Roman influence north of Hadrian's Wall is always tenuous.

383–388: *During wars between rival emperors, Hadrian's Wall is overrun for the last time*

Throughout the 3rd and 4th centuries there are repeated incursions from the north, and the forts along Hadrian's Wall are taken, retaken and rebuilt several times. In the 380s the Wall is overrun once more, and is never rebuilt.

406–410: *Britain is stripped of Roman troops*

Thirty years later the last Roman troops are withdrawn from Britain, leaving the country at the mercy of the Picts, Caledonians, Attacotti and Saxons.

500–550: *Scots settle in Dalriada*
550–600: *Angles settle in the Lothians*
563: *St Columba comes to Iona and preaches Christianity to mainland tribes*

597: *Death of St Columba*

The Scots, a tribe from Ireland, establish settlements on the west coast of Scotland at Dalriada (Argyll) during the first half of the 6th century. During the latter half of the century Angles settle in the Lothians in eastern Scotland. Christianity reaches Scotland in the form of the monastery established on the Isle of Iona by St Columba, an Irish nobleman turned monk. From this first centre of Christianity he sets out to convert the pagan tribes on the mainland, with some success. After Columba's death his work continues, and a large part of Scotland is converted to Christianity at the same time as the re-conversion of England from Europe.

835: *First Norse raids on Scotland*
843: *Kenneth McAlpin attempts unification of Scotland*

920: *Constantine III allies himself with English against Norsemen*

The first raids by Norsemen on the coasts of Scotland are followed by the establishment of settlements. Kenneth McAlpin, King of the Scots, makes the first serious attempt to unite Scotland to resist the Norse and the Northumbrians; he meets with limited success. Eighty years later Constantine III, King of the Scots, allies himself with the English against the spread of Viking settlement. The English eventually capture the Lothians from their kinsmen the Angles, and Constantine then allies himself with the Vikings to eject the English.

937: *Athelstan defeats league of Scots, British and Norsemen at Brunanburgh*

940–946: *Edmund conquers Strathclyde and gives it in fief to Malcolm I*

1016: *Malcolm II defeats Northumbrians at Carham*

1034: *Duncan becomes first king of all Scotland*

(1040–57: *Macbeth*)

(1057–58: *Lulach*)

1058: *Malcolm III succeeds to throne*

1070: *Malcolm III marries daughter of Edward (the Confessor) of England. English influence increases*

(1093–94 and 1094–97: *Donald Bane*)

(1094: *Duncan II*)

(1097–1107: *Edgar*)

(1107–24: *Alexander I*)

1124: *David I succeeds to throne; he continues policy of Anglicisation, and brings Anglo-Norman barons to Scotland. Feudal system established*

(1153–65: *Malcolm IV*)

1165: *William I, the Lion, succeeds to throne*

1173: *William the Lion joins revolt of barons against Henry II of England. Captured at Alnwick, he is forced to swear allegiance to Henry*

1188: *Richard I sells back Scottish independence*

(1214–49: *Alexander II*)

1249: *Alexander III succeeds to throne*

1263: *Alexander III defeats Norsemen at Largs*

1266: *Alexander III marries his daughter to Eric II of Norway, and acquires the Hebrides*

1286: *Alexander III dies and succession crisis ensues*

1290: *Margaret, the Maid of Norway, dies on voyage to Scotland*

1290–92: *First interregnum; Edward I of England claims throne*

1292: *John de Baliol placed on throne as vassal of Edward I of England*

1295: *John de Baliol revolts against Edward in alliance with France*

1296: *Edward I defeats Scots at Dunbar. Second interregnum; Scotland under English occupation*

Athelstan, grandson of Alfred the Great of Wessex, defeats the combined army at Brunanburgh.

Athelstan is succeeded by his brother Edmund as 'King of All Britain'. He conquers Strathclyde and gives it in fief to the Alban king, Malcolm I.

Malcolm II finally inflicts a decisive defeat on the Northumbrians at the Battle of Carham, near Coldstream. The Scots at last control all country north of the Tweed. In 1031 Malcolm swears allegiance to Cnut, Danish King of All England. Three years later he dies, and is succeeded by his grandson Duncan, king of the Strathclyde realm. Although Viking settlements remain in the Western Isles and some northern coastal enclaves, Scotland is united under a single king for the first time. In 1040 Duncan is killed by his general, MacBeath (or MacBeth), who takes the throne.

In 1070 Malcolm III of Canmore, son of Duncan, marries Margaret, granddaughter of Edward the Confessor of England. The match brings an English influence to the court, and Edinburgh and Dunfermline become the main centres. English is adopted as the language of the court and clergy. Malcolm's son David I continues the policy of Anglicisation. He makes grants of land and charters to Anglo-Norman barons as well as to some of his closest associates among the hereditary tribal chiefs, thus bringing the feudal system to Scotland. English clerics acquire considerable influence in the church, and such foundations as St Andrews and Jedburgh are begun under English priests.

William the Lion, King of Scotland, joins the English rebels against King Henry II in the hope of regaining Northumberland. He is defeated at Alnwick, captured, and forced to swear allegiance to Henry. Scotland loses her independence for the first time.

Henry's son Richard I (the Lionheart) sells Scottish independence back to William the Lion for 10,000 Marks— to finance the Third Crusade.

Alexander III defeats the Norse at Largs in 1263, and in consequence adds the Western Isles to the Scottish kingdom. To restore his bankrupt exchequer Eric II of Norway is forced to sell the Hebrides to Alexander, and marries the Scots king's daughter to seal the bargain.

On Alexander's death in a riding accident in 1286 a succession crisis breaks out. The throne is claimed for his granddaughter Margaret—the 'Maid of Norway', still a child, the daughter of Eric—by Robert the Bruce and by John de Baliol, both the latter being indirect descendants of David I through the female line. The Maid of Norway is finally declared queen, with a council of clerics and nobles to rule in her name. Details of the procedure to be adopted by this Regency Council cause persistent disagreement and unrest, and it is 4 years before the council sends to Norway for the infant queen. On the voyage to Edinburgh the child dies, aged 7. Civil war breaks out between the Bruce and Baliol factions.

In this unsettled period King Edward I of England lays claim to the throne himself. He crosses the border, and occupies the country as far north as Perth. In 1292 he acknowledges John de Baliol, his feudal vassal, as king.

1297: *William Wallace defeats English at Stirling Bridge*
1298: *Edward I defeats Wallace at Falkirk; English bowmen play major part in slaughter of 15,000 Scots*

1303: *Wallace returns from French exile and captures Stirling. Edward I invades once again*
1304: *Edward takes Stirling*
1305: *Wallace betrayed, captured and executed*

1306: *Robert the Bruce crowned at Scone as Robert I. He is defeated at Methven and flees to Ireland*
1307–10: *Robert I wins Battle of Loudoun. Death of Edward I on march north. Robert consolidates position by 'the harrying of the Buchan'*

1314: *English under Edward II decisively defeated by Robert I at Bannockburn*

1329: *Death of Robert I. David II succeeds to throne in infancy*

1332: *Earl of Mar defeated at Dupplin*

1333: *Edward III defeats Scots at Halidon Hill*

1341: *Edward Baliol driven from Scotland. David II returns from France*

After 3 years this unpopular puppet king allies himself with France—then at war with England—and revolts against Edward. Edward invades Scotland once more, sacking Berwick and defeating the Scots in a major battle at Dunbar. The Great Seal of Scotland is broken, and the historic Stone of Scone—the Stone of Destiny, upon which all Scots monarchs had been crowned—is taken into England. Edward withdraws, leaving Scotland under military occupation. After his departure a revolt breaks out led by a minor nobleman, Sir William Wallace. He defeats an English force at Stirling Bridge, and rules for a year in the name of John de Baliol. Once more Edward invades, and defeats Wallace at Falkirk. Before the revolt can be decisively crushed, however, Edward is forced to return to England to deal with domestic problems.

In 1303 Edward undertakes a full-scale campaign against Scotland. Wallace is finally captured and executed in 1305, as 'a traitor to England'. Later in that year Robert the Bruce and John Comyn, both members of the old Regency Council, meet at Dumfries in an attempt to unify strategy against the English. They quarrel; Bruce stabs Comyn to death, and is crowned King of Scotland at Scone shortly afterwards. This forces him to take the field earlier than he had hoped; and apart from Edward and his puppet Baliol, the Comyns are out against him. He is defeated at Methven near Perth, and retires in hiding to the island of Ratlin, off Ireland. He returns the next year and triumphs in the Battle of Loudoun. Edward threatens to invade once more, but dies, and the campaign is abandoned. Edward is surnamed 'Hammer of the Scots'.

For the next three years Robert I consolidates his position against the Comyns and other opponents, stabilising his grip on the crown with a fierce campaign in the north-east known as 'the harrying of the Buchan'. In 1310 Edward II of England, a sorry shadow of his mighty father, makes an attempt to retake Scotland; all English troops are ejected, and Robert carries the war into northern England. Edward mounts yet another major campaign, but is defeated at the historic Battle of Bannockburn. Secure on his throne, Robert continues to harry the English for many years, until they are forced to sue for peace in 1328. A treaty is negotiated at Edinburgh and ratified at Northampton; the main clause is the recognition of Scottish independence by the English throne.

In 1329 Robert the Bruce dies, to be succeeded by his 5-year-old son David II. The Earl of Moray is made Regent. Edward III of England decides to fish in troubled waters and send north an army of disinherited or disaffected Scots led by Edward Baliol, son of John. The new Regent, the Earl of Mar, meets them at Dupplin and is defeated. As a result of the victory Edward III claims feudal overlordship of Scotland. Baliol's invasion shows signs of weakening, and Edward hurries north and inflicts another defeat on the Scots at Halidon Hill near Berwick. Edward loses interest in Baliol's cause and returns to continue his wars with the French. The boy king David grows up in refuge in France, and the Regency rebuilds the kingdom during a period of comparative peace. In 1341 David returns home.

Inevitably, David II decides to attack England, strengthened as he is by a close alliance with France. The value of the French connection is cast into some question by the great victory of the English bowmen at Crécy in 1345, but the following year David crosses the border.

1346: *Scots invade England. David II defeated and captured at Neville's Cross*

At Neville's Cross, near Durham, he is defeated and captured on 17th October. He spends the next 13 years a prisoner of the English, who occupy large areas of Scotland once again.

1357: *David II ransomed*
1371: *Robert II succeeds to throne on death of David II; foundation of Stewart dynasty*
(1390–1406: Robert III)

David II is finally ransomed for a huge sum of money and the promise that his heir will be an English prince. This promise inevitably causes internal strife in Scotland; and on his death David is, in fact, succeeded by his nephew Robert Stewart. At 55 Robert II is past ruling effectively, and a period of continuous disorder ensues, lasting until the death of his successor Robert III in 1406. During both these reigns the real power in the realm is wielded by the Dukes of Albany and Rothesay, and in this uncertain climate Robert III sends his heir James to France for safe-keeping. The boy is captured at sea, and remains in prison in England until 1424, while internal warfare rages in Scotland.

1406: *James I succeeds to throne, but remains in English captivity until 1424*

James I is released in 1424, and rules Scotland wisely until his death in 1437. He introduces many effective constitutional reforms, and much legislation. The advantages of his reign are thrown away again upon his death.

1437–60: *James II. Internal warfare between crown and Earls of Douglas*

His son James II faces a long struggle with the powerful Douglases; they are finally defeated at Arkinholm near Dumfries in 1452. The cause of the feud had been the murder of the eighth Earl of Douglas by James, personally, after Douglas had come to Stirling Castle on promise of safe-conduct. For all their defiance of the crown, the Douglases make a major contribution to the recovery of southern Scotland from the English.

1460: *James III succeeds to throne on death of James II at Roxburghe. Protracted struggle with Lords of the Isles ends in victory for the crown in 1476*

By 1460 the only important English possession in southern Scotland is Berwick. In that year James II is killed by a bursting cannon while leading the attack on Roxburghe Castle. James III rules during a period of relative peace, and enlarges the realm by sending his unruly nobles to occupy themselves on an expedition against the Lords of the Isles. The Western Isles are finally subdued in 1476, and on James's marriage to Margaret of Denmark he receives the Orkneys and Shetlands as her dowry. For all his efforts to consolidate the central government of the kingdom, James dies in an internal conflict—he is defeated and killed by a faction of rebellious nobles at the Battle of Sauchieburn in 1488. In the same year the English finally cede Berwick. The nobles give a semblance of legality to their cause by kidnapping the boy heir, James IV, and holding him as titular head of their faction. That this should have been seen as an advantage proves that the very existence of the central authority was now accepted, and that rebellions would in future be against individual kings rather than against the strongly established Stewart dynasty itself.

1488: *James III killed at Battle of Sauchieburn. James IV seized by disaffected nobles*

For all that he is installed by rebellion, James IV proves to be a strong king who establishes a climate of royal authority. His one major error lies in reviving the French alliance. When Henry VIII of England is campaigning successfully in France, James leads 100,000 Scots south in an

1513: *James IV and majority of Scottish peerage killed at Flodden Field. James V succeeds to throne as infant*

invasion of England. In October 1513 he brings unprecedented disaster on Scottish arms; at Flodden Field the Earl of Surrey inflicts a crushing defeat and among the 10,000 Scots dead are the king and almost the whole of his aristocracy. An 18-month-old boy inherits the throne as James V. The war continues sporadically until 1528, when James throws off the influence of regents and advisors. Despite pressure exerted by Henry VIII of England, James maintains friendship with France and obedience to the church of Rome. During his life he makes two French marriages; firstly to Madeleine, daughter of Francis I, and secondly to Mary of Guise, in 1537. His insistence on maintaining the French connection in the face of Henry VIII's hostility divides his kingdom; many of his western and southern noblemen will not support what they regard as a 'French war'. The army which James leads to defeat by the English at Solway Moss in 1542 is provided by Cardinal Beaton and the Catholic clergy. Exhausted and disheartened, James V dies at Falkland a week after the birth of his daughter Mary.

Mary is barely a year old when Henry VIII tries to force a marriage with his infant son Edward; the terms are unacceptable to the regents and the match is abandoned. Henry's furious reaction is a series of violent campaigns in southern Scotland in 1544–45—'the Wars of Rough Wooing'. Scotland's reaction is yet another revival of the French alliance. Cardinal Beaton is assassinated in 1546, and the following year the Scots are defeated at the last battle between the national armies of Scotland and England, the Battle of Pinkie. The Regent, Arran, sends the child queen to France for safety, and she is betrothed to the Dauphin. In 1550 peace is concluded between France and England, and the terms include Scotland joining the pact as well. Despite this treaty French troops remain in Scotland, causing much local ill-feeling. Arran resigns the regency. Mary of Guise attempts to increase the French influence by appointing Frenchmen to high office, and there is a fear that a French prince will be placed on the throne of Scotland. The match between the young Mary and the Dauphin is endangered.

Another cause for unrest during this period is the general ill-feeling against the church. Resentment of church wealth provides fertile ground for religious reformers such as John Knox, and England supports them with finance—eager to assist in the discomfiture of both the Catholic church and its French servants. The formation of a Protestant church in Scotland is marked by the signing of the League and Covenant in 1557, and in 1560 the Scottish Parliament abolishes papal authority and the celebration of mass.

The following year the 18-year-old Mary, recently widowed by the death of the Dauphin, returns to Scotland to find that the 'auld alliance' with France, and the religion to which she belongs, have both been abandoned. Continually at loggerheads with the Reformers led by John Knox, she pushes her claim to the throne of England without success. In 1565 she marries Lord Darnley, but the match is a failure. Her secretary, confidant, and—some said—lover Rizzio is murdered before her eyes at Darnley's instigation. Darnley himself dies under suspicious circumstances, in an explosion which Mary is alleged to

1542: *James V defeated by English at Solway Moss, and dies a week after birth of his daughter, the future Mary, Queen of Scots*

1544–45: *Rejection of projected match between Mary and Edward leads to 'Wars of Rough Wooing'*

1547: *Scots defeated at Pinkie in last battle between national armies of England and Scotland*

1550–54: *Unrest in Scotland over continuing French influence*

1557–60: *John Knox leads Reform party; the League and Covenant is signed, and papal authority is abolished*

1561: *Mary, Queen of Scots returns from France*

1565: *Mary marries Lord Darnley*

1567: *Darnley murdered. Mary gives birth to future James VI, and marries* have plotted. In June of 1567 her son James is born. In the autumn she marries yet again, this time the Earl of Bothwell. Opposition to Mary has been growing steadily among her lords and the Reformers; she is defeated by them at Carberry Hill and forced to abdicate in favour of her infant son, with her half-brother, the Earl of Moray, as Regent. She is imprisoned in Loch Leven Castle, escapes, and is finally defeated a year later at Langside. She flees to England in May 1568, and is confined by Elizabeth I for a total of 19 years. There are several plots against Elizabeth's life, in some of which Mary certainly acquiesces, even if she takes no more active part. In 1587 Elizabeth is finally prevailed upon to have Mary executed, and she is beheaded at Fotheringay on 8th February.

Mary's flight marks the firm establishment of the Protestant faith in Scotland, and in 1567 the Scottish Parliament recognises it as the official religion of the country.

In 1581 the 14-year-old James VI takes over the rule of his kingdom after a succession of inept regents. Almost immediately he is kidnapped by a group of Protestant extremists at Ruthven Castle in 1582, and held prisoner for 10 months. This experience confirms him in his determination to exert his authority over both church and state, and in 1584 he passes the 'Black Acts', giving himself the right to appoint his own bishops. He takes pains to maintain good relations with England, and on the death of Elizabeth I in 1603 he succeeds to the English throne as well, ruling as 'James the First and Sixth of England and Scotland'. On his death in 1625 he is succeeded by his son Charles I.

Charles I alienates the Scots by his inept attempts to standardise the religious practices of the two countries. His new Prayer Book and his policy regarding Episcopacy lead to riots in 1637, and the signing of the new National Covenant in 1638. There are demonstrations by both sides on the border in 1639, ending in the Peace of Berwick. The disillusionment of the Covenanters, or Protestant party, with Charles I leads them to side with the English Parliament when Civil War breaks out in 1642. Nevertheless, because their declared goal is religious rather than any fundamental constitutional reform, it is to the Covenanters that Charles I goes in 1646. He attempts to negotiate an alliance, but discussions break down on the religious issue and he is handed over to his enemies in England. In 1649 he is beheaded, and the Covenanters make their peace with Charles II. In the Second Civil War, Cromwell defeats Scottish forces loyal to Charles at Dunbar on 3rd September 1650. The same year sees the defeat at Carbisdale of James Graham, first Marquis of Montrose; throughout this period he has been one of the monarchy's staunchest and most successful soldiers, despite his personal loyalty to the Covenant, and he pays for it with his life. For 10 years Scotland suffers a relatively benign dictatorship under the Commonwealth. Cromwell's troops slight many castles to prevent their being occupied in any future war.

One of Charles II's first acts on his Restoration is to rescind all enactments of the Scottish Parliament back to 1633, thus bringing about the Covenanter Wars of 1666–90. The Covenanters mount an unsuccessful attack on

Edinburgh in 1666; win a victory over government forces at Drumclog in 1679; and are heavily defeated later that year at Bothwell Brig. The struggle continues under James II, who succeeds to the throne in 1685. James's open Catholicism brings a new fury to the confrontation, but he is forced to flee England in 1688 by the threat of Protestant revolution. William of Orange and James's daughter Mary reign jointly. Supporters of James II in Scotland resist, and win a victory over government troops at Killiecrankie in 1689—but the battle costs the life of Graham of Claverhouse, Viscount Dundee, one of James II's most energetic commanders through the Covenanter Wars. By 1690 the conflict is over; the Presbytery is established once again, and its General Assembly meets for the first time since 1653.

1685: *James II succeeds to throne. Severities against Covenanters increase*
1688–89: *James II deposed. Battle of Killiecrankie*

William's rule is unpopular in the Highlands, and the clans slow to take the oath of loyalty to the new king. In 1692 it is decided—largely by Sir John Dalrymple, Master of Stair—that an example will be made of the Macdonalds of Glencoe, in Argyllshire. Age-old clan hatreds have more to do with this tragedy than political expediency. The Macdonalds are massacred by Campbell of Glen Lyon on 13th February, under circumstances of great treachery and cruelty. This atrocity not only cements the hatred between Campbell and Macdonald, but gives the Jacobite cause a powerful rallying-cry.

1692: *Massacre of Glencoe*

While religious and political struggles continue in Scotland an attempt is made at forcing commercial growth, and a statute is passed for a Scottish overseas trading company on the lines of the West India Company. In 1698, 1,200 Scottish settlers are shipped westwards across the Atlantic and establish settlements on the isthmus of Panama, in Spanish territory. This causes great friction between Britain and Spain, and the settlers are decimated by disease and Spanish attacks. By 1700 the few survivors return to Scotland.

1695–1700: *Scotland's only attempt at overseas colonisation is unsuccessful*

For most of the 17th century the real power in Scotland has been the king and his English Parliament and troops. The Scottish Parliament has provided dignity but little real authority; in the period 1689–1707 this state of affairs alters radically. The most effective—and final—Scottish Parliament restores parliamentary rule to most of Scotland except the Highlands. This rule is deliberately fostered by England, where it is realised that a more genuine part in the government must be handed over to the Scots if the Jacobite cause is to be defeated.

1689–1707: *Last and most successful Scottish Parliament paves way for unification*

After unsuccessful attempts to negotiate a union of the two parliaments in 1689 and again in 1702, a detailed treaty of unification is recognised by both parties in 1707. Within a united kingdom under Queen Anne, much local responsibility and freedom is preserved. No fewer than four uprisings take place in the name of the exiled Catholic Stewart kings in the 40 years after unification. Two minor risings, in 1708 and 1719, are suppressed; the second enjoys Spanish support. In 1715 and 1745 major rebellions cause great turmoil throughout Britain.

1707: *Act of Union*

In 1715 the Earl of Mar, formerly a fervent Unionist but now disillusioned, raises the Highland clans in the cause of the Old Pretender, 'James III or VIII', the son of James II. The rebellion spreads slowly and penetrates only as far

1715: *First major Jacobite rising. Earl of Mar raises standard of 'Old Pretender'*

south as Perth. There Mar meets government forces under the Duke of Argyll, and fights the indecisive Battle of Sheriffmuir. Hopes for a rising in the south fade, and the Pretender arrives only to lead his supporters in their flight back to France.

In 1744 plans for a French invasion of Scotland miscarry, and no help can be expected from France by the Jacobites when they rise once more the following year. Against the disinterest of the south, now feeling the very real benefits of unification, and the small numbers of Highlanders who turn out, are set the personal magnetism of Bonnie Prince Charlie and the weakness of the British army at home due to overseas commitments. Within a matter of weeks Prince Charles Edward is the master of Scotland. He defeats Sir John Cope's army at Prestonpans on 21st September, and by December has advanced into England as far as Derby. The government withdraws troops from Europe who begin to push the Jacobites back. In the course of his retreat the Prince wins a further victory, at Falkirk on 17th January 1746, over General Hawley. The troops of the Duke of Cumberland force him to continue the retreat immediately, however; and in the decisive Battle of Culloden, near Inverness, on 16th April, the Jacobite cause is finally snuffed out by the cannon and skilled bayonet-fighting of Cumberland's redcoats. For his harrying of the defeated enemy, Cumberland earns the nickname 'the Butcher'. Prince Charles Edward escapes to France after many adventures, and dies in 1788; his unfortunate Highlanders suffer under repressive laws and an English military occupation. After years of suffering, however, the wounds of Anglo-Scottish strife slowly heal. With growing prosperity and intellectual stature Scotland gradually comes to feel part of a genuinely united kingdom; and barely 60 years after Culloden kilted Highlanders will be among the most loyal, reliable and admired soldiers in a British army locked in war with France—the 'auld ally'.

1745–46: *Second major Jacobite rising under Prince Charles Edward*

The Castles of Scotland

Aberdour Castle

Aberdour, Fife.
7 miles east of the northern end of the Forth Road Bridge on A921.

This ruined castle, which overlooks the harbour at Aberdour, dates back to the 14th century, when the tower was built on a rhomboidal plan. The free-standing tower was gradually added to until the 17th century, when building was finally completed. These additions explain the four visible building periods, beginning with the 14th-century medieval tower house which was rebuilt in the 15th century and extended to the south in the 16th century. In the 17th century the tower house was extended once more, to the east, but less than a hundred years after its completion Aberdour Castle was burnt and left abandoned.

The barony of Aberdour dates from the 14th century, when Thomas Randolph, Earl of Moray, nephew and supporter of King Robert the Bruce, was given lands by his uncle. These then passed down to the Earl's eldest son (also Thomas) in 1332, and when he was killed at Dupplin in the same year the younger son, John, inherited the estates. In 1342, John granted a charter of the barony to his great friend William Douglas, Knight, and the property has belonged to one or other branch of the Douglas family ever since.

Historical records show that Sir William, too, granted a charter of the lands of Aberdour to his nephew James, later Lord of Dalkeith. Between 1456 and 1458 the fourth Lord Dalkeith (another James) succeeded to the title and lands, and was created Earl of Morton in anticipation of his forthcoming marriage to James I's daughter Joanna, who was deaf and dumb.

At the beginning of the 16th century the barony belonged to John, second Earl of Morton, and in 1513 it passed on to James, the third Earl. In 1538 the Earl and his wife were summoned for not paying the feudal dues on the lands of Aberdour—which was probably a ruse on the part of the king to obtain the lands for himself. The king got his way, but on the death of James V in 1542 the Earl re-established his position. The Earl died in 1548 and was succeeded by his son-in-law, George Douglas, the famous Regent Morton. This powerful man had a hazardous and chequered career, for not long after gaining Aberdour he was involved in the plot to murder Rizzio, the Queen's favourite. Although the resourceful Earl managed to save his own life, the Queen punished him by dispensing with his services as Chancellor. Luckily for Morton the storm blew over more quickly than might have been expected, due to political necessity, and he

was recalled. Nonetheless, Morton was hated by the politicians of the day and he eventually and finally fell from favour in 1580, when he was executed on the excuse that he was involved in Lord Darnley's murder. At this stage the lands and barony of Aberdour were granted to the Earl of Lennox, and Lord Maxwell, the Regent's brother-in-law, took the title of Earl of Morton. In 1587 the Morton lands were again restored to the Earl of Angus by the Duke of Lennox 'for the sake of peace in the realm against the nobles of the same'. During the 17th century, a difficult period for the supporters of the monarchy, the sixth Earl of Morton found himself in financial difficulties and had to sell part of his lands. In 1647 the family moved from Dalkeith into Aberdour Castle, which at this time was very richly furnished, as shown by the 1647 inventory. The walls of the principal rooms were hung with tapestry and had curtains at the windows. The private rooms were furnished with enormous beds, one covered with red silk and gold fringes, another of red cloth with black and yellow lace.

Earl William, the sixth Earl, died in 1648 and was succeeded by his son Robert—who died the following year—and then by his grandson William, the eighth Earl. Aberdour Castle is traditionally believed to have been burnt down in 1715 when occupied by dragoons, but this has never been proved. It is more likely that the castle was partially destroyed in 1688; although the Earl went so far as to obtain estimates for the re-building, he obviously could not afford the necessary £1,144 and so the castle was allowed to stand empty.

The ruins were left to crumble, and were finally abandoned by the Morton family in 1725 when the adjoining property—then known as Cuttlehill, now Aberdour House—was added to the estate. The rebuilt east range of the castle was used as a barrack, school-room, masonic hall and dwelling until 1924, when the castle was put in the care of the predecessors of Historic Buildings and Monuments, Scottish Development Department. The Government restored and modernised the south-east wing to house the custodian—latest of the long line of keepers of this castle.

The site of Aberdour was originally chosen for its considerable strength. Nowadays this is not so obvious. The steep slope to the south has been broken down by 17th-century terracing and to the north by the railway. It is still possible to distinguish the entrance gate with its moulded jambs, the ancient porter's lodge and round tower at the northern angle: but the outer courtyard, which in the 17th century was enclosed by a walled garden to the east, a terrace to the south and an inner courtyard to the west, is now just a car park.

All that survives of the oldest part of the castle—the tower—is the basement and a substantial part of the south-east wall, including three wall slits used for lighting the interior on the ground floor. Access to all upper floors was by the stair in the east angle. Above first-floor level the tower has been rebuilt. Remains show that originally the castle was a tower house type of dwelling with store-room, hall and private apartments built one on top of another and connected by a vertical turnpike stair. The resulting rather imposing structure was fairly simple to build and very strong, able to withstand violent but preferably short assaults.

During the 15th century, the upper part of the tower was obviously rebuilt to provide further accommodation after what may have been a collapse or even partial demolition by the owners. Again, in the 16th century, the living quarters proved inadequate for the needs of the family, and a new range was added which represented a great advance in comfort and convenience on the original tower plan. Finally, around 1610, Earl William Morton had the east range of the castle extended on an L-plan shape with a projecting wing at the south corner. Two small towers project from the north front, one an integral feature of the original building, the other an early addition. The whole of the first floor of the main block was occupied by a picture gallery with connecting passages to the old building; although the fine fireplace has been preserved in the south-east wall, the room's appearance has been changed from the original due to window and roof alterations.

The projecting wing, now the custodian's house connects with the main block only at gallery level. One of the features worth noting at Aberdour Castle is the entresol, which has a hand-painted ceiling worked by skilled local craftsmen using pigments mixed in a glue medium and applied to a surface of chalk and glue. Although the ceiling has faded, it still shows details of the design including flowers, fruits and winged cherubs.

The gardens here are quite remarkable, and include a large beehive-shaped dovecot with north-facing entrance sheltered by a stone weather table supported on projecting corbels. The walls are built in four stages defined by string courses set forward to provide perches for the birds and to keep out vermin. Inside the dovecot, a small flight of steps leads to floor level where there is a central revolving pole to which were attached ladders used to reach some of the more inaccessible of the 600 nests. Beyond and below the dovecot was the orchard, which in 1690 was drained and laid out as gardens.

Open to the public all year, Summer, Monday to Saturday 9.30am–7pm, Sunday 2–7pm; Winter, Saturday to Wednesday 9.30am–4pm, Thursday morning.

Achnacarry Castle

Achnacarry, Inverness, Highland.
12 miles north-east of Fort William off B8005.

The chiefs of the Clan Cameron, the Camerons of Lochiel, have held the castle as their family seat since the mid 17th century. In 1746 the Duke of Cumberland destroyed the original castle because of the then chief's support for the cause of Prince Charles Edward Stuart. The family was sent into exile, returning in 1784 under amnesty. The present house was built in 1805 and completed in 1830. It was further restored in 1952 by Ian G. Lindsay after a serious fire. During the Second World War it was taken over as a training centre for commandos. Not far away is Loch Arkaig, well-known for brown trout fishing.

Not open to the public.

Affleck Castle

Monikie, Angus, Tayside.
9 miles north-east of Dundee off B978.

To the west of Monikie and on the border of the Downie Hills, in a very fertile area, stands this small tower house with its turreted keep. The building is of particular interest in that it has survived the centuries in perfect condition, neither changed by repairs and alterations nor effaced by war or neglect. Built in the 15th century, the castle consists of four storeys and a garret built on an L-plan, with the principal staircase set in one wing. It was constructed in the irregularly shaped local red sandstone rubble but with the angles and openings all very carefully wrought by masons.

The outer arched door has an empty panel above it for armorial achievement, and a niche for the statue of the patron saint. Within the door a short passage leads to the cellarage on the ground floor of the main building, with access on the left to the stair foot. On the storey above the cellars is the common hall of the castle. This is vaulted but has no fireplace or sanitation and has three large windows with benches in each of the bays.

Above this storey, the spiral staircase leads to a second, more comfortable floor which was the lord's hall, and at this point the staircase stops. To get to the upper floors visitors or intruders would have had to cross the hall to the opposite corner where there is another spiral staircase leading to the roof. This type of staircase design was included mainly for security reasons, so that anyone wanting to get to the battlements had to cross the hall in full view, but it also served a second purpose, as the upper part of the 'jam' allowed space for two small rooms including a tiny cell, a latrine and a peep-hole for viewing the hall below.

Above the lord's hall is the solar or withdrawing room which in spite of its small size is exceptionally elegant. The fine large windows have stone side

Affleck Castle

benches and the fireplace, designed in the rich style of the 15th century, has ornately moulded jambs. In the north end wall are large closets which may have contained a latrine and some sort of simple bunk beds.

At the south-east corner of the building is a glorious chapel with an arched opening which looks more like a miniature chancel arch than simply a door. The chapel is vaulted in the finest ashlar and lit by ornate but small windows with trefoiled heads and stepped soles.

In the south-west of the solar, the spiral stair leads up and along the battlements to the cap house at the top of the tower. It is remarkable that though Affleck Castle was designed to provide adequate accommodation, room was never allowed for a kitchen; cooking and serving were presumably done in an outbuilding within the barmkin wall and the food carried across to the hall—except at times of siege, when the lord's hall fireplace would presumably have been used.

The castle was the ancient fortress of the Auchinlecks or Afflecks, who seem to have neglected it, as in 1466 David, Earl of Crawford, subscribed to James III for the deed of property for Affleck. In 1471 this was confirmed by the king. However, the Auchinlecks' good fortunes returned under the patronage of the Earl of Crawford: with the improvement of their finances they began to take more interest in the estate, and built the existing tower house in the late 15th century. The earliest records of Affleck are of the 'castell and fortalice' in 1501. Affleck Castle is now in the care of Historic Buildings and Monuments, Scottish Development Department.

Not open to the public.

Airlie Castle
Kirriemuir, Angus, Tayside.
5½ miles north-east of Alyth off A926.

Situated on the brow of a ravine, the castle has been the home of the Earls of Airlie, titular heads of the Ogilvy clan, since 1431. In 1639, during the reign of Charles I, the Earl of Airlie left Scotland to join the king's supporters and while he was away the castle was seriously looted and eventually burnt down. During the Jacobite rebellions of 1715 and 1745 the castle was again attacked, and Lord Ogilvy forced to flee to France for refuge. In 1792, after his return, he rebuilt the castle. It has since been restored yet again in this century by the twelfth Earl of Airlie, with particular attention given to the stonework, ironwork and construction of a new wing.

One of the particular points of interest at this

castle are the gardens, where the topiary work portrays the battle formations at Waterloo. These gardens were a favourite haunt of the late Queen Mary, who often visited her friend Mabel, Countess of Airlie, grandmother of the present Earl.

Open to the public by appointment only.

Allardyce Castle
Inverbervie, Kincardine and Deeside, Grampian.
20 miles south of Aberdeen on A92.

Standing on the north bank of the Bervie Water and about 1 mile above Inverbervie's Jubilee Bridge is Allardyce Castle. It is thought that it was built around 1662, the time of the marriage of Lady Mary Graham to Sir John Allardyce. The multi-turreted stair tower at the castle is a particularly fine example of the peculiarly Scottish art of label-corbelling, which can best be described as both ornamental and functional, consisting of stone brackets which support projecting battlements or turrets.

Not open to the public.

Alyth Castle
Alyth, Perth and Kinross, Tayside.
5 miles north-east of Blairgowrie off A926.

Near the town of Alyth lie the ruins of the reputed Alyth Castle, where legend has it that Guinevere, wife of King Arthur, was imprisoned by the ancient Picts. All that remains of the ruins is a large fallen stone wall and some ramparts.

Not open to the public.

Ardtornish Castle
Ardtornish, Lochaber, Highland.
2½ miles south-east of Claggan off A884.

A ruined castle built in the 14th century on the brow of a cliff overlooking the sea and backed by yet more cliffs. For many hundreds of years the estate belonged to the Lords of the Isles.

Not open to the public.

Ardvreck Castle
Inchnadamph, by Lairg, Sutherland, Highland.
On A837 at Loch Assynt.

Perched on a rocky spur on the shores of Loch Assynt are the ruins of Ardvreck Castle. Built about 1591, the castle consisted of three storeys with a gable passage serving the upper window ports. The castle was the clan centre for the Macleods of Assynt, who owned this area. James Graham, Marquess of Montrose, after losing the battle of Carbisdale, gave himself up to the Macleods of

Assynt at Ardvreck Castle. He was handed over to the Covenanter authorities in Edinburgh, tried, hanged and his body dismembered and displayed in public. Ardvreck Castle was subsequently destroyed in 1672, during a raid by the Mackenzies.

Not open to the public.

Armadale Castle
Sleat, Isle of Skye, Highland.
Less than 1 mile from Armadale pier, on A851.

The castle looks over the Sound of Sleat, from Skye to Knoydart on the mainland of Scotland. It was built in 1815 by Gillespie Graham for Lord Macdonald of Sleat. The castle, now a stabilised ruin, was in the neo-Gothic style and served for many years as the seat of the High Chief of the Clan Donald and is now the focal point of the Clan Donald Centre. The cottage end of the castle has been restored and houses a museum and theatre. There is a ferry service from Armadale to the mainland.

Open to the public all year, daily. Refreshments available.

Arnage Castle
Ellon, Aberdeen, Grampian.
4 miles north-east of Ellon off A948.

Arnage Castle is at the centre of the area of Aberdeenshire traditionally called the Buchan. Built by the Cheyne family in 1380, the castle is a good example of the work of Thomas Leiper, a master mason. The Cheyne family, who were of Norman origin, lived at Arnage until 1643. In 1702 the castle and its lands became part of the property of the Provost, John Ross. His family continued as lairds of Arnage until the mid-1930s.

The castle itself stands in wooded surroundings in the Vale of Ebrie, a tributary of the famous trout river the Ythan. The building is constructed on the conventional Z-plan with its towers at opposite ends to the main keep. A further wing was added in the 19th century.

Not open to the public.

Auchindoun Castle
Dufftown, Banff and Buchan, Grampian.
3 miles south-east of Dufftown on A941.

The castle dates from the late 15th century and is built on the L-plan tower style. The design is attributed to the Earl of Mar, James Cochrane. It stands on a bluff above the River Fiddich, famous for its malt whisky distilleries, and is visible from a great distance along the road from Cabrach. The present building is surrounded by prehistoric earthworks of unknown origin. Auchindoun Castle was held for many years by members of the

Gordon clan, who aroused the hatred of the Mackintoshes to such an extent that they eventually defied the stronger Gordon clan and set fire to the castle. Nearby is the site of the Battle of Carron where, in 1010, King Malcolm II routed an army of Scandinavian invaders.

Not open to the public.

Auchterarder Castle
Auchterarder, Perth and Kinross, Tayside.
12 miles south-west of Perth on A9.

Built in the 11th century, the castle stands just north of the town. The only sections of the building still remaining today are the donjon keep and its surrounding moat. Originally the seat of a royal barony, the castle was also a royal residence until Robert the Bruce gave the castle and the freedom of the burgh to Sir William Montefacts, who included it in the dowry of his daughter Marie when she married Sir John Drummond. The castle then passed into the family ownership of the Earls of Perth.

Several major points of Scottish history occurred in and around the castle: it was here that John Knox negotiated the Treaty of Perth in 1559—which granted the first official recognition of protestant-ism in Scotland—with Mary of Lorraine, widow of James V. In 1716 the Earl of Mar ordered the town of Auchterarder to be burnt, with several others in the district. This was to prevent shelter being taken by the Duke of Argyll and his troops; but it caused the local people such hardship that they would no longer agree to support the Jacobite cause. This is now a private house.

Not open to the public.

Ayr Castle
Kyle and Carrick, Strathclyde.
30 miles south of Glasgow on A77.

Nothing remains of the original stronghold, built by William the Lion in 1202. In the 12th century the church of St John was built in the centre of the town, but this, too, is much reduced. In 1652 Cromwell built a citadel which took in a large part of the structure of the church, and parts of the 17th-century walls remain. Little has been done to preserve or restore the site. At a much later date a tower was built in honour of the Scots patriot Sir William Wallace, and his statue may be seen today.

Not open to the public.

Ayton Castle
Ayton, Berwickshire, Borders.
7 miles north of Berwick-on-Tweed on A1, take the Ayton turn off. The castle entrance is in the village.

The most outstanding feature of the town of Ayton is its castle. This large red sandstone building was constructed in 1851 on the site of an older castle which was burnt down—accidentally—in 1834. The present building is in Victorian baronial style and according to local tradition was built with no plan, no architect and purely on the whims of the then owner. Because Ayton is the first centre one reaches on crossing the border from England to Scotland on the A1, the old castle had been a natural meeting place for envoys during the many wars between England and Scotland. The new castle is still privately owned and occupied.

Open to the public, May to September, Sundays, 2–5pm.

Balbegno Castle
Fettercairn, Kincardine and Deeside, Grampian.
13 miles north-east of Brechin off A94.

About 1 mile south of Fettercairn stands Balbegno Castle, built in 1570 in Gothic style by James Wood. It has a fine rib-vaulted hall and painted plaster severies (vaulted compartments) which are rare features of the tower houses of this period. The builder, James Wood, was a descendant of the famous Scottish seafarer Admiral Sir Andrew Wood, who is reputed to have defeated an English naval squadron in the Firth of Forth.

Not open to the public.

Balbithan Castle
Kintore, Aberdeen, Grampian.
12 miles north-west of Aberdeen off A96.

Balbithan Castle lies in a secluded glen on the bank of the River Don opposite the royal burgh of Kintore, and near the road from Inverurie to Hatton of Fintray. This lovely old turreted house was built by William Chalmers around 1560. Rumour has it that a cannon ball fired from the tower of Hallforest (on the far side of Kintore) fell in the courtyard of Old Balbithan, and the Chalmers laird was so furious that he vowed he would build a castle where 'neither friend nor foe would find him'. Major alterations and additions took place between 1600 and 1630.

Balbithan was plundered by Covenanter forces in 1640, and Montrose met here with his leaders during his northern campaigns, but the spot has few other notable historical associations.

Old Balbithan has disappeared completely. The new castle was built on the L-plan, and is one of the most interesting examples of the Scottish castle to be found today, as the basic plan has been extended and includes a projecting wing or jamb of unusual proportions. In 1860 the whole roof was lowered by one storey.

Balbithan is three storeys high with a possible earlier attic tucked under the roof. The ground floor consists mainly of kitchen, pantries and storage cellars, and the south wing, possibly the oldest part of the building, contains a spiral service stair and mural chambers. In this end of the building is a 'garden room' which may have been the servants' hall but which has since been made into one of the most attractive rooms in the house. Beyond it a narrow service stair leads up within the wall to the great hall, which is now a library and which has at some stage been partitioned to make an extra bedroom. There are wall chambers in both rooms and an aumbry in the wall just beyond the library door. The second floor, containing 'the new drawing room'—which was later made into three bedrooms and is now again a long gallery—has been altered a great deal over the years. At some period the ceilings were all raised by two feet but unfortunately no plans or documents can be found to solve the mystery of when and why the height of the roof was changed.

The Chalmers family sold Balbithan in 1690 and from then on it was mostly owned by Gordons until 1864. On the death in that year of the last heir entail, Mr Benjamin Abernethy Gordon, it was sold to the Earl of Kintore and became a part of the Keithhall Estate. The present owner, Mrs N. McMurtrie, has taken great pains with the programme of restoration and preservation.

Open strictly by appointment.

Balfluig Castle
Alford, Aberdeen, Grampian.
25 miles from Aberdeen off A944.

Built around 1556 on account of the unsettled state of the surrounding country, Balfluig is the seat of the Forbes barony of Alford, and above its main door can be seen the date of its construction. The present owner, Mr Mark Tennant, restored the castle in 1968.

Not open to the public.

Balgonie Castle
by Markinch, Fife.
4 miles north of Kirkcaldy off B921.

The castle stands on the precipitous south bank of the River Leven, 1 mile south-east of Markinch. The tower was probably built during the latter half of the 14th century. The castle was enlarged by several of the lairds from 1496 to 1702. Today the tower is still inhabited. Balgonie was the home of Field-Marshal Sir Alexander Leslie (first Earl of Leven) Lord General of the Scottish Covenanting Army. In 1716 the castle was occupied by Rob Roy McGregor and 200 clansmen. The castle is undergoing major restoration.

Open to the public, all year, Thursday to Sunday 2–5pm or by appointment.

Ballindalloch Castle
Ballindalloch, Moray, Grampian.
13 miles north-east of Grantown-on-Spey on A95.

The castle is one of Scotland's most romantic, set in the magnificent surroundings of the Spey valley. It is one of the most outstanding examples of baronial architecture in northern Scotland and was probably constructed in the 16th century but the exact date of origin is unknown. The earliest date known is 1546, carved on a stone lintel in one of the bedrooms. The castle was built on the traditional Z-plan and its most unusual and interesting feature is the original front entrance which was cleverly designed to fill a space between the steep rock face and the end of the retaining wall of the bridge over the river. In the 17th century, the caphouse and water tower were added, with a further two wings being built on in the 19th century.

Open to the public, May to September, Sundays only 2–4pm.

Balloch Castle
Balloch, Dumbarton, Strathclyde.
15 miles north-west of Glasgow.

Balloch Castle, sometimes known as the Castle in the Park, was built about 1800 from a design by Lugar for John Buchan of Ardoch, who owned Balloch. In 1830 it passed to Gibson Scott, who improved the grounds; and its was later taken over by A. J. Denniston Brown, great-grandson of a Provost of Glasgow, John Brown.

The building overlooks Loch Lomond, and has been owned since 1915 by the Glasgow Corporation, who set aside 200 acres as public park for the citizens of Glasgow and retained the beautiful gardens laid out by the original owners.

The actual castle is not open to the public.

Balmoral Castle
Crathie, Kincardine and Deeside, Grampian.
8 miles north-west of Ballater on A93.

A private residence of Her Majesty the Queen, used by the Royal Family as a summer holiday estate.

The early medieval fortified manor on the site was called Kindrochit, and was a favourite hunting lodge of King Robert II. In 1390 Sir Malcolm Drummond was given royal permission to erect a tower at Kindrochit. The estate passed into the hands of the Earls of Huntly, and appears again in the records of 1484. At this date a tax return was made for the estate 'Bouchmorale', as it was then called. The Gordons of Huntly kept the castle in their hands until 1662 when it passed to the Farquharsons of Inverey, who in turn sold it to clear a bankrupt estate in 1798.

Queen Victoria's attention was first drawn to Balmoral when John Clark, the son of her doctor Sir James Clark, visited Sir Robert Gordon, then the owner, around 1845. At this time the Royal family holidayed at Ardverikie on Loch Laggan, where they were bored by what seemed to be perpetual rain. On hearing the glowing reports of Balmoral, the family obtained a tenancy on the estate when Sir Robert Gordon died suddenly. The Prince Consort, Prince Albert, finally bought the estate in 1852 for £31,000, and during the next four years William Smith of Aberdeen was employed to rebuild the castle in white granite as a typical castellated Scottish baronial mansion.

The dominating feature is still a square tower rising to 80 feet, topped by a round turret. The largest room is the ballroom, on a lower level than the rest of the building. The castle is designed to accommodate eighty-four people. Balmoral is situated against a magnificent backdrop of wooded hills rising towards mountains over 3,000 feet high.

Gardens, grounds and exhibition in the castle ballroom are open to the public, May, June and July, Monday to Saturday 10am–5pm. Refreshments available.

Balvaird Castle
Strathmiglo, Fife.
6 miles south-east of Bridge of Garn off A91.

The castle lies in the valley of the River Eden a short distance north-west of the village of Strathmiglo, part of which is known as the 'temple-lands', having belonged originally to the Knights Templar and later to the Knights of St John. The castle is reputed to have been built in the reign of James V. It was built on a 15th-century L-plan, with certain improvements over a normal castle of this type— these being a larger than normal keep and a square stair tower, two features usually only found in L-plan castles built in the 16th century. Some of the more outstanding features of the castle are the particularly fine fireplace in the hall; three large windows with stone seats; and aumbries or cupboards carved in the Gothic style to store (or display when opened) plate, silver and other valuables. The decoration of the castle was probably enriched originally with gilt and colourwork in the form of heraldic devices, but little sign of this remains today.

Visits by appointment only.

Balvaird Castle

Balvenie Castle

Dufftown, Moray, Grampian.
Off A941 to Craigellachie and close to the station.

The castle stands above Dufftown and the River Fiddich, and is believed at one time to have been called Mortlach Castle, *c.* 1296. Built in the 13th century, it is one of the oldest examples of a stone castle in these parts. It consisted of a quadrangular court measuring 150 by 130 feet, surrounded by high walls with towers at the west and north corners, and probably one at the east where the 16th-century round tower now stands. The castle was protected by a wide ditch 30 or 40 feet out from the walls, and part of this fosse still remain on the south-west and north-west sides. The north-east side was altered from the original 13th-century plan, probably during the 16th century, when the fosse was replaced by a cultivation terrace.

Balvenie, like so many other Scottish castles, has been changed and added to over the years. Originally the living rooms were at the north-west and south-east sides of the courtyard, made of wood and stone and obviously burnt down at some stage. Repairs to these probably took place in the late 14th and early 15th centuries, and at the same time stone vaults were added. In the 16th century the northern half of the main building was demolished and rebuilt to suit the family better. This final alteration by John Stewart, the fourth Earl of Atholl, changed the building from a stern fortalice to a stately dwelling with enclosed court-yard; but the evidence of split and blistered freestone shows that once again the castle was destroyed by fire.

Looking at the castle from the outside, the two building periods are clearly visible. The well-proportioned round tower of Atholl illustrates fine mouldings and detailed stone-work—proof of the local mason's skill. The building was on three storeys with an attic above, and the windows in this section are of particular interest. Each of those on the second floor has a corbelled bow-shaped sill and all were built with moulded canopied lintels. The windows are also glazed with leaded lights in the upper part and an oak transom and shutter below, and had wrought iron grilles for protection. At the corner of the building is the round tower with its conical roof of slate, while the rest of the façade is covered with a steep pitched roof terminating in gables at the end of the building. Near the top of the wall are panels which held three coats of arms. These included the Royal Arms, the arms of John Stewart, and the Earl's coat of arms impaled with those of his wife, Lady Elizabeth Gordon, daughter of George, fourth Earl of Huntly.

On both sides of the arched entrance doorway of this building are gun loops set within splayed mouths. These are let into the wall at intervals and are typical defensive features of the period. The older part of the front facade incorporates part of the wall of the first period building, with later work, probably dating from the early 15th century, above it. The south-west gable shows signs of having had a tall gable chimney and also on this side at first floor level is evidence of a projecting garderobe of an earlier date. The arched entrance doorway and the doorways at the entrances from the courtyard to the two stair towers are all intricately moulded and carved. At the front of the main entrance is a strong double-leafed yett or grille of wrought iron, the only one of its kind remaining in Scotland, while the arched pend of this entry includes stone benches and has a small vaulted guardroom opening off it.

The main building with its two prominent round stair towers is probably the most imposing section of the building when seen from the outside. Inside the Stewart building there are four vaulted apart-ments at ground level including the hall, with-drawing room, a room in the tower and a fourth in the angle between the stair tower and curtain wall. Each room has a fireplace and mural garderobe, and three of them are lighted by small high windows set in the outside walls with gun loops at a lower level. A small wheel stair joins the tower room with the vaulted cellar below.

The second floor and attic were designed as private rooms and extra bedrooms were situated in the upper floors of the older part of the main building. In the 15th century, the kitchen buildings were against the south-west curtain wall and the ruin of the kitchen fireplace flue is still there today on the inner face of the curtain. The fireplace seems to have had a double arch and within its recess was an oven, whilst a smaller oven stood in a small space to the south-east where one can still see the stone sink. Nearby was the brew house with its brew cauldron, and to the north-west of the kitchen a stairway led to the first floor of the buildings on the north-west side of the close. In the 15th century this section of the castle as well as the main building was altered and parts demol-ished. Three vaulted cellars were made with a hall above them, and at the same time the upper part of the enceinte wall was rebuilt around the well. Balvenie Castle passed into the hands of the Douglas family at an unknown date, although authentic references in the early 15th century mention James Douglas, second son of the third Earl and later seventh Earl of Douglas, first of Avondale and Lord Balvenie, as owner. When he died in 1440 he was succeeded by his son William, who was fatally stabbed in the Castle of Stirling by James II, 12 years later. His brother James, ninth Earl of Douglas, set out to avenge the murder and after a brief reconciliation with the King returned to open rebellion. In 1455, 'The Black Douglases' were defeated at Arkinholm, and forfeited their estates to the Crown. These included Balvenie, which was then placed in the care of Patrick Lyon, Lord Glamis. Four years later John Stewart, afterwards first Earl of Atholl, was given the castle on condition that 'one red rose was to be rendered, if demanded, at the principal seat of the Atholl family on St John the Baptist's day'. A century later the custom still continued—although payment had been increased to two red roses.

The castle remained in the hands of the Stewart Earls of Atholl until the 17th century, and during this time they added the handsome building to the south-east side of the site. In 1595 John, fifth Earl of Atholl, died and in 1610 his four daughters gave up their interest in the estates to the Crown. The castle then became the property of James, Lord Innermeath, second Earl of Atholl, but not for long; during the next 5 years it was acquired first by John, eighth Lord Saltoun, then by Sir James Stewart of Killeith, afterwards Lord Ochiltree, and then by Robert Innes of Innermarkie. Robert Innes had a difficult time during the next few years defending himself against his unruly neighbour, but his ability was obviously recognised for in 1628 he was made a baronet of Nova Scotia.

Balvenie Castle was often the scene of fighting during the 17th century. In 1635 the district was continuously under attack by the Macgregors and in 1644, after the Battle of Fyvie, the Marquis of Montrose marched to Balvenie to allow his men a few days rest out of reach of Argyll's cavalry. Five years later a band of Royalists was defeated at Balvenie; eighty men were killed and nearly 900 taken as prisoners. Among them was probably Sir Walter Innes, the owner of the castle.

In 1658 Balvenie had to be sold to Colonel Sutherland of Kinminity in order to pay the heavy debts incurred by the Innes family during the Civil War. Later, Arthur Forbes claimed the lordship of Balvenie but his claim was not recognised for some time, and because of his high-handed actions he was put in the Tolbooth prison in Edinburgh. On his release Forbes met Alexander Duff of Branco, whom he employed at his agent. At the same time this cunning man bought up many of the Forbes debts and finally took possession of Balvenie himself in 1687, although legal settlement was not completed until 1743.

In 1715 William Duff, who succeeded his father and who lived at Balvenie, was enlisted to prevent the 'High and Low Countrie Jacobites' from joining forces. Duff refused, but wrote 'I shall maintain the castle against the rebels, and not quit it but with my life'. Duff was subsequently suspected of treachery because of his action—or inaction—but there is no proof of this. He left to serve in the army of Prince Eugene of Hungary, and on his return in 1718 he killed himself. The estate passed to the Crown once more and was bought by William Duff of Dipple, the uncle and heir of the late William. In 1722 he died, leaving the castle to his son, another William, who later became Lord Branco and then Earl of Fife.

In 1928 the trustees handed over the castle to the predecessors of Historic Buildings and Monuments, Scottish Development Department.

Open to the public, every day, 24 March to 30 September, weekdays 9.30am–7pm, Sundays 2–7pm.

Bamff Castle
Alyth, Perth and Kinross, Tayside.
Off A926.

Now called Bamff House, it is the family seat of the Ramsays who have held it since 1232. This castle lies 3 miles out of Alyth. It consists of a fortified tower, dating back to 1585, and various further additions which date from the 18th century.

Not open to the public.

Barcaldine Castle
Benderloch, Argyll, Strathclyde.
15 miles north of Oban on A82.

The castle lies to the south-west of the township of Barcaldine, and from it there is an excellent view over Loch Creran. It was built in the late 16th century by Duncan Campbell of Glenorchy, in the baronial style and in a position particularly well-suited to defence. The building remained the property of the Campbells of Barcaldine until 1842 when it was sold; it was later bought back, as a roofless castle, by the family and restored to its former glory during the period 1896 to 1910. The castle today is still the seat of the Campbell baronets of Barcaldine and is occupied by the family.

Open to the public by appointment only.

Barholm Castle
Barholm, Gatehouse-of-Fleet, Castle Douglas, Stewartry, Dumfries and Galloway.
10 miles south-east of Newton Stewart on A75.

This roofless tower castle stands in a striking position among farm lands and above the coastal road overlooking the sea. It was built in the 16th century, around 1570, and its main claim to historical fame is that for a short while John Knox, the Protestant reformer, hid here.

Not open to the public.

Barra Castle

Old Meldrum, Aberdeen, Grampian.
Off A981 about a mile south-west of the road to Inverurie.

The castle stands immediately west of Barra Hill, site of Robert the Bruce's famous victory in 1307 over the Comyns under the Earl of Buchan, his traditional enemy.

The castle itself is a 17th-century stone mansion with a second wing which was added later in the mid-Georgian period. The buildings are on three sides of a square, the fourth side of which is closed by a wall carrying decorative stone vases. Barra Castle today is the home of the Irvine family of Drum who are related to the Ramsays of Barra and who were responsible for adding the new wing in 1755 and completing the present rather complicated but elegant castle.

Open by appointment only.

Beaufort Castle

Beauly, Inverness, Highland.
4 miles south-west of Beauly off A831 and A833.

The existing Beaufort Castle was built in typical baronial style in about 1880. Prior to this there had been a much older castle on the same site; Castle Dounie, built about 1400. This was destroyed by the Duke of Cumberland in 1746 as part of his pacification programme in the Highlands after his victory over Bonnie Prince Charlie at Culloden; but there are still ruins in the terraced garden of the present Beaufort Castle which were part of the original building.

Beaufort Castle itself has suffered many mishaps, and in 1936 was badly damaged by fire and then rebuilt with the addition of a new wing. Both buildings have been the seat of the Frasers of Lovat, many of whom have been famous in Scottish and British history. Simon, Lord Lovat, an extra-ordinary character remembered for his political changes of course, was finally executed on Tower Hill in 1747 for his support and participation in the Jacobite rising of 1745. He is still affectionately remembered in Scotland for his last words in reply to a Cockney woman, who screamed from the crowd watching him on his way to the gallows 'You'll get that nasty head of yours chopped off, you ugly old Scotch dog!'—'I believe I shall, you ugly old English bitch!'. The present Lord Lovat was a famous leader of commando troops in the Second World War.

Not open to the public.

Benholm Castle

Inverbervie, Kincardine and Deeside, Grampian.
Near Inverbervie off A92.

Benholm Castle is basically a 15th-century tower built on the classical tower form and crowned with a parapet and angle bartizans. The modern mansion was added comparatively recently.

Formerly the stronghold of the Keiths, Earls of Marischal, the castle was the site of a famous jewel theft which took place in 1620; the unlikely culprit turned out to be the widowed countess of the fifth Earl of Keith.

Not open to the public.

Black Castle

Moulin, Pitlochry, Perth and Kinross, Tayside.
24 miles north of Perth on A9.

The ruins of Black Castle stand to the east of the picturesque village of Moulin above Pitlochry. It was built by a nephew of Robert the Bruce, Sir John Campbell of Loch Lochow, in 1320. The castle is said to have stood in a very strong defensive position originally, in the middle of a shallow lake and joined to the mainland by a stone causeway. The ruins show a rectangular layout and evidence of corner drum towers.

Not open to the public.

Blackness Castle

Blackness, West Lothian, Lothian.
On the south shore of the Firth of Forth, 15 miles west of Edinburgh off A904.

The castle stands on an outcrop of rock and dominates the village of the same name on the south shore of the Firth of Forth.

In medieval times Blackness was a notable port, due to the fact that the royal burgh of Linlithgow was so near. Although there is no mention of the castle until the 15th century, the Viponts had owned the area since before 1200. In the 15th century George Crichton owned these lands, but during the minority of James II the Douglases seized the castle for a short while until the Crichtons recovered it once more. In 1452 Sir George Crichton was Governor of Stirling Castle and was later made Earl of Caithness, but for some reason appears to have resigned his estates in the following year. His son, James Crichton, was so furious at the loss of his inheritance that he took Blackness Castle and imprisoned his father until forced to surrender by the king. From this time the lands by Blackness became a part of the Queen's jointure until 1465, and the castle was often used as a prison. In 1543 Cardinal Beaton was imprisoned here, and in 1544 the Earl of Angus. Blackness was handed over to the French in 1548 when they arrived to help the Scots; when Mary, Queen of Scots fled to England in 1568 the castle held out for her at first, but Alexander Stewart, the Captain, eventually joined the Regent and gave up the castle. In about 1600 the captaincy passed from the Stewarts to the

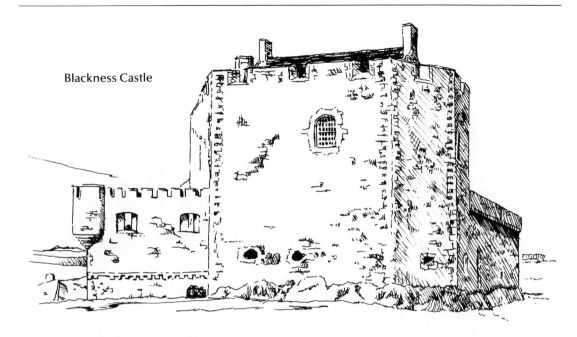

Blackness Castle

Livingstons, who held the castle for over a century until it was captured by General Monk in 1654.

During the 18th century the castle was occupied by a small garrison of troops and in the 19th century it was used to hold powder and stores. Since then the castle has been handed over to the care of the Government, who have restored it to its 17th-century outline. The main doorway to the castle is fitted with an iron yett, and behind this a passage leads to the kitchen and vaulted gun chambers on the lower floors and a large hall on the second floor. Around the castle is a 16th-century barmkin wall which was widened and strengthened internally during the 17th century to make space for a gun platform to the east. Around the courtyard were the usual lean-to buildings including barracks, stables and brewhouse, and in the centre is the 'main mast' tower. This is the oldest part of the castle and dates from the 15th century. Later, around 1667, a turnpike was added at the north-east corner so that the tower could be used as a prison. One horror of Blackness Castle is the pit prison beneath the tower chamber; this feebly lit and miserable hole contains a drain which was cleansed by the tide.

Open to the public, April to September, weekdays 9.30am–7pm, Sundays 2–7pm; October to March, weekdays 9.30am–4pm, Sundays 2–4pm.

Blair Castle
Blair Atholl, Perth and Kinross, Tayside.
Situated at Blair Atholl on A9.

The castle stands at the confluence of the fast-flowing Tilt and Garry rivers in countryside re-nowned for its beauty. Within sight of the castle the scenery changes from grassy valleys to wooded hillsides blending into precipitous rock faces, and culminating in the summit of Ben-y-Gloe at 3,671 feet.

The baronial castle was built in 1269 when David Strathbogie, Earl of Atholl, returned from the Crusades to find that his neighbour, John Comyn, had begun to build a castle nearby. The oldest part of the castle still standing is called 'Cummings' tower and probably dates from the original building.

The castle has been altered considerably over the years; in 1530 the third Earl added a large hall with vaulted rooms beneath it, and in 1652 the castle was captured and damaged by Cromwell's troops which led to a great wave of renovation, rebuilding and alteration.

In 1703, Queen Anne made the second Marquis a Duke, which led to more renovations and additions to keep up social appearances. In 1745 more damage and violence occurred when the Jacobites, led by Bonnie Prince Charlie, occupied the castle. In the following year, while the castle was occupied by government troops, a younger brother of the Duke, who was a Jacobite sympathiser, laid siege to the castle, making Blair Atholl the last castle in the British Isles ever to be besieged. Because of the damage caused by these events the second Duke, as an act of humility to the Sovereign, docked the castle of its battlements and two storeys, turning it into a plain white house. In 1872 the architect David Bryce restored it in full baronial style, adding the front entrance.

The interior is still decorated in sumptuous 18th-century style and the rooms are furnished with

Blair Castle

extremely fine examples of the period including outstanding pieces of Chippendale and Sheraton craftsmanship. There is on display a collection of Sevres porcelain, and paintings by well-known artists of the period, such as Lely and Zoffany. Certain rooms hold collections of weapons and armour illustrating the various periods of history and military campaigns, and in all, thirty-two rooms are open to the public. This particularly fine example of a Scottish castle is still inhabited by the Duke, who retains the only private army in the British Isles today, the Atholl Highlanders.

Open to the public, Easter week, Sunday and Monday in April, every day from 3rd Sunday in April until 2nd Sunday in October, Monday to Saturday 10am–6pm, Sundays 2–6pm. Refreshments available.

Boghall Castle
Boghall Farm, Biggar, Lanark, Strathclyde. 28 miles south-east of Edinburgh on A702.

The castle was situated to the south of the town in marshland, but only a small part of it remains. It was at one time the seat of the Fleming family, protectors of the burgh of Biggar.

Open to the public by arrangement with the farmer.

Borthwick Castle
Midlothian, Lothian. 10 miles south of Edinburgh on A7.

Set in a picturesque valley, the castle is protected on three sides by the Gores and North Middleton waters. The south side was originally guarded by curtain walls with flanking towers, but only one of these remains and now serves as the gate-house.

The castle was built by the first Lord Borthwick in 1430 and is a particularly good example of the tower-house design. It stands today, complete and virtually unaltered, never having been added to since it was first erected. Borthwick Castle is still considered by experts to be at least a hundred years in advance of its contemporaries in design. The main tower stands over 100 feet high and the walls are 12 to 14 feet thick. The living quarters of the castle, the kitchen, great hall and solar, are on the first floor. Above these are three floors of other private rooms and beneath the great hall are vaulted storage chambers.

Borthwick Castle owes its good state of repair to the fact that it generally escaped the ordeals of siege warfare except when, in 1650, Cromwell laid siege and bombarded the castle with his cannon. The damage was only slight and led to the only rebuilding in the castle's history. Borthwick was visited by Mary, Queen of Scots and her third husband Bothwell in 1567. They were blockaded here by Morton and the rebel lords but the pair escaped separately, Mary disguised as a boy.

During the Second World War the castle was the repository of the official public records of Scotland, but it is still owned by the Borthwick family.

Not open to the public.

Bothwell Castle
Bothwell, Lanark, Strathclyde.
9 miles south-east of Glasgow near Motherwell.

The castle stands a mile to the west of the old Bothwell Bridge over the Clyde—the only span of the river until 300 years ago. This area of Strathclyde is steeped in history; the Romans used the valley as a means of approaching the west end of their wall, and at Uddingston nearby, Bronze Age urns were discovered.

It was built in the 13th century by the family de Moravia, later Murray, and is one of the largest and finest stone castles in Scotland, with a handsome round stone keep. The walls are upward of 15 feet thick in many parts, and over 60 feet high in the sections facing the river. Due to its position, size, and strength the castle has been involved in many of the major events of Scottish history, particularly in the struggles for independence. When John de Baliol was defeated Bothwell Castle was held by Stephen de Brampton for Edward I, and in 1298–99 was besieged by the Scots continuously for more than 14 months. In 1301 Edward I recaptured the castle once more with an army of 6,800 men, necessitating the building of a bridge across the Clyde 'for the passage of the army'. After its capture the castle became the headquarters of the Earl of Pembroke, Aymer de Valence, Warden of Scotland, who gave his name to the 'Valence' tower.

In 1336, while the English were occupying the castle, a period of restoration took place and Edward III made Bothwell his headquarters for a month or so. The castle was occupied by the English for a second period in 1337 but Sir Andrew de Moray, the Warden of Scotland, to whom the castle belonged, recaptured it after a short siege. He then demolished the building in accordance with Bruce's famous 'Testament' which urged the Scots to destroy their castles and rely on a 'scorched earth' policy to defend their lands. Bothwell Castle apparently lay derelict until about 1362 when the barony was acquired by 'Black Archibald the Grim', third Earl of Douglas and Lord of Galloway. It became his favourite seat, and a second restoration was begun. After this the castle settled into a more peaceful period and in 1455 reverted to the Crown on the forfeiture of the 'Black Douglases'. It was given to James, second Lord Crichton, but

his son William again forfeited the castle in 1484 and it was then granted to Sir John Ramsay of Balmain by James III. Once again the castle changed hands and was bestowed on Patrick Hepburn, Lord Hailes, who in turn exchanged it for the barony of Hermitage in 1492. Thus Bothwell passed into the hands of the 'Red Douglases'; and in 1584 the Countess of Angus, who was living at the castle, was ordered to surrender it because of her nephew's connection with the rebellion.

In 1669 Bothwell was taken over by Archibald Douglas, first Earl of Forfar who towards the end of the century extended the castle by building a Palladian-style mansion to the east of the castle. This mansion was demolished in 1926. Lord Forfar pulled down a part of the original castle in order to build the mansion and it was only completed much later by the second Earl, who died at Sheriffmuir in 1715. He was the last of the Douglas line, and after a famous law-suit the title of Baron Douglas of Douglas was awarded to Archibald Stewart, son of Sir John Stewart of Grantully and Lady Jane Douglas, a sister of the first Duke of Douglas. The estates finally devolved on the Countess of Home, and although the ruined castle still belongs to the Earl of Home, in 1935 it was placed in the care of the predecessors of Historic Buildings and Monuments, Scottish Development Department for safekeeping. It has since been repaired and the serious damage threatened by nearby coal mines halted.

Bothwell Castle is built round a large rectangular courtyard enclosure bounded at the west end by a mighty donjon or keep with its own moat. The courtyard is surrounded with a curtain wall defended on the south side by four towers and with an entrance on the north side. With the walls were many buildings, including a hall and chapel. However, only the foundations of the large square tower at the north-east corner survive in today's ruins, with portions of the west and south walls. The great circular donjon has been deliberately wrecked at some stage and one half thrown into the Clyde.

The demolition and restoration of Bothwell is very clear in the west curtain where the part that adjoins the donjon is original work up to the line of buttresses against and upon which the rebuilding has been based. On the donjon's south side there is some primary work still left, consisting of the curtain wall with the prison tower attached and a postern beyond this. From this point the long south curtain is all of a later date. All the buildings so far mentioned were built in the 13th century and make up one of the grandest pieces of secular architecture surviving in Scotland from the Middle Ages, and equal to the best contemporary work in England and France.

Bothwell Castle is still much of a puzzle from the point of view of dating the rebuilding and additions made to the basic 13th-century plan. Apparently the only parts of the original scheme that were completed were the donjon and south-west curtain or wing wall, including the prison tower and postern. Here the work stopped around the time of the Wars of Independence, until it was later restored once again.

The donjon tower—one of the finest pieces of castellar construction in Scotland—was originally 65 feet in diameter with a surrounding moat partly hewn out of live rock, 25 feet in breadth and over 15 feet deep. The entrance to the donjon was through a fine pointed doorway reached by a timber bridge across the moat, with drawbridge connections at the inner end. Behind the donjon drawbridge was a portcullis or yett and then a zig-zag passage leading to the lord's hall. This had a wooden floor, moulded with wall-ribs, suggesting a wooden vault on the lines of a chapter house. To the left of the hall entrance is a doorway onto a spiral staircase to the basement below and the rooms above. The staircase is sited in this position so that anyone wanting to go in or out of the donjon would be visible as he passed through the hall. The basement was used for storage and contained a 20 foot well. Above the hall were two unvaulted storeys including latrines and a passage which led to the prison tower.

As this castle was used both in times of war and peace, it was designed with an eye to convenience as well as defence. The basement was the store, then came the lord's hall with the retainers' hall or garrison on the next floor. Topping it all were the lord's private rooms. These were connected to the prison tower by a fighting deck and external tower so that the lord could escape in times of trouble.

Open to the public, all year, Saturday to Wednesday, Summer 9.30am–7pm, Sundays 2–7pm; Winter 9.30am–4pm, Sundays 2–4pm. Closed 25 and 26 December and 1 and 2 January, Thursday and Friday.

Boyne Castle
Whitehills, Banff and Buchan, Grampian.
East of Portsoy off B9139.

The ruined Boyne Castle stands near the village port of Whitehills in fertile farming land overlooking the east coast of Banff. To all appearances it would seem a typical medieval courtyard fortress, but in fact it was built in the late 16th century and is described as a 'sham' castle. Originally equipped as a fortified establishment for defence by firearms, it comprises an oblong courtyard surrounded by 5-foot thick stone walls with four round towers, one at each corner. Along the front face is a large ditch, while the main entrance consists of a raised and walled causeway defended by two drum towers.

Open by appointment.

Braemar Castle

Braemar Castle
Braemar, Kincardine and Deeside, Grampian.
½ mile north-east of Braemar on A93.

The castle stands on a hill above the Dee; it is a five-storeyed L-plan tower house built by the Earl of Mar, John Erskine, in 1628. It was designed ostensibly as a hunting lodge, but probably also served as a sign of power and prosperity to counterbalance the growing threat of the Farquharsons. Its main features include a round central tower, spiral staircase, unusual star-shaped defensive curtain wall, barrel-vaulted ceilings, massive iron yett and underground pit prison.

In 1689, during the Claverhouse campaign, the castle of Braemar was seized and burnt by the celebrated 'Black Colonel', John Farquharson of Inverey, and it stood for about 50 years as a burnt-out shell. It was later rebuilt by the Government and garrisoned with English troops to keep the Highlands in check. The garrison added ramparts in the above-mentioned star-shape, the latest type of layout for an artillery fort, developed by the famous French military engineer, Vauban.

Inside the castle one can see the dungeons and living rooms, the walls of which are covered with graffiti carved by bored English soldiers. At an even later date the present 'gingerbread' battlements were added when the turrets were raised a storey higher.

The castle still belongs today to the Farquharsons of Invercauld.

Open to the public, May to 1st Monday in October, Saturday to Thursday 10am–6pm.

Brechin Castle
Brechin, Angus, Tayside.
10 miles north-west of Forfar on A94.

Brechin Castle is situated not far from the cathedral and dates from the 13th century, when it was an extremely well fortified stone building designed on the same lines as Bothwell Castle. It probably originally comprised a round stone keep and high straight walls with corner turrets, but was rebuilt in 1711 by the Earl of Dalhousie. His descendant, the current Earl, still lives at the castle today. Both of them were descended from Sir Thomas Maule, who is famous for his heroic defence of the castle against Edward I of England in 1303.

Not open to the public.

Brodick Castle
Brodick, Isle of Arran, Strathclyde.
1½ miles from Brodick pier on A841.

The original structure dated from the time of the Norse occupation of the island, but of the existing castle only the north wing dates from the 14th century, with further additions in the 19th century. Brodick Castle was built mainly in the classic L-plan style and in the ancient seat of the Dukes of Hamilton. It was occupied for a time by Cromwell's troops in the 17th century. The last private owner was Mary, Duchess of Montrose, daughter of the twelfth Duke of Hamilton. On her death in 1957 the castle and its 600 acres of estate passed into the hands of the National Trust for Scotland. Visitors to the castle will find excellent collections of silver, porcelain and paintings, all family heirlooms of the Dukes of Hamilton.

A National Trust for Scotland property.

Open to the public, Easter to September, daily, castle 1–5pm, gardens 10am–dusk. Refreshments available.

Brodie Castle
Forres, Moray, Grampian.
4 miles west of Forres on A96.

The castle lies north of the village of Brodie and is the traditional seat of the Brodie of Brodie, whose family have owned the surrounding land since the mid 11th century. The castle itself dates from the 15th century with additions in the 16th century, and is built on the tower house plan. In 1645 it was burnt down by Lord Gordon, while he was leading part of the Marquis of Montrose's northern campaign for Charles I. Parts of the building survived and were rebuilt, with a further addition being made in 1840.

The castle is today the home of a fine private collection of Dutch, Flemish and English paintings. A particular point of interest about Brodie Castle is that it is the seat of one of the oldest untitled landed families in the United Kingdom, the head of which is addressed simply as 'Brodie' without any prefix or title.

A National Trust for Scotland property.

Open to the public, Easter weekend and May to September, every day, 11am–6pm, Sundays 2–6pm. Refreshments available.

Broughty Castle
Dundee, Angus, Tayside.
2 miles from Dundee off A92.

Situated in the once-wealthy jute producing district of Scotland around Broughty Ferry, a suburb of Dundee, lies Broughty Castle. In 1454 the fourth Earl of Angus was granted permission to build a 'fortalice', and in 1490 Lord Gray was allowed to extend this into the castle and fortress of Broughty Castle. Since then the castle has changed hands many times. In 1547 it was captured by the English fleet under Sir Andrew Dudley after the Battle of Pinkie, near Musselburgh, and in 1550 it was recaptured by the Scots with help from the French. Just over a century later, in 1651, the castle was captured once again, this time by General Monk, before he stormed Dundee. It was then left abandoned, for in 1787 Robert Burns mentioned the ruins of 'Broughty Castle' in his diary. In 1855 the castle was bought for £1,500 by the War Office and reconstructed as a coastal fort by Robert Rouand Anderson; and in 1969 the tower house was opened as a Branch Museum by Dundee Corporation, illustrating the past glories of the whaling industry.

Open to the public, all year, Monday to Thursday and Saturday 10am–1pm and 2–5pm, 1st Sunday July to last Sunday September, 2–5pm.

Buchanan Castle
Drymen, Stirling, Central.
At Drymen near the south end of Loch Lomond off A81.

Set in a glorious position on rising foothills over-looking Endrick Water as it approaches the foot of Loch Lomond, the castle is surrounded by remind-ers of history, and particularly of the famous Rob Roy MacGregor. In 1713 an unenthusiastic force of volunteers from Glasgow was sent here to find Rob Roy and collect the reward of £1,000 offered for his capture. The men had second thoughts about the venture, and fled rather than carry on with their searches. In 1716, Rob gathered 100 MacGregors and marched through the area on his way home to Inversnaid. On his way he stopped at Drymen and 'proclaimed the Pretender and tore the gauger's books'.

Though much reduced from its original size of over 100,000 acres, Buchanan estate is still very large. The 19th-century castle and the remains of the previous castle (destroyed by fire in 1850) together with the surrounding wooded park land laid out by 'Capability Brown', have now been swallowed up by the golf course. The original old House of Buchan, seat of the chiefs of that Ilk, was the site of the first castle. In 1682 the Grahams bought back the castle from the Laird of Buchan. The Marquis of Graham, son of the present Duke, still lives in the district.

Not open to the public.

Buittle Castle
Dalbeattie, Stewartry, Dumfries and Galloway.
¼ mile off A745 near Dalbeattie.

Although the present castle is only of 16th-century origin, it is built on the site of a much older structure where the ancient Celtic Lords of Galloway had their seat. In 1282 the heiress, Devorgilla, wife of the Norman noble John de Baliol, signed the charter to found Balliol College from the original castle. John de Baliol, known as 'Toom Tabard'

(empty coat) to his subjects when he became a vassal king of Scotland, was born here in 1249. 2½ miles north of Buittle Place is the 80-foot Mott of Urr, a well-preserved Saxon or early Norman artificial mound within a fortified enclosure.

Open to the public, every day, daylight hours.

Burleigh Castle
Milnathort, Perth and Kinross, Tayside.
Off M90 between Milnathort and Loch Leven on a side road.

The castle lies 1 mile east of the village of Milna-thort, of plaid-making renown, and dates from around 1500. The structure is roofless but still a fine example of the tower house plan, with an angled tower and a corbelled square cap house which was added in 1582.

The castle was the seat of the Balfours, and was given to the family by James II in the early 16th century. The property later passed into the hands of the Grahams of Kinross, and is mentioned by Sir Walter Scott in his novel *Old Mortality*.

Open to the public at all reasonable times.

Cadzow Castle
Hamilton, Lanark, Strathclyde.
Off A71 at Hamilton.

Set in the High Parks area to the south of the town of Hamilton, above the River Avon, the castle is surrounded by tall oak trees which are thought to have witnessed the rites of the Druids. During the 12th and 13th centuries the castle was the home of the Kings of Scotland, including David I. Later the castle seems to have been the property of the Comyn family, but during the reign of John de Baliol the lands fell once again into the hands of the Crown.

After the Battle of Bannockburn (1314) Robert the Bruce granted Cadzow to the Hamilton family, who built the present castle, which is now in ruins. This typical tower house of 1540 was erected for the then-Duke of Hamilton, who was also Duke of Chatelherault in France—a title granted by Henri II. His French associations gave Cadzow Castle a continental air, unusual in Scottish castles.

In 1570 the castle was besieged by Sir William Drury, commander of the English troops who was assisting Lennox in his fight against the Hamiltons and others of the Queen's friends. The Captain of the castle, Arthur Hamilton, refused to surrender for two days but eventually agreed on condition that the lives of the garrison were spared. In 1579 the castle was besieged again by Regent Morton's troops, and was dismantled and left as a ruin.

Open to the public all year round, 9 am–7 pm. Permits obtainable from the Estate Office, 18 Auchingramont Road, Hamilton.

Caerlaverock

Caerlaverock Castle
Bankend, Nithsdale, Dumfries and Galloway.
7 miles south-east of Dumfries on the B725.

Situated on a sloping shelf of sandstone overlooking the estuary of the River Nith, the general
appearance of the structure is one of stark desola-
tion. According to some sources the ruins of this
castle date from 1220, but the official guide suggests that a more likely date would be 1290.
Certainly there was a castle at Caerlaverock in 1299
though no-one knows by which side it was built. It
is generally agreed that because of its situation—
close to the shore of Solway and guarding a
landing-place—it was built as an English bridgehead
for the invasion of Scotland. In 1300 Edward I of
England laid siege and badly damaged the structure
and in a rhyming account of the siege, written in
French, there is a description of the castle buildings: 'In shape it was like a shield, for it had but
three sides round it, with a tower at each corner,
but one of them was a double one, so high, so long
and so wide, that the gate was underneath it, well
made and strong with a drawbridge and a suffi-
ciency of other defences. And it had good walls
and good ditches filled right up to the brim with
water. And I think you will never see a more finely
situated castle, for on the one side can be seen the
Irish Sea, towards the west, and the north the fair
moorland, surrounded by an arm of the sea, so
that no creature born can approach it on two sides
without putting himself in danger of the sea. On

the south side it is not easy for there are many
places difficult to get through because of woods
and marshes and ditches hollowed out by the sea
where it meets the river.'

This description fits the plan of the castle per-
fectly. It is three-sided in the shape of a shield of
1300, with a tower at each angle except at the north
where two towers flank the gateway. There is also
a wet moat and, to the south, several gullies, now
overgrown. Inside the castle are still some visible
remains of the original building. These are in the
gatehouse, the outside of the west tower up to
twelve courses of the parapet, and in the masonry
in the inside at the base of the eastern tower. It is
probable that Murdoch's Tower is also of this date
plus the first few courses of the curtain from this
tower to within about 20 feet of the gatehouse.

The English held Caerlaverock until 1312 by
which time Edward I, 'Hammer of the Scots', had
died and been succeeded by his son Edward II. At
this time Sir Eustace Maxwell was keeper of the
castle for the English, and he had a difficult task
keeping both English and Scots masters happy. In
1312 he was repaid a debt of £22 by the English
king, who thought this would gain his allegiance
but almost at once he declared for Robert the
Bruce, King of the Scots. The castle was instantly
besieged, but held out, and later Maxwell dismantled it on Bruce's orders—the Scots' policy
was to destroy buildings rather than leave them to
be taken over by the enemy at a later stage.

This was not the end of Caerlaverock's part in

the history of Scottish independence. In 1347, a year after the English victory over the Scots at Neville's Cross, Herbert Maxwell delivered hostages to the castle after submitting to the English king. In return he was given letters of protection for himself, his men and the castle. During this period a great deal of the present building was constructed. Murdoch's Tower was added, with probably the south-east tower and the curtain wall between them plus the west curtain for 20 feet south of the gatehouse.

According to the chronicles, in 1355 or 1356, Roger Kirkpatrick recaptured and wrecked the castle once more; but in another entry in the same chronicle, Roger was said to have been killed by James Lindsay 'at the castle of Caerlaverock'. We only know for sure that the castle was partially demolished, but not until after Roger Kirkpatrick's death. Lack of historical records suggests that after this the castle was deserted for at least two generations. This theory is supported by the existence of another fortfied medieval site a short way south, which seems to have been the residence of the lords of Caerlaverock after their main castle had been gutted.

It is presumed that Caerlaverock was used once more as a residence and fort by 1425 as Murdoch, Duke of Albany, who is said to have given his name to the Murdoch Tower, was imprisoned here. Certain types of masonry, including nearly square stones found in the central part of the west curtain as well as in the western tower of the gatehouse, are proof of rebuilding taking place in the 15th century. According to a historian of the Maxwells, the bartizan of Caerlaverock was completed around 1460 by Robert, second Lord Maxwell, who succeeded his father, the first Lord, in 1452. This is all quite possible as the bold machicolated parapets on the gatehouse, the parapet on Murdoch's Tower and the additions to the front and rear of the gatehouse to improve defence and add extra accommodation, all appear to be of 15th-century origin. The additions changed the gatehouse into a tower house and at the same time, or soon afterwards, a range of buildings was erected in the courtyard beside the west curtain to provide further accommodation.

During the 16th century the castle was at the centre of the troubles between England and Scotland. In 1542 James V was at the castle, but in 1545 it was surrendered peacefully to Henry VIII of England. It was later besieged and regained by the Scots. In 1570, the English are reputed to have been harrying the district and 'threw down' the castle. There is no sign of this destruction, but in 1593 Lord Maxwell made 'great fortifications and has many men working at his house', and it is likely that part of the work included the additions of the wide-mouthed gunports—a typical Scots method of using cannon in castles.

In 1607, despite Lord Maxwell's renovations, Caerlaverock Castle was described as a 'weak house of the Barons of Maxwell'. Nevertheless, Robert Maxwell, the first Earl of Nithsdale, added a fine new block of buildings in the Renaissance style beside the east curtain in around 1634. The Maxwells lived here peacefully until 1640 when, after a 13-week siege, the castle was handed over to a man named Finch. In the inventory for the furniture he counted eighty beds—proof of the splendour of the estate. The ruined castle was no longer habitable—and was left abandoned. It has passed by inheritance through the Herries family to the present Duke of Norfolk, the sixteenth, who placed it in the care of Historic Buildings and Monuments, Scottish Development Department.

Open to the public, every day, Summer 9.30am–7pm, Sundays 2–7pm; Winter 9.30am–4pm, Sundays 2–4pm.

Cairnbulg Castle
Fraserburgh, Aberdeen, Grampian.
Off A92 near Fraserburgh.

This castle stands on the right bank of the water of Philorth by a small copse, 2 miles east of Fraserburgh. Until recently there was some doubt as to the original construction date but recent discoveries have pointed to the castle being built by the Comyns, Earls of Buchan, around 1260. The lower portion of the original rectangular keep is of this period, but this was destroyed by Robert the Bruce during his campaign against the Buchans. Another theory is that the castle was built in 1380 by Sir Alexander Fraser and his wife Joanna, younger daughter of the Earl of Ross. However, it is known for certain that at some stage the Frasers of Philorth, the founders of Fraserburgh, owned the castle; they reconstructed the keep in the tower style, the main part of this structure being 70 feet high, with a smaller tower butting on to it. At a later stage, around 1545, a further round tower was built on to cope with the advent of gunfire in siege-craft. Separating this round tower lies the modern main section, extensively rebuilt in 1897 by Sir John Duthie, the old castle having been abandoned in 1799. Lord Saltoun, chief of the name of Fraser, bought back the castle in 1934.

Not open to the public.

Cakemuir Castle
Tynehead, Midlothian, Lothian.
15 miles south-east of Edinburgh off A68.

A building of 15th-century origin, built more as a residence than as a fortified structure, but retaining some military features: it is basically of tower house style, and there are guard positions on the parapet of the original structure. The main walls are over 6 feet thick. Of particular interest is a fine example of a spiral staircase. The building is privately owned and occupied.

Open to the public by appointment only.

Carbisdale Castle
Lairg, Sutherland, Highland.
5 miles south of Lairg on A836.

The 'castle' is no more than a folly on the south shore of the Kyle of Sutherland. It was completed in 1914 and is built of local grey whinstone with the rooms and galleries decorated to depict different historic periods.

Not open to the public. Youth hostel.

Cardoness Castle
Gatehouse-of-Fleet, Stewartry, Dumfries and Galloway.
1 mile south-west of Gatehouse-of-Fleet on A75.

This castle, now mainly in ruins, stands on a rocky outcrop in a commanding position above Fleet Bay. The site has been changed from what was originally an ideal defensive position by the building of a coastal road, which makes access far easier. Few traces of the less important buildings to the south and east remain, but the rectangular tower is still quite well preserved.

This tower, built in the 15th century on an oblong plan, consists of the ground floor with entresol and three upper storeys. The entrance, which was in the south wall, was probably guarded by an iron yett and wooden door. On the west side of this entrance was the guardroom, which was really only a small recess built into the passage and lit by a loophole. Also off the main entrance was a second passage leading at the east end to the turnpike stair.

The ground floor has been made into two cellars and in the corner of one are circular recesses or what may have been fodder troughs or pickling tubs. In the vault of the ground floor is an entresol with mural chambers built on the south and east walls, each containing a trap—one a 'murder hole' overlooking the entrance and the other allowing sole access to a pit prison. The great hall is situated on the first floor and contains a fine late Gothic fireplace with decorated aumbry on one side and salt box on the other, the usual stone seats at two of the windows and four mural chambers with garderobes.

On the floor above were two rooms, of which only a partition remains—the floors are missing. The western of these rooms, which contains a large carved fireplace, could be reached by a straight stair from the turnpike, while the eastern room could be entered both from the straight stair and directly from the turnpike. It is still just possible to judge the floor level of the attics above from the moulded corbels on the west wall, and there are also signs of a former wall walk, protected by a crenellated parapet.

South of the tower is an almost level platform which at an earlier date was probably enclosed to form an outer bailey. Evidence of other buildings in this courtyard still exists and suggests that there was a kitchen here and quarters for retainers.

Cardoness Castle was for centuries the ancient seat of the McCullochs of Galloway who acquired the land in 1450, but it later passed to the Gordons.

Open to the public, every day, Summer 9.30am–7pm, Sundays 2–7pm; Winter 9.30am–4pm, Sundays 2–4pm.

Cardross Castle
Cardross, Dumbarton, Strathclyde.
On A814, 4 miles north-west of Dumbarton.

The castle stands near the mouth of the River Leven on the outskirts of Dumbarton and 3 miles east of the village of Cardross. It was the place where Robert I—the Bruce—spent his declining years, and where he died in 1329. Sir James Douglas set out from Cardross with the heart of the dead king, which he had requested should be buried in the Holy Land. Douglas fell in battle against the Moors in Spain, but the heart was eventually returned to Melrose Abbey.

Not open to the public.

Carnasserie Castle
Kilmartin, Argyll, Strathclyde.
Off A816, 2 miles north-west of Kilmartin.

Carnasserie Castle stands in a commanding position on a hill above the road, north-west of Kilmartin. The structure, now partially in ruins, was built in the latter half of the 16th century and comprised a tower house with adjoining hall-house. It is considered to be an excellent example of domestic architecture of its time, which also includes certain fortification features. In times of trouble the square tower at the east end of the building, with its wall walk, parapet wall and rounded turrets which project outwards over each corner, was most useful for keeping a lookout and conducting the defence. The walls, too, were built with an eye to defence and contained small gun ports which would take hand-guns.

The house itself is typical of a medieval minor Scottish castle, and architectural details show a classic French Renaissance influence in the same building. This produces a most attractive effect: for example, the string courses which run round the building, stepping up and down in some places to follow the structural changes in level and in other parts to give extra decorative effect, are not just simple rounded mouldings but are much more delicate, similar to the classic cornice. The corbelling, too, is far more refined and attractive than is common in castles of this period. The quality of workmanship is particularly evident above the entrance doorway. Here were three carved panels holding heraldic arms depicting God, King and Campbell, all intricately worked.

Inside the castle were the usual vaulted cellars on the ground floor and a kitchen with a large open fireplace, big enough to take an ox. Bread was baked here in an oven opening off the fireplace. There are also signs of the system of water supply to the kitchen; this came from the outside through the wall and along a stone water channel, poured through a carved stone head and was guided into a suitable receptacle. Over the kitchen and cellars was the long hall. It was reached by a wheel stair within the the small square tower built at the west end. The hall was originally lit by high windows but larger windows were put in at a later date and the originals blocked up. It is more than likely that at one stage the hall contained a timber screen to give more privacy and protection from draughts. At the west end of the hall is the tower, with a room on the first storey opening into the great hall. This room could be reached by a wheel stair which continued up through the other storeys to the wall walk and down as far as the ground floor. Set in the thickness of the south wall of the tower is yet another but straight stair which leads from the first storey retiring room to the cellar below, which probably contained a wine supply. The other rooms in the tower were bedrooms which presumably had timber beams with designs and scenes from parables and fables painted in oil or tempura colour on them. The walls would have been hung with imported French and Flemish tapestries and the beds covered with woven fabric while the castle was occupied; these would have made the rooms seem totally different to the stark cells of today. Outside, the courtyard contained outbuildings which have almost disappeared.

Carnasserie was the home of John Carswell, the first Protestant Bishop of the Isles and Rector of Kilmartin. He published in 1567 the first translation of John Knox's 'Liturgy' in Gaelic, which was the first book to be published in the Gaelic language of Scotland. The castle was captured and demolished in 1685. The present ruins are now in the care of Historic Buildings and Monuments, Scottish Development Department.

Open to the public every day.

Carsluith Castle

Creetown, Wigtown, Dumfries and Galloway.
On A75 about a mile south of Creetown.

The castle stands in farming country on the coast of Wigtown Bay, beside the main road and overlooking the sea. Built in the 16th century on the usual L-plan, the now roofless tower house varies slightly from other castles built in this style. The difference lies in the fact that Carsluith Castle's staircase jamb was added later, in 1568, and the original tower had an open parapet with angle-towers.

The Brouns of Carsluith owned the castle. In fact the family are still as prominent in and around Knockbrex, on the other side of Fleet Bay, as they were when the castle was built. The family also owned land and stock near New Abbey, which is further east near Dumfries. Two Abbots of New Abbey, the well-known Abbot Gilbert Broun and his predecessor, were both Brouns.

The castle is now in the care of Historic Buildings and Monuments, Scottish Development Department.

Open all the year, 9am–8pm in Summer, and during daylight hours in Winter.

Caskieben Castle

Inverurie, Aberdeen, Grampian.
Just off A96 at Inverurie.

Situated on the south-east outskirts of the town and ancient royal burgh of Inverurie, in a great farming region and not far from the Bass, site of an important motte and bailey stronghold. The ancient castle of Caskieben is conjoined to the two-in-one structure of Keith Hall, only viewable from the outside and consisting of a large Restoration mansion. Built on the Z-plan and still in very good condition, the castle is dramatically different to the Restoration mansion which the first Earl of Kintore built in front of it in the Palladian style. The south-facing, crested front of the hall has a classical balustrade supporting urns and standing between square pavilions topped by pointed 'helmets'.

The surrounding park land was originally landscaped by Capability Brown. Caskieben Castle is also remembered for its association with the Latin poet known as the 'Scottish Ovid', son of George, the seventh Johnson Laird of Caskieben. He was born in the castle, which was then the family seat, in 1587.

The mansion is the home of the Earls of Kintore.

Not open to the public.

Cassillis Castle

Maybole, Kyle and Carrick, Strathclyde.
On A477, 10 miles south of Ayr.

Set in an area with a reputation for footwear manufacture and agricultural implements (and of interest to Burns students, as the poet's father and mother first met at Maybole), the castle dates from the 14th century. It was built originally as an oblong tower; in the 17th century a square tower was added with an unusual round, hollow newel. This type of staircase, built in straight flights and landings around a flat inner wall instead of revolving round a circular post or column, made a great difference to castle design and improved on the older wheel stairs.

The area around Cassillis Castle was held by the Cassillis Kennedys, who, it is said, owned no less than twenty-eight baronial mansions in the parish. An ancient legend tells that a Countess of Cassillis was imprisoned in the castle because of her association with Johnny Faa, King of the Gypsies. John Kennedy, her husband and sixth Earl of Cassillis, got home in time to catch the pair, hung Johnny Faa, and imprisoned his Countess for life. The tale is romantic but dubious, as surviving letters from John Kennedy to his wife prove that they were happily married for over 20 years.

Not open to the public.

Castle Campbell
Dollar, Clackmannan, Central.
1 mile north of Dollar off A91.

In the picturesque Dollar glen a mile north of the town of Dollar, perched on a rocky outcrop, stands Castle Campbell. The situation is one of the finest of all the Scottish castles, with a breathtaking view down on to the plains of the Forth. The castle is in the tower house style dating from the 15th century, other buildings and additions to the main house were made in the 16th and 17th centuries. There is a possibility that there was a Norman castle on this site during the 12th century; this is suggested by the grassy mound on which the tower stands, which could be the motte which was a feature of early Norman castles. There are also signs of a defensive ditch.

The present tower is the oldest of the remaining buildings and was built in the late 15th century. In the early days it stood alone inside a protective wall known as a barmkin, but today it is almost impossible to distinguish the original enclosure. In the 16th century the present enclosure and extra accommodation were added round the walls, and at the same time an outer garden was made to the south of the enclosure, outside the wall. This was reached from the castle through a vaulted passage and gate in the south wall. Towards the end of the 16th century, alterations took place in the eastern range. A wheel or turnpike stair tower was built against the tower, a loggia which still stands was added, and a vaulted entrance gateway was flanked by two gunports. Due to the site restrictions—rock foundations and lack of space—

the castle was destined never to alter very drastically, and it is thought that the existing wall follows the line of the first barmkin while the courtyard and buildings occupy the bailey of the 12th-century castle.

The tower is characteristically 15th century, built on a simple oblong plan with massive walls rising to an overhanging parapet 60 feet above the ground. Inside are four floors set one on top of another, of which three are vaulted; the ground, the first and the top. The tower has two entrances, one in the west wall at ground level and the other in the south wall at first floor level. The opening in the west wall has a round arched doorway leading to a barrel-vaulted passage and then on through a pointed arched doorway to the vaulted ground floor chamber. This was originally lit by two narrow slit windows; one still remains, but the other has been converted into a doorway which in turn leads to a turnpike stair, added in the 17th century at the same time as the east range of buildings.

In the south-east corner of the original tower wall is a pit prison entered through a trap door in the floor above and hardly discernible from ground level outside except for the presence of a narrow slit window.

From the north side of the entrance a straight stair rises within the thickness of the wall to the first floor principal rooms. At its foot was a door with draw-bar which in times of trouble would have been wedged across the back of the door to prevent intruders from forcing their way inside. The floor in the entrance passage has been lowered 3½ feet, possibly during preparations for the building of later courtyard dwellings.

The ground floor of the tower was a cellar or storeroom. On top of this was the great hall with its two entrances—one from the straight stair just mentioned, and another from a first floor doorway in the south wall. This was originally reached by an outside staircase which was pulled down during the late 16th or early 17th century, to make room for the new turnpike. On the right of the entrance, a small lobby leads to the prison below. Covering most of the east wall of the hall is the fireplace with a high small window set beside it in the wall. On the opposite wall is a similar window but most of the light came from a third window in the south wall which has been enlarged at some stage. This leaves the north wall, which shows remains of a buffer recess in the stonework.

The second floor, which is the only storey not vaulted, is reached from the new turnpike through the end of a small lobby. It has a fireplace on its north wall, and to the right-hand side of this an aumbry or wall cupboard. Two windows, one in the west and an enlarged one in the south wall, light this floor. Within the thickness of the walls to the right of the fireplace is an L-shaped garderobe or latrine chamber containing a seat, chute and a recess for an oil lamp.

The turnpike stair leads on up to the third floor where a small mural chamber with slit window opens into the main great chamber. Here a fine barrel-vault covers the whole of the room, supporting the roof of the tower above. This vault is embellished with an intricate system of transverse ribs, crossed by ridge ribs, running from end to end. The ribs, and two ugly mask heads in Renaissance style on the under side of the vault, suggest that this vault was added during the late 16th century or early 17th. To carry out this conversion the south window had to be blocked up and another made in the north wall. Only the east window with its wall-seating remains the same as in the original design—the west window was enlarged in the 16th century.

The roof of the tower was first designed with crow-stepped gables and parapet walk overhanging the wall face and carved on a single corbel course. At the angles were projecting roundels and both roundel and corbel course were set with grotesque gargoyles in the shape of beasts. In the 19th century the original roof was altered and a concrete one substituted. The courtyard entrance in the north was built in the late 16th or early 17th century. Its doorway is flanked on either side by gun ports and was designed to take a long bar-pole. On the east side of the entrance passageway, set in the wall, is a stone bench and locker, and on the west side is the doorway of the guardroom, which has a lean-to roof and which occupied the south-west corner of the courtyard. The site of the south range of buildings was first excavated to gain a level foundation which explains why the basement in this section is below courtyard level. It has five vaulted cellars each lit by a narrow slit window and was entered from an outside corridor or gallery, also below courtyard level.

The west end of this range opens onto the garden. On the first floor was a fine suite of rooms including the great hall with a porch and staircase at its east end and handsome fireplace in the north wall. Five large windows lit this hall and gave a superb view to the south. The eastmost window was enlarged, in fact it is quite possible that all these windows were insertions of a later date. The two east chambers contain garderobes, and from the evidence of burnt timber on this floor it would be sensible to presume that the garderobes were added in the 17th century when a general restoration seems to have taken place at the time that the east wing was erected.

Above the hall was another suite of rooms and on top of that an attic storey. The north side of the building was treated not as just something to look from but more as something to look at, yet still the east range is the most sophisticated part of the castle buildings.

Built in the late 16th or early 17th century, the courtyard façade is finished in fine ashlar. Each storey is clearly defined and the whole decorated by moulded string courses and neatly paired windows.

At the north end is the turnpike stair which was originally designed to give access to both the old tower and the new east range. Between it and the south range is an open arcade or loggia of arches, and above this were covered galleries lit by two pairs of windows. Finally, on the ground floor, are two barrel-vaulted chambers. This range was lived in until quite recently which accounts for the modernisation of the upper floors.

The castle was originally the stronghold of the Stewarts of Lorne and Innermeath, and came into the hands of the Campbells of Argyll by marriage. In 1457 Colin Campbell was created first Earl of Argyll and it was probably he who built the tower known as the 'gloume'. This successful man became Lord High Chancellor of Scotland in 1483, having several times acted as ambassador to England and France and holding the positions of Master of the King's Household and Justician of Scotland south of the Forth. In 1463 he was among the commissioners appointed to negotiate a truce with Edward IV of England and later a treaty of alliance with the same king in 1474, whereby James, Prince of Scotland, was betrothed to Cecilia, Edward's youngest daughter. Colin Campbell continued successfully in politics, and in 1489–1490 James IV changed the name of the castle from Castle Gloom to Castle Campbell by an Act of Parliament. Colin died in 1493 and was succeeded by his son, Archibald, who was slain at Flodden in 1513.

Archibald, the fourth Earl, greatly distinguished himself at the Battle of Pinkie (1547) and at the siege of Haddington (1548). He also became one of the first of the Earls to embrace the reformed faith, and in 1556 it is believed that John Knox stayed at the castle as the Earl's guest. Some say that Knox's famous 'dispensation of the sacrament of the Lord's Supper' took place outside the castle, but in all probability this ministration took place in the chapel of the castle.

During the 17th century the Scots became increasingly bitter over the Union of the Crowns whereby James VI, an absentee monarch, transformed monarchy into a despotism. Later, his son, Charles I, was just as unpopular because he tried to impose unwelcome religious policies upon his Scottish subjects. United in their determination not to endure episcopacy, the Scots agreed on the National Covenant of 1638.

Both Argyll and Montrose took part in the fighting which followed with the king's forces. Meanwhile, civil war was looming in England, and when both King Charles I and the English Parliament asked for Scotland's support, the country was sadly rent by divided loyalties to king and faith. Montrose took up arms for King Charles even though he agreed wholeheartedly with the National Covenant.

In 1639, Archibald, the eighth Earl and first Marquis, gathered an army in opposition to the threatened invasion of Scotland by Charles. In 1640 the Treaty of Ripon temporarily settled the troubles and the next year Charles visited Scotland. In 1644, however, the troubles blew up again, and Montrose defeated the Covenanters at Tippermuir. Argyll and the Earl of Lothian were sent against him, but at Inverlochy the two men met and Argyll was disabled, his forces routed and he was forced to take refuge in his galley on the loch. In 1645 the Covenanters again suffered at the hands of Montrose at the battle of Kilsyth; but at Philiphaugh, a month later, Montrose was finally and irredeemably defeated. In 1650 Montrose was brought to trial, but Argyll refused any part in the proceedings, saying that he was too prejudiced to be a judge.

In 1645 Montrose attempted but failed to take the castle, even though he spoilt the surrounding countryside and caused much hardship to the local people. In 1648 there are records of the fact that Argyll had a garrison in the castle under William Blackburn. In 1654 the castle was taken and burnt by Cromwell's troops under General Monk. Shortly after this the castle was garrisoned by English troops. The Bishops of Dunkeld, from whom Colin Campbell originally leased the land, continued as superiors of these lands until the 17th century.

From the time of the tenth Earl and first Duke, the lands were held directly from the Crown. George, the sixth Duke, sold the castle in the early 19th century and at this time the building was reported to be in a tumbledown condition. In 1948 Mr J. E. Kerr of Harvieston offered the castle and glen to the National Trust for Scotland. Castle Campbell is now maintained by Historic Buildings and Monuments, Scottish Development Department, and the surrounding glen approaches are owned by the National Trust for Scotland.

Open to the public, April to September, weekdays 10am–7pm, Sundays 2–7pm; October to March, weekdays 10am–4pm, Sundays 2–4pm.

Castle Cary
Castlecary, Clackmannan, Central.
At the junction of A80 and A803.

The Antonine Wall passed close to the present site of the town of Castlecary, and the remains of one of the principal staging posts built by the Romans on the wall was excavated here in 1902. Prior to this a considerable amount of building material in the Roman fort had been removed for other purposes.

It is likely that some of this stone was used in the actual castle of Cary. This fort was further mutilated in 1841 when the main Edinburgh/Glasgow railway line was built directly through the site. Just to the south-west of the Roman ruin stands the existing castle, built in the late 15th century above the Red Burn by the Livingstone family, following a raid on their lands by the Flemings of Cumbernauld.

The Baillie family, descendants of the famous house of Baliol, owned the castle from 1640 until it was burnt by a raiding party of Highland clansmen during the Jacobite rising. During the Baillies' occupation an adjoining wing known as the hall house was added to the tower with its large square keep of five storeys. Sometime soon after, the castle is thought to have been taken over by the Dundas family, the Earls of Zetland, who restored it to its present state. Positive dates are difficult to establish as no record seems to have been kept. It is known that in the 18th century, Lizzie Baillie eloped with her lover—a Graham—by jumping out of an upper tower window, so perhaps the Dundas family took over later in that century.

The castle is said to have two ghosts; General Baillie, Montrose's opponent at Kilsyth; and Lizzie Baillie, looking for her father, as the news of her elopement is said to have killed him.

Castlecary, although by no means remote, is difficult to find and reach due to the building of the modern motorway between Glasgow and Stirling, which has transformed it from an historical centre of communication to a modern-day backwater.

Open by appointment only.

Castle Craig
Black Isle, Ross and Cromarty, Highland.
Off B9163 on the peninsula Black Isle.

Castle Craig is today the ruin of a 15th-century tower house of which only the oblong tower remains. This tower is situated on a cliff overhanging the sea, and the gaunt ruin emanates an aura of desperate loneliness. The castle was at one time the seat of the Ross clan, particularly of Bishop Ross, who chose this solitary spot not for quiet reflection but rather with a healthy regard for physical security.

Open by appointment only.

Castle Dounie
Beauly, Inverness, Highland.
4 miles south-west of Beauly off A831.

The ruins of Castle Dounie can be found in a terraced garden belonging to the present Beaufort Castle. The castle was built in about 1400 and was the first major seat of the Frasers of Lovat, a family originally descended from Norman–French stock. This building was destroyed by the Duke of Cumberland in 1746 as part of his pacification programme in the Highlands after his victory over Bonnie Prince Charlie at Culloden.

Not open to the public.

Castle Forbes
Alford, Aberdeen, Grampian.
Off A944 across the Bridge of Keig on the north side of the River Don.

Set in the fertile Howe of Alford, this is the traditional seat of the Premier Baron of Scotland.

Not open to the public.

Castle Fraser
Sauchen, Inverurie, Aberdeen, Grampian.
3 miles south of Kemnay off B993.

Castle Fraser, in rolling Scottish countryside, is in a state of full preservation and still inhabited today. It is one of the most outstanding examples of castle building in Scotland.

Approached today by a broad walk sheltered by magnificent sycamores, the castle was built originally in the early 15th century as a square tower and main block; in the 17th century a round tower and extension were added to complete the

Castle Fraser

Z-form. Two very famous castellar masons were involved in the building of Castle Fraser. These two, Thomas Leiper and I. Bell of Midmar, were responsible for at least five of the best-known castles in Scotland beside Castle Fraser, including Cluny and Craigievar.

An outstanding feature of the main tower block is the false surround of stone gun barrels. These have no practical use but add to the impression of fortfied strength. The great hall of the castle is also superb. The castle was originally built for the Laird, Michael Fraser, and when he died, building stopped temporarily. It was begun again in 1600 when the original plan by Leiper was completed by the addition of the lower part of the main block and a round tower at the south-east corner. Between 1610 and 1620 Bell was commissioned to add another storey and garret to the Michael Tower and main block. At the same time he added three extra storeys to the round tower and an armorial frontispiece carved in deep red freestone, carrying the royal arms above those of the Frasers. Inset at the base of a tablet of stone he placed the inscription 'I. Bell 1617'.

A National Trust for Scotland property.

Open to the public, May to September, daily 2–6pm. Refreshments available.

Castle Grant

Grantown-on-Spey, Badenoch and Strathspey, Highland.
On A95 at Grantown.

Castle Grant, seat of the Grant clan, Earls of Seafield, gives its name to Grantown, usually designated as 'on-Spey' to distinguish it from Granton near Edinburgh. The Grants of Grant descended through twenty-five generations from Sir Laurence Le Grant, who was Sheriff of Inverness in 1258. In the time of Robert the Bruce the Grants acquired the lands of Inverallan in Strathspey where for a time they lived in a mansion house to the south-east of Castle Grant.

The castle dates from the early 15th century but was altered and had wings built on to the south at a later date. It is austere, and was described by Queen Victoria in her *Journal* as 'a very plain looking house, like a factory'. The oldest portion of the building is the tower which bears the name 'Barbie's Tower', after an unknown chatelaine by the name of Barbara who is said to have refused to marry the man her father proposed for her and was consequently locked up in a cupboard known as the 'blackness'. However, no skeleton was found when the cupboard was opened in 1880.

There are other legends apart from that of Barbara. There was the piper who swore he could march and pipe all the way from Inverness and then three times round the castle without a rest.

Apparently he failed of his boast, as his heart gave out on the third circuit of the castle. Then there is the story of a champion boatman, who travelled to London and proved himself the fastest boatman on the Thames.

The castle has always belonged to the Grants, except for a short while in 1747 when the Jacobites occupied it while Sir Ludovick Grant was away. The castle today is not complete, as parts of the building have been destroyed by fire. The eighth Earl, who died in 1885, left the estates to his mother and it was she who planted the extensive woods surrounding the territory. In 1911 she died, leaving the estates in trust, ultimately to revert to the Earls of Seafield. The present Earl inherited the castle in 1969 from Nina, daughter of the eleventh Earl, James Ogilvie Grant, who was killed in action in 1915. The castle is currently undergoing extensive renovation.

Currently not open to the public.

Castle Haven

Borgue, Stewartry, Dumfries and Galloway.
Off A75 near Borgue.

The so-called Borg Castle at Haven stands overlooking Wigtown Bay. In the distance, on a clear day, the Isle of Man can be seen from this spot. The origins of this structure date back to the Iron Age. Built on a D-shape, the 'castle' consists of very thick (20–25 feet) walls surrounding a space of perhaps 60 by 35 feet. The wall contains the usual galleries found in brochs and duns of this period. Surrounding the stone structure is a further earthwork of the same shape.

Public access across the fields.

Castle Kennedy

Stranraer, Merrick, Dumfries and Galloway.
3 miles east of Stranraer off A75.

All that remains of this 15th-century castle are some ruins and the gardens which surround the present day Lochinch Castle. These stand on a peninsula between the Black and White Lochs. It was originally the seat of the Kennedy family, passed to the Stairs in the 17th century, and was eventually destroyed by fire in 1716. The gardens are worth visiting, as they were laid out by the second Earl of Stair, who was inspired by Versailles. Today, after a long period of neglect, they have been restored to their original beauty and contain many rare plants. The gardens belong to the Earl and Countess of Stair.

Open to the public, April to September, daily 10am–5pm. Refreshments available.

Castle of Kinord
Dinnet, Aberdeen, Grampian.
On A93 at Dinnet.

The village of Dinnet has two points of historical interest nearby, both on Loch Kinord. The first is Crannog Island—probably built for defence reasons and dating from the Bronze Age. It is unique as an early example of man's civil engineering capabilities. This artificial island was formed by a large raft of logs and brushwood on which were built up layers of stone and earth held together by intersecting timbers. The process continued until the structure sank in position and it was then anchored by log piles sunk all round.

Nearby, on Castle Island, stand the ruins of Castle Kinord, a medieval peel tower which played its part in a decisive period of Scottish history during the War of Independence. This happened after the defeat of the English forces at the Battle of Culblean in 1335. Part of these defeated forces took possession and refuge at Castle Kinord under Sir Robert Menzies, but capitulated after a siege which damaged the castle extensively.

Not open to the public.

Castle Law
Abernethy, Perth and Kinross, Tayside.
Off A913 at Abernethy.

Castle Law fort stands on high ground looking over the town of Abernethy a mile to the southwest. Traditionally, Abernethy is regarded as a centre of the Pictish domain and was possibly the capital of the Pictish kingdom.

The fort comprises three banks of concentric ramparts, the centremost of which surrounds a level area approximately 100 yards in diameter. The outer two rings were in the nature of reinforced ditches. The main structure of the inner ring, the oldest part of the fort, is of clay with timber ties and facings of stone. Evidence of the timber is shown by characteristic staining in the clay and the channels in the stonework. In the centre ring was the main dwelling, built against the outer wall. This is shown by the depression 4 to 5 feet deep and 6 feet wide, in the form of a passage, widening into a circular chamber with a surrounding gallery. The internal diameter of this beehive-like chamber was probably somewhere around 35 feet. The gallery itself is cut largely out of living rock. There are holes left which were presumably sockets for jambs or doors of wood or stone.

Entrance to the fort was by a causeway, 25 feet wide across the outer two barriers. This was not straight but staggered, for defence reasons. Traces of a massive timber gateway were found here where the causeway met the inner ring.

The inhabitants of this fort were, as already mentioned, early Picts, and its period of occupancy was from the first millennium B.C. to the second century A.D. The span of this occupation is shown by finds including Bronze Age brooches and remains of a later date, such as fragments of glass and a buckle of Rhenish origin, the latter showing Roman influence. A short distance to the northeast, excavations have revealed the remains of a Roman legionary fort. The fort is in the care of Historic Buildings and Monuments, Scottish Development Department.

The site is freely accessible.

Castle Leod
Strathpeffer, Ross and Cromarty, Highland.
On A835 between Dingwall and Contin.

Castle Leod stands to the north of the village of Strathpeffer and was built on a typical L-plan with corbelling on the tower. It dates from the 14th century. In the 17th century, Sir Rory Mackenzie inherited the castle from his father and made many alterations, including the main access and the top storey. A further addition was built in the years 1912–1914. The castle is set in wooded parkland, noted for its fine trees, amongst which are two enormous Spanish chestnuts, planted in 1550 by Sir John Mackenzie, ancestor of Sir Rory. The largest of these trees has a girth of more than 30 feet at its base. Traditionally, Highland Games take place in the grounds of the castle on the first Saturday of August every year.

Open only to members of the Mackenzie Clan with proof of sponsorship by a Mackenzie society.

Castle Menzies
Weem, Perth and Kinross, Tayside.
A little beyond Weem on B846.

Set in the 19th-century centre of wool manufacture at Aberfeldy, and not far from Weem, is Castle Menzies. The area around Weem has some of the finest stands of hardwood trees in Scotland including beech, oak, sycamore, Spanish chestnut and ash, reaching from 80 to 104 feet high.

The castle was built in the 16th century by the Menzies clan, when their original seat, Comrie Castle, near Coshieville, was burnt down. Further additions were made in the 19th century, adhering as nearly as possible to the original L-plan tower style.

The interior of Castle Menzies is similar in style to the Castle of Elcho in that the rooms were built adjoining each other with little or no corridor or passage space. The exterior of the building was passage space. The exterior of the building was designed so that the eye was attracted upwards to the rich corbelling and crow-stepped gables and other roof ornamentation and not distracted by the shape of the walls, which were kept purposely simple. Castle Menzies stood neglected for many years, but is now in the care of the clan society.

Open to the public, April to September, Monday to Saturday 10.30am–5pm, Sundays 2–5pm.

Castle of Mey

John O'Groats, Caithness, Highland.
7 miles west of John O'Groats off A836.

The castle has belonged to H.M. Queen Elizabeth, The Queen Mother, since 1952. It stands in a commanding position above the seashore overlooking the Pentland Firth and the Orkney Isles. The building maintains much of its original striking appearance and atmosphere, with its towers and turrets very typical of the style of the late 16th century. The Z-plan indicates that it was probably built between 1566 and 1572 by George, the fourth Earl of Caithness. Various further additions and alterations were made during the 17th, 18th, 19th and 20th centuries. In due course the castle passed to the family of the Sinclairs of Mey, who in turn succeeded to the Earldom of Caithness in 1789, and the castle became the seat of the earldom until 1889. It was originally known as Castle of Mey, but was for a period called Barrogil Castle. On purchasing the castle and policies in 1952 the Queen Mother gave the castle back its original name.

Not open to the public, but the gardens are open on three days in the summer under Scotland's Garden Scheme.

Castle of Park

Glenluce, Merrick, Dumfries and Galloway.
Off A747, 1 mile west of Glenluce.

Overlooking the sandy shores of Luce Bay and a little to the west of Glenluce stands the Castle of Park, with a distant view of the Isle of Man on a clear day. Built in 1590 by Thomas Hay of Park, this tall, imposing castellated mansion was constructed of stone from the nearby ruins of Luce Abbey. Thomas Hay was the son of the last Abbot of Glenluce, and obtained the lands at the time of the Reformation. The building is in excellent condition, having recently been restored, and is now in the care of Historic Buildings and Monuments, Scottish Development Department.

Not open to the public, but may be viewed from outside.

Castle Stalker

Creagan, Argyll, Strathclyde.
Off A828 near Creagan.

The castle stands on an island in Loch Laich, which leads into Loch Linnhe. It was built at the beginning of the 16th century on a typical tower-plan and was used originally as a hunting lodge for James IV. The builder of the castle, Duncan Stewart of Appin, presented the hunting lodge to James IV to ingratiate himself with his royal relative. The estates fell into ruin when the Stewarts of Appin took part in the rising of the '45 and the property was forfeited and placed in trust by the Government to Colin Campbell of Glenure, in the same district. It is this character whose assassination was made famous in the story of the Appin murder in Robert Louis Stevenson's novel *Kidnapped*. After lying in ruins for two centuries the now-restored Castle Stalker is well worth visiting, especially in fine weather, as the surrounding scenery is particularly beautiful.

Open by appointment only from Easter to September.

Castle Stuart

Petty Parish, Dalcross, Inverness, Highland.
Off A96 on B9039.

Dalcross is interesting in having a touch of the old and the new. The town's main claim to fame nowadays is that it is the site of the airport for the city of Inverness. About a mile to the west of the airport stands Castle Stuart, built by the third Earl of Moray in 1625 on estates that he had purchased from the Mackintoshes. The Petty Church at Dalcross was the traditional burying place of the chiefs of the Mackintoshes.

This tower-plan building was only occupied during the 17th century, after which it fell into disrepair until 1860. The thirteenth Earl of Moray then attempted to restore the building, but only rebuilt the roof. In 1951 a Mr Colin Mackenzie took a lease on the building and re-established it as a dwelling. The most interesting point about Castle Stuart is that even though it stood unoccupied for so long, it represents one of the best surviving examples of an early 17th-century gentleman's house. The castle is now a private dwelling.

Not open to the public.

Castle Sween

Kilmory, Argyll, Strathclyde.
Off A816, left at Cairnbaan and left again at Bellanoch to the end of Loch Sween.

On the west coast of the Knapdale peninsula is Castle Sween. It was probably built in the middle of the 12th century and is the earliest stone castle in Scotland built after the Norman style, with large angle buttresses. At some later date, an oblong tower house with pointed loopholes and a cylindrical tower adjoining it were added. The castle today is in ruins, having been destroyed by one of Montrose's commanders, Sir Alexander Macdonald, in 1647.

The castle retains its original proportions, however, and an excellent idea can be obtained of this important stage in Scottish castle building from this one example. It is in the care of Historic Buildings and Monuments, Scottish Development Department.

Open to the public, every day. Refreshments available.

Castle Tioram
Ardmolich, Inverness, Highland.
Off A861 near Ardmolich.

Castle Tioram stands at the eastern neck of the Ardnamurchan peninsula on a prominent outcrop of rock which itself is at the dry end of a long spit of sand jutting into Loch Moidart.

The castle was built in the early 13th century by the Macdonalds of Clan Ranald. The main part of the structure is the curtain wall, which is over 30 feet high and 8 feet thick with rounding at the corners, characteristic of the period. At a later date, turrets were added to these walls. At the beginning of the 17th century a range of stone dwelling-houses was added to the inside of the south wall, and a high tower with corbelled angle turrets. In 1715 a Macdonald of Clan Ranald ordered the structure to be burnt when he set out to join the Jacobite rising, and no-one has lived in the castle since that gallant but hopeless gesture more than 250 years ago.

Not open to the public.

Castle of Old Wick
Wick, Caithness, Highland.
At the junction of the A882 and A9.

High on a rocky promontory cut off from the land by a man-made ditch stands the Castle of Old Wick. The other three sides of this structure are formidably defended by the cliffs which fall sheer to the sea. The castle itself is in the form of a simple rectangular keep of probable Norse origins. There is no ground level entrance and the lower floors and basement were lit very poorly by narrow slits. Judging by the large entrance in the wall, something like 15 feet off the ground, it would seem that access was by an external staircase or bridge of timber.

The earliest recorded inhabitants of the castle were the Cheynes family and during their tenure it was known as Castle Oliphant. The most notable recorded event in the castle's history was its capture in 1596 by the master of Caithness, son of the fourth Earl of Caithness; he was himself extricated from the castle and imprisoned for 6 years, after which he was executed.

Open to the public at all times except when the adjoining rifle range is in use.

Caterthuns, Brown and White
Bridgend, Angus, Tayside.
5 miles north-west of Brechin off the road to Bridgend.

The Brown and White forts of Caterthun are of uncertain origin but are thought to date from the middle Iron Age, around 300 B.C.

'Brown Caterthun' stands alone and consists of six circular lines of defence; the largest and outer ring has a diameter of approximately 1,000 feet. This consists of a rampart and external ditch; the rampart has eight entrances, as does the second line of defence, which is only a wall without a ditch. Inside these rings are two more ramparts with an intervening ditch and then a far greater rampart faced with rock. Finally, the innermost of the six defence rings consists of a dry stone wall with a single entrance. The detailed history is naturally not known, but from the number of defence lines it is clear that the fort was rebuilt and added to on numerous occasions.

'White Caterthun' stands a mile to the south-west of Brown Caterthun and is an oval fort crowning a hilltop. This structure is one of the most imposing ruins of its type in Britain. The outer wall (approximately 20 feet thick) and a low rampart encircle the fort proper, covering an area of some 500 by 250 feet. Inside this outer rampart stand the remains of a huge stone wall which originally would seem to have been 14 feet thick. The remains of these two walls are in a collapsed state and for the most part the strewn rock of both walls is interspersed, forming a belt of jumbled stone 100 feet wide. Outside the outer rampart are the remains of two more ramparts, and traces of a further two which were probably never completed.

The site is freely accessible.

Cawdor Castle
Cawdor, Nairn, Highland.
Between Nairn and Inverness on B9090 off A96.

Set near the shores of the Moray Firth in delightful scenery is Cawdor Castle, which dominates the village of the same name. It is one of the best known of all the castles in Scotland due to its association with Shakespeare's *Macbeth*, a story which belongs in fact to legend, as the real Duncan met his death in 1040, long before the castle was built. Most of the existing building is comparatively modern, 17th century, but the central tower-keep dates from around 1454 when James II granted the Thane of Cawdor a Royal licence to fortify the existing tower which was built between 1370 and 1380. He did this on condition that he and his descendants could retain the right to enter the castle at any time.

In the early days the tower-keep stood alone, surrounded by a dry ditch and reached by a drawbridge and protected by an excellent example of an iron yett or portcullis. The entrance to the keep itself at this early date would have been by a retractable timber stair to the first floor level, where today an arched window fills the space of the original door.

The keep was at first four floors high and the chambers in the tower were vaulted in stone to protect them from being burnt out from below. At the top of each corner of the tower is a rounded turret set out from the parapet with a cap-house, which makes this older section seem to be of a later date. In the 16th century major additions were made to the castle, comprising a curtain wall and further living accommodation; and in the 17th century the north and west wings were much

enlarged and a great deal of mural carving added, bringing the castle to its present and final stage. The Thanes of Cawdor, whose family name was actually Calder, lived in the castle until approximately 1510, when it passed into the hands of the Campbells by the marriage of Muriel Calder to Sir John Campbell, the third son of the second Earl of Argyll. This marriage started a new line of Campbells of Cawdor. The Campbell family continued as lairds at Cawdor and immediately after the '45 rising were said to have given sanctuary to the famous Simon, Lord Lovat, during his flight from the Duke of Cumberland's occupying troops. The castle was uninhabited for 100 years after the Jacobite uprising, when the lairds moved south and settled on family lands in Wales. It is today a fine example of castle architecture in Scotland, as it has been virtually untouched since then.

Open to the public, May to September, daily 10am–5.30pm. Refreshments available.

Claypotts Castle
Broughty Ferry, Dundee, Angus, Tayside.
1 mile north-west of Broughty Ferry on the Dundee-Arbroath road.

Claypotts Castle stands somewhat incongruously in the suburb of Broughty Ferry, the town of Dundee's seaside resort, on lands from which it

Claypotts Castle

takes its name. The earliest historical reference to Claypotts is in 1365, when a document dated to the thirty-sixth year of David's reign confirms a charter of liberties given for the Abbey of Lindores by Alexander II in 1247. It is evident from this document that the lands of Claypotts must have been given to Lindores before 1247. This seems to be all that is known of the area until the early 16th century, when John Strachan or Strathauchin was recorded as leasing lands from the Abbot of Lindores in 1511. John Strachan, who was related to the Strachans of Carmyllie, was also recorded as having stolen seven horses and wagons with his brother Gilbert and four others. Nonetheless, Gilbert Strachan's career does not seem to have suffered from the publicity as he progressed from vicar of Strathmiglo to Canon of Aberdeen and eventually became rector of the university.

John had two sons, John and James. John succeeded his father and inherited Claypotts, while James followed his uncle into the church and also became a rector of the university. When John died, he too was succeeded by his son John. In 1544 it is presumed to have been John, brother of James, who was said to have had the property confiscated for failing to attend a muster at Leith. This apparent threat was never carried out as the Strachans definitely remained at Claypotts. In 1547 the nearby Broughty Castle was occupied by English troops after a token resistance. Although no mention of Claypotts was made at this stage, it is more than likely that it too was attacked. In 1549 the siege was lifted, but the Strachans obviously felt the wisest plan was to fortify their home to deter further attacks.

John Strachan, presumably the second John Strachan of Claypotts, who married Enfame Durhan —a neighbour's daughter—and had seven children, is often mentioned in documents. He is named as one of the curators or guardians of John Thornton on his marriage to Isobel Strachan of Carmyllie in 1557. In 1560 he served on a jury in Forfar, and in 1570 he and his son Gilbert witnessed a charter given by James Strachan at Claypotts. It was this John who between 1569 and 1588 built Claypotts Castle.

In 1593 the second John Strachan died and was succeeded by his son Gilbert who died not quite a year after his father. The third John Strachan of Claypotts was still a child at the time and his mother, with the help of her brothers, tried to take over the castle, but the plot failed and she was fined and forced to surrender her claim.

In the 17th century the Grahams of Ballunie took over the tenure of the land and the Strachan family moved to a farm near their lands of Skryne at Dalhousie not far from the Strachans of Carmyllie. In 1601 the family sold Claypotts to Sir William Graham of Ballunie who owned the lands to the west and north of Claypotts at Gotterston, Warries-

ton and Ballunie. Sir William transferred the lands in 1616 to his son David who then sold them in 1620 to Sir William Graham of Claverhouse. David was probably the last owner of Claypotts to actually live at the castle. Graham of Claverhouse was a prominent figure in the locality—a burgess of Dundee, Justice of the Peace and representative for Forfarshire at the Parliament of 1633. In 1640 he bought Glen Ogilvie as his family house, and on his death in 1642 was succeeded in turn by his son George, his grandson William and great grandson John. John Graham of Claverhouse was a famous soldier, statesman and loyal supporter of the Stuarts; however, he had little to do with Claypotts, being brought up at Glen Ogilvie and making his home at Dudhope. He was tragically killed on the battlefield of Killiecrankie, and the Claverhouse lands subsequently reverted to the Crown. In 1694 they were granted to James, second Marquis of Douglas, by the new king for services rendered. By now the lands included the estates of Ballewny, Miltoun of Craigie, Warrieston and Gotterston, the lands of Claypotts and a pendicle in North Ferry with fishing upon the Tay. The Marquis died in 1700 and was succeeded by his son.

In 1703 the third Marquis was made Duke of Douglas, but in 1761 he died childless and his lands passed to his nephew after a bitter legal battle. Archibald's right to inherit was questioned by the curators of the Duke of Hamilton on the grounds that Archibald was illegitimate. This accusation was, however, never proved, and in 1709 Archibald was made Lord Douglas of Douglas. In 1827 Archibald, Lord Douglas, died and was succeeded by three of his sons in succession and later by his daughter Jane. Her daughter Lucy Elizabeth inherited the lands from her mother and was succeeded by her son, the twelfth Earl of Home. Claypotts still belongs to the Homes, but in 1926 they placed it in the care of Historic Buildings and Monuments, Scottish Development Department.

The castle was built in the 16th century in the shape of a rectangular block with round towers at two of the diagonally opposite corners—known as the Z-plan style. The main stair was built in one of the angles between the south tower and the central block and a domestic stair was put in a corresponding position between the central block and north tower.

Claypotts is particularly worth a visit if only to see the square garret chambers which corbel out over the drum towers. The chamber at the north end is built firmly on its tower, but at the south end the curving wall of the tower projects about a foot below the garret storey. The simplicity of the ground floor of the castle, with its wide-mouthed loopholes, contrasts dramatically with the decoration of the dormer windows and of the cornice at the top of the wall. The castle was built mainly for comfort and convenience, with only the essential defensive features including short lengths of parapet walk, and a loophole in the kitchen. This particular feature in the back of the kitchen fireplace was inserted to give all-round defence to the castle.

On the ground floor of the castle is the entrance with a moulded matrix of an heraldic panel above the doorway. Inside are the usual vaulted cellars, then the hall on the first floor and private rooms above. A passage leads from the entrance to two vaulted cellars, the main stairway and the kitchen. Here are the remains of the arched fireplace with its massive chimney, with small beehive oven to one side and crude sink on the other. The nearby stream was obviously used to supply water as there are signs of a rainwater store under the stairway. The left-hand cellar leads through to the domestic stair and to a third store in the north tower.

The hall on the first floor opened off an ante-chamber formed by a screen. At the north-east corner of this room a doorway opens on to the domestic stair which in this case runs continuously from ground floor to attic. This is unusual, as in most castles of this period the staircase stops at the first floor and continues upwards in some other part of the building. This ensured that any intruders had to cross an open space such as the main hall before gaining access to the upper floors of the building.

An interesting feature of the floors above the main hall is the presence of two fireplaces at opposite ends of large rooms. This would seem to indicate that it was intended to increase the number of rooms by the use of wooden partitions. The castle is in good repair, including the original roof.

Open to the public, April to September, weekdays 10am–7pm, Sundays 2–7pm; October to March, weekdays 10am–4pm, Sundays 2–4pm.

Cluny Castle
Sauchen, Aberdeen, Grampian.
Off A944.

Cluny Castle is a large, modern and picturesque neo-baronial pile dating from 1830, when it was built by John Smith, the architect. The existing building incorporates part of a 17th-century Z-plan castle built by I. Bell for Thomas Gordon in 1604. From existing drawings it is easy to see that modern Cluny Castle covers what was probably one of the best examples of Z-plan tower castles in Scotland. Its architect also designed and built Craigievar.

Open to the public on application to the owners.

Colquhonnie Castle
Strathdon, Aberdeen, Grampian.
Off A97.

The ruined castle stands on the right bank of the River Don at Strathdon; it was never completely finished. Building was started on this intended tower house at the beginning of the 16th century, but work finally stopped a few years later after three of the lairds had been killed by fatal falls whilst overseeing the building.

Not open to the public.

Comlongon Castle
Clarencefield, Nithsdale, Dumfries and Galloway.
7 miles west of Annan on B724 off A75.

Comlongon Castle was built in the 15th century and is a typical example of the rectangular tower house, with the usual stark exterior and no projec-tions. The castle design stuck to the original conception of a tower house plan, with each floor covering the complete ground floor plan of the tower. Entrance is by the vaulted basement to the usual hall on the first floor. The overall impression is one of grim strength.

Open to the public, every day, March to October, 10am–5pm.

Comrie Castle
Coshieville, Perth and Kinross, Tayside. A short distance from Keltneyburn, off A827.

Now in ruins, Comrie Castle stands at the bridge across the River Lyon not far from Coshieville Inn, where in the 18th century, cattle-drovers from the north and north-west stopped on their way to the Falkirk and Crieff meeting places. The castle, original home of the Clan Menzies, is thought to have been built in the 14th century by Thomas Menzies, who died in 1380. It was burnt down in the 16th century.

Not open to the public.

Corgaff Castle
The Lecht Pass, Aberdeen, Grampian.
Off A939, north of Crathie.

Situated at the end of the Lecht Pass, which connects Strathdon with Strathavon, and facing the steep climb up from Cockbridge, is Corgaff Castle, twin of Braemar Castle. It was built in the 16th century, around 1537, as a hunting seat by Thomas Erskine, Earl of Mar. Since 1435 both the lands and dignity belonging to the Earldom had been annexed by the Crown, but in 1507 the forest of Corgaff (with other Mar lands) was granted to Alexander, later first Lord Elphinstone, by James IV. The second Lord Elphinstone ceded the lands of Corgaff to his eldest son Robert on his marriage, and they then passed into the hands of the Forbeses as vassals of the Elphinstones.

In 1571, during a feud between the Forbeses and Gordons, Adam Gordon of Auchindoun set fire to the castle, burning alive Margaret Campbell, wife of the Forbes laird, with her family and servants. The Erskine Earls of Mar recovered the lands some years later and restored the keep, but in 1689 the castle was burnt down again by Jacobites. It was held by them in 1745 as an arms store until, in 1746, Lord Ancrum took it from them with an army of 400 men. In the meantime in 1716 Lord Mar forfeited the lands, which then passed back to the Forbes. Around 1748 Corgaff Castle was bought by the Government as a base for Hanoverian troops who were employed in disarming the Highlands and establishing order in this wild district.

Originally the castle was built as a tower house, with two vaulted cellars in the basement, a lofty vaulted hall on the first floor with adjoining kitchen and an upper storey and garret. After the fires in 1571 and 1689 most of the castle still stood intact except for the roof and upper wooden floors. In 1748 the nucleus of the castle, the tower, was remodelled as a fortified post for the Hanoverian troops. At this stage, wings, known as 'pavilions', were added to each gable wall, plus a star-shaped loop-holed curtain wall similar to the one at Braemar Castle. The castle is now in the care of Historic Buildings and Monuments, Scottish Development Department.

Open to the public by appointment only.

Corthally Castle
Carnwath, Clydesdale, Strathclyde.
On B7016, north of Carnwath.

Corthally Castle is now nothing but a ruin of which only the moat and the extent of the inner and outer courts can be traced. It is thought to have been built by the Douglas family in the 12th century, and became the property of the powerful Somerville family in 1317 when William Somerville married Janet Douglas and received the lands of Carnwath and the Castle of Corthally. Until 1602 the Somervilles, with their seat at Corthally, were one of the most powerful families in Scotland. Kings James III, IV and VI all visited the castle, which was famous for its excellent hunting and lavish hospitality.

The present ruin is situated on part of the land around Woodend Farm.

Open to the public on application to Woodend Farm.

Craig Castle
Lumsden, Aberdeen, Grampian.
Near Lumsden off A97.

This forbidding castle, which can best be described as a cliff-like block of masonry, is situated 60 feet above the Burn of Craig. It was built by the Gordons in the 16th century in the L-plan tower-house style, with tiny windows and a battery of gun-loops which presented daunting problems for would-be attackers. Additions were made to the castle in 1726, 1832 and 1908. Over the door of the castle are three panels carrying coats of arms. The doorway itself has a massive iron yett, which opens on to a vaulted vestibule whose ceiling ribs meet in a large foliated central boss decorated with the Scottish Royal Arms. Shields in the corbel caps of two of the ribs bear the three boars' heads of the Gordons and a carving of the five wounds of Christ.

A spiral staircase in the tower has sixty-three steps over 4 feet wide, lit by loopholes in the north wall. The first floor contains the great hall, with a piper's gallery and helmet bearing the coat of arms and initials of Francis Gordon, the seventh laird, and his wife. These armorial bearings from 1516 to the present day have recently been repaired and tinctured under the care of the present owner.

Not open to the public.

Craigie Castle
Craigie, Kyle and Carrick, Strathclyde.
About a mile south-west of Craigie off A719.

This little-known ruined castle, of considerable interest, dates from the early 13th century, and is surrounded by a ditch. It had at one time a rib-vaulted hall consisting of three bays over an unvaulted basement, but experts have found traces of an earlier hall which had a crenellated parapet rising flush with the main wall-face. In the centre of one wall was a round-arched doorway, and opposite this a late medieval fireplace, added in the 15th century, was built over another round-arched opening. It is now quite difficult to determine the original plan but signs suggest that it was originally a simple rectangle of suitable size for a building such as an early hall-house. Experts believe that Craigie Castle was originally a hall-house of the late 12th or early 13th century with a wide crenellated parapet enclosing a saddle-back roof. During the 15th century it is likely that these crenellations were built over and a new hall fashioned on the walls of its predecessor.

Not open to the public.

Craigievar Castle
Alford, Aberdeen, Grampian.
6 miles south of Alford on A980.

Set in secluded hilly country south of Alford is the fairytale castle of Craigievar, built in 1626 as an L-plan tower house for the flamboyant Forbes laird known as 'Willie the Marchant of Aberdeen', brother of the Bishop of Aberdeen. The simplicity of this seven-storey tower contrasts dramatically with the explosion of delicately corbelled turrets and conical cap-like roofs. It is, unlike other castles of its time, tall and slender, rather like an upended matchbox; rising from a smooth lawn, it is virtually unaltered since the day it was first built. The castle has been continuously occupied, by the Forbes and later the Forbes-Sempill family, from its earliest days, which may account for its almost perfect condition. The castle and some 30 acres of ground were bought from the Forbes-Sempill family and presented to the National Trust for Scotland in 1963.

The castle can only be entered by one route. Potential assailants would have had a difficult task tackling first the ramparts, then the heavily studded outer door with its iron grid behind, and lastly another studded double door on the stone stair leading to the great hall. Inside the castle are superb examples of richly moulded plaster ceilings, particularly in the great hall, where a great groined vault illustrates the decoration of raised panels, heraldry, foliage, classic portrait medallions and elaborate pendants, all in plaster relief. They were the work of a London craftsman who also worked at Muchalls a few years before.

The fireplace at Craigievar is surmounted by an

Craigievar Castle

immense armorial tablet of the Royal Arms and in the same room is a musicians' gallery as well as the original timber-screen. Off this hall is a withdrawing room, and upstairs the 'Queen's bedroom' with yet another beautifully decorated ceiling and a canopied bed. The rooms on the higher levels, reached by the turnpike stair, are remarkably light for a building of this time, due to the many windows set in the turrets. Even the servants' quarters are still charmingly furnished with box beds in arched timber frames.

Craigievar is a 'homely' sort of castle in spite of all its period perfection, and fortunately the trees surrounding it still flourish and give this dream-like building a secluded and dignified setting.

A National Trust for Scotland property.

Open to the public, May to September, daily 2–6pm.

Craigmillar Castle
Edinburgh, Midlothian, Lothian.
3 miles from the centre of Edinburgh off the Old Dalkeith Road.

The famous Craigmillar Castle lies just beyond Duddingston in the parish of Liberton on the southern outskirts of Edinburgh. Because of its size, strength and nearness to Edinburgh, Craigmillar was a popular haunt of the Stuart kings who enjoyed its comfort and convenience. It was they who caused it to be remembered for some of the darkest and most sinister happenings in Scottish history.

This 14th-century building, only partly ruined, was built on a massive but simple L-plan on the southern verge of a 30-foot rock which falls away from the base of the tower in a steep cliff. The central tower measures 53 by 49 feet on the longest sides, and is built of close-textured reddish grey rubble. An attacker would have had a difficult time storming the castle, as once he had made his way round two sides of the tower he would then have had to cross a timber decking over a sunken ditch, and afterwards tackle the iron yett as well as the outer door of the portal. Inside the tower a narrow vaulted passage leads to the basement and to a newel stair which leads to the upper floors of the house. The passage and stair take up all the wing in this section.

The main building has a large vaulted store sub-divided by a wooden loft, of which the tower half is again divided with a secondary stone partition. The main openings to this cellarage are narrow loops, though doors have been made in the walls at a later date to give access to the additional buildings that adjoin this tower. One inner door closes the cellars while another shuts off the newel stair. The vaulted hall on the first floor of the main building has a large, richly moulded fireplace at its upper end and includes three large windows with stone seats. These were altered during the

Craigmillar Castle

16th or 17th century and leaded glass put into the upper sections and wooden shutters fitted below. Beside the fireplace, a door opened into a small privy which has since been converted into a passage leading to the newer buildings. At the north-east corner of the hall is a mural closet which experts suggest may have been built over a pit or prison, as happened at Comlongon Tower in Nithsdale.

The stair from the basement stops at hall level on a landing which has to be crossed to reach the second flight which then carries on up to the roof. This arrangement was planned as a defence measure but had the other advantage of leaving space in the wing free for three private rooms which could be entered from the newel stair. The room at hall level was originally a kitchen but was made into a living room at a later date when a newer kitchen was built.

In 1427 a quadrangular curtain wall was built round the tower house to form a courtyard about 120 by 80 feet. Made of coursed rubble with occasional oyster-shell pinnings, the wall is cornered by stout round towers and topped by one of the best preserved machicolated parapets to be seen in Scotland. Only the north-eastern tower, which faced the main approach to the castle, is provided with cannon openings which look rather like inverted keyholes. The rest of the wall was serviced by large round openings set high in the towers to take large guns. In the north curtain of this wall is the plain arched main entrance with a stone slab depicting the Preston Arms and the name Craigmillar. Overhead on the battlements stands the lion rampant of Scotland—a special concession to the Lord of Craigmillar, who as tenant-in-chief was entitled to place it above his own arms.

Other additions were made to the original castle over the centuries. In 1544, after the castle was burnt by Hertford, the east range, containing cellars, kitchen , private room and bedchambers, was added. In 1661 the western range was reconstructed by Sir John Gilmour, President of the Court of Session. This was designed slightly differently to the usual 17th-century wing in that the principal apartments of kitchen, dining room and withdrawing room were all on the ground floor and opened into one another without a corridor. All these additions improved the comfort of the castle but did nothing to help the defensive integrity of the old tower house. However, about the time of its restoration in 1544, a precinct wall was built round the castle, enclosing an area of about 1¼ acres. The entrance to this yard lies in the north wall and is flanked by a round tower at the north-east corner which is deceptively fitted up as a dovecot but bristled with gun-loops. The precinct is divided into an outer court in front with gardens either side. Also included in the courtyard were farmyard offices and an external chapel built of grey and red freestone with crow-stepped gables.

Although Craigmillar has been altered drastically over the years, the traditional and conservative layout of the castle remains the same, resulting in what is now a castle of the high Middle Ages—an extremely strong fortress home able to withstand almost any form of attack.

Historically, Craigmillar Castle is even more interesting than architecturally. In 1347 the barony was acquired by the Preston family who founded the castle. In 1544 the castle was partially destroyed by the English forces but was still occupied, for in 1566 the young Queen Mary fled here for peace and quiet from the turmoil of Holyrood and Rizzio's murder. Also at Craigmillar the famous 'band' was signed between Argyll, Huntly, Bothwell, Maitland and Sir James Balfour, which resulted in Darnley's murder. It has never been established whether the Queen was involved but certainly she was in residence at the castle when the plot was hatched. In 1572 civil war broke out following Queen Mary's abdication and Craigmillar Castle was garrisoned by the Regent Mar—against Edinburgh. In 1660 the barony of Craigmillar was bought from the Prestons by Sir John Gilmour, one of the most upright judges of his time. It was his descendant, Sir John Little Gilmour of Craigmillar and Liberton, who, in 1946, handed over the property to the care of the predecessors of Historic Buildings and Monuments, Scottish Development Department.

Open to the public, April to September, weekdays 9.30am–7pm, Sundays 2–7pm; October to March, weekdays 9.30am–4pm, Sundays 2–4pm.

Craignethan Castle
Crossford, Clydesdale, Strathclyde.
5 miles north-west of Lanark off A72.

This partially restored and extensive ruin lies in a dell overlooking the River Nethan, and was formerly known as Draffen Castle. It was built in the 16th century by one of Scotland's most talented and devious nobles, Sir James Hamilton of Finnart, the Bastard of Arran—assassin, traitor, King's Master of Works and apparently a man of some taste.

The original keep, guarded on three sides by cliffs, was later added to and was one of the most important of the tower houses in Scotland. However, it was not very cleverly designed from a defensive viewpoint—the gunners manning posts on three sides of the castle would have discharged their shot into space, and on the fourth side, the steep slope down to the castle only improved the attackers' chances. It seems that the gun-ports were fashionable additions rather than essential defensive items. They may have been included to frighten the enemy rather than inflict real damage.

Craignethan Castle was the chief stronghold of the Hamiltons, who supported Mary, Queen of Scots, and because of this the castle was frequently under attack from Protestant party opponents. In 1579 it was partially destroyed by the Protestant party but was rebuilt again in about 1665 by the Hays. The oldest part of the castle still standing is the large tower house with its very ornate details, but the outer walls and towers are also exceptionally well preserved. Craignethan is regarded as the model for Tillietudlem in Scott's novel *Old Mortality*. It is in the care of Historic Buildings and Monuments, Scottish Development Department.

Open to the public daily, Summer, weekdays 9.30am–7pm, Sundays 2–7pm; Winter, 9.30am–4pm, Sundays 2–4pm; closed 25 and 26 December and 1 and 2 January.

Craigston Castle
Turriff, Aberdeen, Grampian.
4 miles north-east of Turriff off A947.

The renaissance-style Craigston Castle was built between 1604 and 1607 by John Urquhart, the Tutor of Cromarty, guardian of his grand-nephew Sir Thomas, father of the great Sir Thomas Urquhart, who translated Rabelais. Like so many things undertaken by the Urquharts the castle was highly original. It consisted of a tower, with two wings added in the 18th century, attributed to William Adam. On the first floor there is the original great hall 30 feet broad by 21 feet high and linked to an anteroom by handsome double doors.

Set in the 18th-century doors, walls and shutters of the two rooms are a series of carved oak panels dating from early in the 17th century. In the 'Queen's room' there is an oak chest which belonged to John Urquhart.

Open to the public by appointment only.

Crathes Castle
Crathes, Banchory, Kincardine and Deeside, Grampian.
3 miles east of Banchory on A93.

The original castle was built on lands which were given to Alexander de Burnard by King Robert and formed the nucleus of the Barony of Leys. Crathes Castle dates from 1553, when the double square tower was built in Scottish baronial style with turrets and battlements. Apparently the castle was finally completed in 1596 when it is thought that the Bells, a famous family of Aberdeenshire masons, remodelled the upper parts. During the 18th century a three-storeyed east wing was added and later a Queen Anne wing which was destroyed by

fire in 1966 was rebuilt to house an information centre.

On the first floor of this 16th-century castle is the vaulted tower room—the original Great Hall with its curved Elizabethan fireplace, built from granite. In the late 1930s the walls were stripped bare by the late Sir James and Lady Burnett to expose the original stonework and return the room to its austere 16th-century dignity. Here, beside the greatest family treasure—the horn of Leys, which it is believed was given by Robert the Bruce to the Burnetts in 1323—are works by Jameson, the father of Scottish portrait painting, and a portrait of Bishop Burnett, aider and abetter of Dutch William (King William III) and author of a famous book *History of My Own Times*. Also in the hall at the upper end, facing the fireplace, was once a dais where the laird and his family dined.

The greatest features of Crathes are the bedroom ceilings on the second and third floors. These were discovered in 1877, hidden under a layer of

Crathes
Castle

Juras Maccabeos

Crathes Castle *(detail from ceiling)*

lath and plaster for over a century. The present blazingly colourful ceilings, painted by Jacobean artists in the Chamber of the Muses, the Chamber of Nine Worthies, and the Green Lady's Room, are well worth seeing. Between the ceiling joists the boards are painted with symbolic figures, and on the sides of the joists are inscribed descriptive jingles explaining the pictures and offering words of wisdom. At the top of the house, the Long Gallery runs across the whole breadth of the building from east to west and has a spectacular oaken ceiling carved with heraldic shields.

Crathes is well worth a visit, particularly for garden enthusiasts, who will find the magnificent 18th-century formal gardens set out with some of Britain's finest plant collections. The Irish Yew hedges which divide the garden into units are around 260 years old and the lime avenues are possibly even older. Each enclosure has a different personality and colour scheme, from the Pool Garden with its purple-foliaged plants, to the spectacular yellow-flowered witch-hazel and Eucryphia in another section. There is a Visitor Centre housing a well-stocked shop and two permanent exhibitions on the castle, family and surroundings.

A National Trust for Scotland property.

Open to the public, every day, mid-April to September (weekends in October), 11am–6pm. Refreshments available.

Crawford Castle
Crawford, Clydesdale, Strathclyde.
¾ mile from Crawford on A74.

This ruined castle on the bank of the Clyde was last occupied at the end of the 18th century when it was destroyed and much of the masonry used to build the present house. The castle was first mentioned in 12th-century documents but almost certainly it was built before that. The surrounding area is particularly rich in Roman army camps which were sited here because of the important river crossing at Crawford. In fact, the road on which the castle stands is called Camps Road and leads to Camps Reservoir and Campshead.

Crawford Castle belonged to the Carmichaels, Lindsayes and eventually the Dukes of Angus Home before reverting to the Crown of Scotland. At one stage it is thought to have been used as a hunting seat by James V, father of James I and VI of England and Scotland. His wife was Margaret of France, and a story is told of the 'Scottish Dessert' promised by James V when his French companions complained of the lack of vegetation and generally bleak aspect of Crawford Moor. The king is supposed to have replied that he would provide them with a dessert for dinner that night 'richer than anything produced in France'. He gave each astonished guest a plate full of Scottish gold coins produced in Crawford parish.

Wallace was reputed to have taken the castle from English hands, but the truth is uncertain. We do know that James V repaid the hospitality shown by his Seneschal Carmichael by making his daughter pregnant.

Not open to the public but can be seen from the roadside.

Crichton Castle
Crichton, Midlothian, Lothian.
2½ miles west of Pathhead on A68 from Edinburgh.

Crichton Castle stands majestically on a bare site above the valley of the East Lothian River Tyne. The solid rectangular tower house, with hall on the first floor, is thought to have been built late in the

14th century as a three-storey block, of which the top storey has since been removed. Below the hall is a vaulted basement, lit by narrow loops. On the first floor is the main entrance in the north-west corner with a newel stair which leads to the upper storeys and no doubt at one stage went on up to the roof. A second stair leads down to the basement, to what was a loft in the basement vault and to a dismal cramped pit with only a tiny air-slit. Above this prison are what once were the kitchen quarters, reached by a third stair from the hall. On the west side of the tower house was a fortified barmkin which screened all the outbuildings and which swept round below the present western buildings. Sometime during the 15th century, Chancellor Sir William Crichton, who was a guardian of James II during his minority, added a keep-gatehouse on the south side of the barmkin. This contained three storeys and included its own hall on the first floor, staircase, buttery, cellar and upper hall. During the following years the barmkin was destroyed and replaced by a close-set quadrangular mansion enclosing a narrow courtyard; and in the second half of the 15th century an inferior western wing was added.

The final building work took place in the 16th century when the north wing of the castle, which still stands today, was added. In 1585 the notorious Earl of Bothwell and his Countess Margaret Douglas rearranged the ground floor cellars of the north wing and made a second kitchen with service stair on the first floor. East of the kitchen they added a well-lit and spacious dining-room with two turret chambers. Crichton Castle at this stage had four kitchens, but even more unusual was the striking contrast of the newer buildings to the older portions of the fortress. Bothwell's additions were elaborately Italian Renaissance in style, and it is thought that they may have been copied from the Palace of Ferrara.

Crichton is doubly important as a fine architectural example of castellar building which shows definite foreign influence in the construction. Although it is certain that the master mason responsible for the south wing was a Scotsman, the diamond façade and Italianate character of the internal arcade are most likely the work of an Italian architect whom Bothwell may have brought back in 1581. When completed, Crichton became one of the ablest and most remarkable pieces of house-planning in Scotland, and it remains so today. The original tower house was obviously abandoned at a fairly early stage and either left to fall into ruins, or perhaps had the top storey removed to unify all the building periods. Bothwell was never very concerned about preserving the original tower and for many years historians failed to recognise its existence, believing the south-west six-storeyed narrow tower to be the nucleus of the castle.

South of the castle stands a roofless building which was not a chapel, as one would expect, but a stable with quarters for grooms overhead. Around and about are signs of yet more buildings.

The earliest record of the barony of Crichton dates back to the 13th century when John de Crichton received a charter of the barony from Robert III. It is possible that he began to build a great tower, but his son, the famous Sir William Crichton, is the more likely of the two to have extended the castle and added the keep-gatehouse in the 15th century. It was this man who lured the young Earl of Douglas and his brother to the famous 'Black Dinner' at Edinburgh Castle in 1440. The unsuspecting lads were lavishly entertained, unaware of the conspiracy against them. At the end of the dinner they were dragged out and murdered. In the civil war which followed, the Chancellor was besieged in the Castle of Douglas by the furious Douglases, while one of their followers, John Forrester, marched to Crichton Castle, stormed it and apparently demolished the buildings. It was presumably after this event that the Chancellor remodelled and extended the castle.

William, third Lord Crichton, was also held at the castle by Royal forces for his part in the Duke of Albany's conspiracy against James III in 1483. He managed to escape but his lands and castle were forfeited and given by the king to Sir John Ramsay, his favourite. Sir John became Lord Bothwell and Treasurer of Scotland, but he died an 'obscure and traitorous spy' in the pay of England after Sauchieburn in 1488. Again the castle and estates were forfeited and granted by James IV to Patrick Hepburn, Lord Hailes, who was created Earl Bothwell. In 1559 the castle was besieged and captured by the Earl of Arran because of Bothwell's actions on behalf of the Catholics against Queen Elizabeth and the Protestant lords. Two years later the wedding took place here of Lord John Stewart, a natural brother of Queen Mary, but in 1567 the castle was forfeited for the third time when the notorious Earl of Bothwell, Queen Mary's husband, was found guilty of actions against the Crown.

James VI transferred the title and estates to a kinsman, Francis Stewart, a cultured ruffian who thrived on violence and uproar, and it was he who brought an Italian architect to decorate Crichton Castle in such an exotic way. In 1593, after the wild Earl's forfeiture, the castle was ordered to be razed to the ground, but the threat was never carried out, and after many further changes of ownership, and eventual deterioration into ruins, Crichton was placed in the care of Historic Buildings and Monuments, Scottish Development Department.

Open to the public, every day, April to September, 9.30am–7pm, Sundays 2–7pm; October to March, weekends only, Saturdays 9.30am–4pm, Sundays 2–4pm.

Crookston Castle
Crookston, Glasgow, Strathclyde.
3 miles south-east of Paisley.

On the banks of the White Cart river are the ruins of Crookston Castle. As far back as 1130 there was a castle here, probably on the same site and built by Robert Croc. In 1330 the lands were given to Stewart of Darnley, whose descendants took the title of Earls of Lennox and built the present castle in the latter part of the 14th century. According to legend, Mary, Queen of Scots and Henry, Lord Darnley, son of the Earl of Lennox, were betrothed here; and it is certain that they stayed here after their marriage in 1565.

Built as a tower house surrounded by an oval-shaped perimeter defence consisting of a ditch and wide bank (which is thought to be of 12th-century origin), Crookston Castle, which is under the guardianship of Historic Buildings and Monuments, Scottish Development Department, was the first property presented to the National Trust for Scotland by Sir John Maxwell in 1931.

Open to the public, April to September, weekdays 10am–7pm, Sundays 2–7pm; October to March, weekdays 10am–4pm, Sundays 2–4pm.

Culzean Castle
Maybole, Kyle and Carrick, Strathclyde. 12 miles south of Ayr off A719.

Standing on a cliff-top overlooking the lower Firth of Clyde is this magnificent structure, the Castle of Culzean (pronounced 'Cu-lain'). It was built between 1772 and 1792 by Robert Adam for the Earl of Cassillis, chief of the Kennedys. This Georgian building is on a site associated with the Kennedys for many centuries and is probably built round an ancient tower of their original castle. Two superb features are a magnificent oval staircase and a round drawing room. A flat in the castle was reserved for General Eisenhower as his Scottish residence, at his convenience. The castle is surrounded by one of Scotland's first Country Parks, which includes a walled garden dating from 1783. The home farm buildings have been converted into a restaurant, shop, visitor centre and information point. There are various other attractions on the estate such as a deer park, woodland walks, swan pond and adventure playground.

A National Trust for Scotland property.

Open to the public, every day, 1 April to 31 October, April and October 12 noon–5pm, May to September 10am–6pm.

Dalhousie Castle
Bonnyrigg, Midlothian, Lothian.
Off A6094, 5 miles south of Bonnyrigg.

This mansion dates from the 12th century but has since been modernised and converted into a hotel. The first Marquess of Dalhousie, a famous Viceroy of India, lies buried nearby at Cockpen.

Not open to the public.

Dalquharran Castle
Dailly, Kyle and Carrick, Strathclyde.
Off A77 at Girvan.

Set in the Girvan valley is this little-known castle, it was built in the heart of the Kennedy country in the 16th century. It is one of a group of five castles including Killochan, Bargany, Penkill and Kilkerran. The roof was removed in 1967 and the castle now lies derelict.

Not open to the public.

Dalveen Castle
Dalveen, Nithsdale, Dumfries and Galloway.
Off A702, 5 miles from Carron Bridge.

The only remaining sign of a castle at Dalveen is a stone built into the wall of a farmhouse in 1836 bearing the Douglas arms and the date 1662. It was once an important Douglas stronghold standing on the right bank of the River Carron, not far from a wild pass over the Lowther Hills from Crawford to Durisdeer which dates back to Roman times. The pass was the scene of a famous rescue, when a party of Covenanters who were being taken for trial at Edinburgh escaped.

Not accessible to the public.

Darnaway Castle
Darnaway, Forres, Moray, Grampian.
4 miles west of Forres turn off at 'Thistle' signpost to Darnaway Visitor Centre.

Set in the exceptionally beautiful surroundings of Darnaway Forest is this imposing mansion which was built in 1810 to incorporate fragments of the earlier 15th-century castle built by Randolph, Earl of Moray and Regent of Scotland. The 15th-century banqueting hall, 90 by 35 feet with an arched oaken roof, stands to the rear of the modern structure.

In 1664, Queen Mary held court here and later it became a favourite haunt of James IV who gave it to his mistress, Lady Janet Kennedy. It is one of the seats of the Earls of Moray, and contains a grim painting of the 'Bonny Earl' gashed with wounds.

Open to the public, Wednesday and Sunday, June, July and August, 1.15–5pm. Refreshments available at the nearby Darnaway Visitor Centre.

Delgatie Castle

Turriff, Banff and Buchan, Grampian.
2 miles east of Turriff off A947.

Standing in wooded grounds not far from Turriff is the tower house home of the Hays of Erroll. The original 13th-century stone keep with its four-storey tower —each floor was connected with an internal ladder—was slowly added to over the centuries and in many different stages. By the 16th century Delgatie Castle had been extended three times and was completely rebuilt on an L-plan. In 1594 the castle was besieged after the Battle of Glenlivet, and the west wall breached; this damage was restored in 1597. The present chapel and kitchen were built on to the main tower in the 17th century, and in 1720 further additions were made including the Long Drawing Room on the north side.

From 1940 to 1945 the castle was occupied by the army; when they left, the castle stood empty until 1951 when restoration work started.

Delgatie and Towie Barclay Castles have many common features, as both were rebuilt by the same master mason in the 16th century and they belong to a group of Aberdeenshire castles built for families closely related and united by loyalty to Mary, Queen of Scots and the Catholic religion.

In the solar or laird's private room at Delgatie, the ribs of the groin-vaulted roof meet in a central boss bearing the arms of Gilbert Hay, Earl of Erroll. Two of the other rooms have painted ceilings and the ceiling in the Tulip Room is decorated with proverbs on the beams interspersed with colourful armorial paintings. The castle contains a fine collection of armour including many Eastern weapons, coats of mail, a Genoese crossbow and a knight's helmet dated around 1350. Here also is a two-handed sword of about 1400 and a fine Scottish broadsword and dirk used at Culloden.

The castle has been in the possession of the Hays for nearly 700 years. The family is said to have gained its name from the Battle of Luncarty near Perth in about 971, when three giant men held a narrow pass against invading Danes. For this they were given the name Haye (in Gaelic, *Garadh*) which means palisade or wall, as they stood like a wall, using ox yokes as weapons, defending the pass. Historical records show that a century later two Hays came over with William of Normandy to conquer the English. By 1150 the same family had become large landowners in almost all the counties of Normandy (which then included England) and had reappeared in Scotland.

Robert the Bruce rewarded the Chief of the Hays with the office of Hereditary Lord High Constable of Scotland for his part in the War of Liberation. The office may be described as combining the duties of Commander-in-Chief, Home Secretary and Earl Marshal, and is still held by the Earl of Erroll today. The clan suffered a terrible blow when the chief, the third Earl of Erroll, Lord Hay of Yester, Sir Gilbert Hay of Delgatie and eighty-seven other chieftains and officers of the name, with all their men between the ages of 16 and 60, were killed beside their king at Flodden Field on 9th September, 1513. In 1650 Hay of Delgatie, a professional soldier who was Montrose's chief of staff, was executed with him and buried at his side in St. Giles Church. During the 1715 and 1745 Jacobite uprisings the Hays suffered again for their loyalty and many of the families left Scotland to settle in France, Sweden, Saxony, Italy and Poland. Nowadays they are spread all over the world.

Open to the public at any time, but only by previous appointment.

Dirleton Castle

Dirleton, East Lothian, Lothian.
In the village of Dirleton off the A198, Edinburgh to North Berwick road.

Not far from the wide village green of Dirleton, in a lovely flower garden, stands one of the most picturesque castle ruins in Scotland. The oldest buildings, a group of towers, are thought to have been built in 1225 for John de Vaux, seneschal of the Queen Marie de Coucy, and are among the first examples of a 'clustered donjon' in this country. Other additions were made to the castle in the 14th and 16th centuries; of these original buildings a three-storey Renaissance portion still stands with the three drum towers, part of the walls, a 16th-century circular dovecot and 17th-century bowling green.

In 1298, the castle was besieged by Edward I but in 1311 it was retaken by the Scots. In 1650 it fell to Cromwell's troops, and was destroyed by General Lambert.

Dirleton Castle was a compact and powerful building crammed on to a restricted site and combining powerful defences with excellent accommodation. The three large towers were built of dressed ashlar and rose from long spreading bases from the edge of the rock. The largest tower housed a polygonal lord's hall and beneath this was the garrison post. Another round tower, and a square tower set between the two complete the group. Originally a fourth interior tower helped form an inner courtyard from which an outside stair led to the solar on the first floor. In the main entrance at Dirleton was a covered passage, fortified by two portcullises and two pairs of timber doors. Sadly, very little of the castle remains except for the donjon and the splayed bases of two corner towers, but it is well worth a visit, if only to see what is thought to be the prettiest village in Scotland.

Dirleton Castle

The castle is in the care of Historic Buildings and Monuments, Scottish Development Department.

Open to the public, April to September 9.30am–7.30pm; October to March 9.30am–4.30pm.

Dornoch Castle
Dornoch, Sutherland, Highland.
Off A9 to Dornoch.

Dornoch Castle, set high on its stone pile, overlooks the town; it is now a hotel. It was built about 1250 by Sir Gilbert—formerly Bishop Gilbert of Moravia —who in 1224 founded Dornoch Cathedral, and was designed primarily as a palace for the Bishops of Caithness. In 1550 the castle was rebuilt leaving only the original great stone vaults which now support the massive north tower and turret stairs. In 1814 the upper storeys of the main wing were renovated once more.

Open only to the hotel's guests, mid April to end October.

Douglas Castle
Douglas, Clydesdale, Strathclyde.
On A70, 1 mile east of Douglas, 12 miles south-west of Lanark.

Douglas Castle stood near the site of the present-day town of Douglas, the centre of the coal-mining area. It was definitely standing in 1307 when history records Sir James Douglas as trapping the English garrison while they were at worship in the chapel, and thereby recapturing his castle. It suffered an ironic fate—it was demolished between 1938 and 1948 due to a coal seam opening below it.

The castle's main claim to fame was as the seat of Sir James Douglas, who was one of Robert the Bruce's foremost commanders during the king's guerrilla campaign to regain his Scottish crown. Aside from his patriotism, Douglas was notorious for his acts of terrorism. After Robert the Bruce's wars, during which the castle was badly damaged, it was rebuilt, and immortalised by Sir Walter Scott as his *Castle Dangerous.*

Public access every day.

Doune Castle
Doune, Stirling, Central.
Off A84 from Stirling to Callander.

Doune Castle stands on a promontory above the banks of the River Teith immediately to the east of the village of the same name. The exact building date is uncertain but ancient records mention the castle being built as a royal palace in the late 14th century by Robert Stewart, Duke of Albany and Regent of Scotland, in the reign of Robert III. The existing castle has never been finished. No doubt

Doune Castle

it was primarily built as the chief seat of the Earldom of Menteith, but obviously the site was chosen with an eye to defence; in the Middle Ages, two great routes from Edinburgh to Inverlochy and from Glasgow to Perth met at Doune, and since Roman times the Teith valley has been looked on as a gateway to the mountains. Doune Castle therefore made an excellent base for whoever controlled the route to the Highlands. At the same time it is possible that Doune had a third purpose—to deter the Lord of the Isles from taking the Earldom of Ross, which Albany claimed on behalf of his son, Earl of Buchan.

In 1420, when Albany died, his estates and political power passed to his son Murdoch Stewart, second Duke of Albany. He ruled feebly for 4 years when James I returned to Scotland. In 1425 Duke Murdoch, his son Alexander and his father-in-law the Earl of Lennox, were beheaded on Heading Hill, within site of Doune. They were accused of 'Roboria' (unconstitutional violence) by the king, who confiscated the property and used it as a royal residence, state prison and sometimes as a dower house of the Queens of Scotland. Both Mary of Gueldres and Margaret of Denmark, queens of James II and III, spent much of their widowhood at Doune and so did Margaret Tudor, wife of James IV. Mary, Queen of Scots and her son James VI occasionally visited the castle, as the suite of rooms above the kitchen, known as 'Queen Mary's apartments', indicate.

In 1528 Sir James Stewart, brother of Lord Methven, third husband of Margaret Tudor the Queen Dowager of Scotland, was made Steward

and Chamberlain of Menteith and Captain of Doune Castle. In 1570, during the civil wars that took place on the Queen's flight to England, Doune Castle was besieged and captured by Regent Lennox, who agreed that it should not be demolished. In spite of his alleged support of Queen Mary's cause in 1570, Sir James Stewart was made Lord of Doune, and his son and heir James married a daughter of the Regent Moray. In 1592 James VI made this second James, Earl of Moray. Doune Castle has remained in the hands of the Earls of Moray ever since. In 1581, Sir Robert Drummond of Carnock, the King's Master of Works, organised repairs to the castle and at the same time a dyke was built round the wood of Doune. In 1593 the king, hearing of a conspiracy being hatched against him at Doune by the Earls of Atholl, Montrose and Gowrie, rode from Linlithgow with some 300 horsemen and caught Gowrie and Montrose. Atholl escaped to Blair Castle and the other two nobles were kept alive on Lord Hamilton's intervention.

In 1645 the castle was occupied by Montrose, but apart from a brisk skirmish in 1654 it saw little action and suffered little damage. In 1689 it was garrisoned by the Government, and in 1703 Sir Colin Campbell nailed up the door of Doune Castle to keep out Episcopalian preachers.

In 1715 part of the nearby Bridge of Doune was blown up by the Duke of Argyll to prevent the Earl of Mar and his men from crossing the river, but although the castle was still garrisoned by the Government it played no part in the Jacobite rising. However, in 1745 it was seized by Jacobites and used by them as a prison. Many estate accounts show that Doune Castle was repaired in 1605, 1717, 1718 and 1738. Nevertheless, by the end of the 18th century it had been completely unroofed and remained as a shell until 1883–86, when it was restored by George Philip Stuart, fourteenth Earl of Moray.

The existing castle has apparently never been completed. Built of brown sandstone rubble, the main mass of castle buildings is concentrated at the front, facing the attacking direction. Behind this the castle tails off into a simple screen wall or curtain.

The front structure is divided in two. At the north-east corner is the gatehouse and the self-contained residence of the lord containing the hall and a suite of living rooms with a private chapel. Alongside the building is a second, larger hall entered from the courtyard and originally not joined to the gatehouse. To the left of the gatehouse, the castle 'tails off' into a wall 40 feet high by 7 feet thick. On the south side of the castle is a low outer wall outside the great curtain, which would have been built to delay attackers and prevent them bringing up guns against the main wall. Inside the wall is the postern gate with its guest rooms and kitchen tower, which has a huge fireplace 18 feet wide by 9 feet deep. From the door in the kitchen tower, or from the one in the keep-gatehouse, it is possible to reach the wall walk which had a parapet on both front and rear so that the curtain could be defended against attackers, both outside or inside the courtyard. From the wall walk there are some magnificent views over the surrounding countryside.

Open to the public, April to September, every day 9.30am–7pm, Sunday 2–7pm; October to March, Saturday-Wednesday 9.30am–4pm, Sundays 2–4pm.

Drum Castle

Culter, Aberdeen, Grampian.
10 miles south-west of Aberdeen off A93 to Royal Deeside.

Set in pleasant grounds is the massive tower of Drum Castle which was built around 1286 to guard the Royal Forest of Drum. It was one of the first and certainly amongst the most famous of medieval Scottish tower houses. It was built by Richard Cementarius as a simple rectangle with battlements and rounded corners, 70 feet high; and in 1323 the king gave it to William de Irvine, his armour-bearer and clerk register, whose descendants have owned it ever since.

In 1619 a Renaissance mansion with dormer windows and crow-stepped gables was added and linked to the original tower. The former banqueting hall of the tower, now entered by a doorway

made through the 9-foot thick walls of the Jacobean wing, is a great vaulted chamber which occupies a complete storey of the keep. The ceilings are decorated with shields bearing the arms of families linked to the Irvines. Above this hall is another vaulted chamber reached by a wheel stair which rises from the first floor up to the battlements. The Jacobean wing at Drum is worth a mention. Here, a stone-flagged, vaulted passage leads along the length of the basement: and in the drawing room, which was once the great hall of the 1619 castle, hang Raeburn portraits of a former laird and his wife, a Reynolds and a fine Gilbert portrait. The castle is set in extensive gardens planted with many rare trees and shrubs.

A National Trust for Scotland property.

Open to the public, May to September, every day 2–6pm. Refreshments available.

Druminnor Castle

Near Rhynie, Aberdeen, Grampian.
North of A941 junction with A97 about 1 mile off the main road.

Druminnor Castle was built in the 15th century on lands granted to Duncan Forbes in 1271. From this earlier date the Forbes family lived in a timber-built motte and bailey stronghold at a site called Castlehill until 1440. In the 15th century the first Lord Forbes employed John of Kenlock and William of Inverkip from Renfrewshire to build the present castle.

The castle today is only a fragment of its original size but the surviving 'palace house' on the basement ground floor, together with staircase, first floor and remains of the present second floor, are thought to date back to 1440. In this section of the castle is the famous 'happy room' which takes its name from the 15th-century inscription—believed to have been written by King James II—part of which includes the words 'happy room'.

In 1571 the Forbes were defeated in the Battle of Tillyangus by the Gordons, and the castle was sacked. In the rebuilding which followed, the round stair with its heraldic panels, gun-loops, crow-stepped gables and attic windows, was added. The castle was once again restored in 1966.

Open by prior appointment only.

Drumlanrig Castle

Thornhill, Dumfries and Galloway.
3 miles north of Thornhill off A76.

Drumlanrig Castle, which stands high above the Nith valley, is a 17th-century red sandstone building. The original castle was built by Sir James Douglas of Drumlanrig between 1513 and 1578, but was completely destroyed and later rebuilt in the period 1645–88 to the design of Sir William Bruce for the first Duke of Queensberry, now Buccleuch. The Duke was so astounded by its cost that he occupied it for only a day. Nevertheless, Drumlanrig is most impressive; with its grandly sweeping forecourt it looks more like a great English 'stately home' than a typical conservative Scottish castle. Now one of the Buccleuch residences.

Open to the public, every day except Friday, May to August, Sundays 2–6pm. Refreshments available.

Drummond Castle

Muthill, Perth and Kinross, Tayside.
2 miles north-west of Muthill where A822 joins A9.

Drummond Castle stands about 2 miles to the north-west of the village of Muthill on a rock high above the magnificent gardens. The 15th-century nucleus of the castle is its lofty keep which stands apart from the modern mansion, well-known for its pictures and fine gardens. The castle was badly damaged by Cromwell, and again in 1715 by its own chatelaine, the Countess of Perth, to prevent the Hanoverians from using it. This is the Scottish seat of the Drummond-Willoughbys, Earls of Ancaster, who descend in the female line from the early Drummonds.

Only the gardens are open to the public.

Duart Castle

Craignure, Isle of Mull, Argyll, Strathclyde.
4 miles south-east of Craignure on A849.

Standing high on the rocks above the eastern entrance to the Sound of Mull on the island of Mull, in the Inner Hebrides, is Duart Castle, home of the chiefs of the Macleans of Duart. The keep was built in the 13th century, probably by Lachlan Lubanach Maclean of Duart, but the curtain walls seem older and suggest an even earlier castle. Later additions were made to the castle in both the 16th and 17th centuries, and in 1912 what was left of Duart was restored by the architect Sir John Burnet for the then chief, Sir Fitzroy Maclean.

Duart Castle is protected by a great, window-less, curtain wall, 30 feet high and almost 10 feet thick which surrounds the residential buildings set around two sides of a courtyard bounded on the seaward side by the great tower of the keep. Beyond the curtain wall was a deep fosse cut in the rock to give further protection.

Maclean means 'Son of Gillean', after a 13th-century ancestor, Gillean of the Battle Axe, whose lineage can be traced through a Celtic abbot of Lismore and the Royal house of Lorne of the ancient Gaelic kings of Dalriada. It seems that the Maclean chiefs had become related to the rulers of

the Isles, and the story is told that Lachlan Lubanach Maclean kidnapped his bride's father to force his approval of the match, and in doing so slew the Mackinnon chief. This deed made him even more popular, for the Lord of the Isles granted him more lands on Mull where previously the Mackinnons had ruled. In establishing himself and his line, Lachlan Lubanach Maclean had to obtain a papal dispensation to legalise his marriage to Mary Macdonald, daughter of the Lord of the Isles, as they were too closely related.

For a long time the Macleans of Duart feuded with a rival branch of their clan, the Maclaines of Loch Buie, and many strange tales are told of these struggles. It is recorded that Hector Mor Maclean of Duart (grandson of the chief who fell in 1513 with the 'flowers of the forest' on Flodden Field) supported Ian 'the Toothless' Maclaine of Loch Buie in suppressing a rising led by Loch Buie's only son 'Ewen of the Little Head', who was slain. His ghost 'the headless horseman' still rides abroad whenever a Maclaine of Loch Buie is about to die. It is said that Hector Mor then interned Ian the Toothless on the island of Cairnbuig, away from all ordinary women, so that he could have no heir, but allowed him an ugly and misshapen maid-servant, by whom Ian had a son 'Murdoch the Stunted', who escaped to Ireland and after many adventures returned to become ancestor of the later Maclaines of Loch Buie.

While Macdonald held the Lordship of the Isles the Macleans were his ardent supporters, even when Macdonald's son Angus Og, supported by the Clan Donald chieftains, rose in rebellion against his father. At this time Macdonald was still a semi-sovereign prince and his nobles took titles such as 'Lord Maclean and the Master of Duart'. In 1505 King James IV challenged Hector Odhar Maclean of Duart, but the Macleans continued to support the rightful Lords of the Isles against Scotland—and later England—until the last Macdonald claimant died in 1545. After this the Macleans slowly submitted to the Scottish crown while struggling with different branches of the Clan Donald to fill the title of Lordship of the Isles. For this reason they entered an uneasy alliance with the mainland Campbells of Argyll, and in some cases intermarried. These marriages were often unhappy; for instance, Lachlan Cattanach Maclean of Duart became bored with his wife, Lady Catherine Campbell, Argyll's sister, because she had not provided him with a son. So he marooned her on a dangerous rock which was covered at high tide and, thinking she was drowned, told the Campbells she was dead. Unfortunately for him she had been rescued by fishermen and taken to the Earl of Argyll. In 1523, another brother, the Thane of Cawdor, surprised the Maclean of Duart and murdered him in his bed. The next chief was Lady Catherine's step-son, Hector Mor Maclean of

Duart, who extended the great tower of Duart Castle. In 1540 he was kidnapped by James V. Another famous 16th-century Maclean lady was Catherine Maclean, Duart's sister and Argyll's widow, who then married the O'Donnell ruler of Tirconail, but was captured by the O'Neill, ruler of Tyrone, who made her his mistress. She was therefore a Scottish dowager and an Irish Queen in distress, and she had sons by both Calvagh O'Donnell and Shane O'Neill.

By far the most distinguished of all the Maclean chiefs was the Herculean Sir Lachlan Mor Maclean, who as a youth on his mother's remarriage, murdered eighteen of the guests and imprisoned the bridegroom, Maclaine of Ardnamurchan, thus regaining his estates. Later he saved Argyll's army after its defeat by the Earls of Huntly and Erroll at Glenlivet, where he captured Erroll's standard. Sir Lachlan Mor was killed in 1598, and from then on the Macleans seemed to lose power to the Campbell's.

In 1604 Duart Castle was surrendered to the King's Commissioner and 5 years later Hector Og Maclean of Duart, with most of his Hebridean chiefs, was kidnapped by the King's Lord Lieutenant. He was released only after he had agreed terms; the destruction of all his galleys, the banning of all firearms and two-edged swords, and the compulsory education of his children under Privy Council direction. Hector moved back to Duart Castle with eight gentlemen. In 1631 the chief heir was made a Baronet of Nova Scotia; although he lived at Iona for a while, he later moved back and enlarged Duart Castle and it was probably he who built the residential quarters in the north wing of the castle courtyard.

Throughout the 17th century civil wars the Macleans remained loyal to the Stuart kings and took part as staunch Jacobites in the risings of the 18th century. Under Montrose, they played a major part in the harrying of the Campbells and for a short time lost the castle to the enemy. Later, Argyll, who had bought up most of the Maclean's debts, took over the castle and it was not until 1911 that the chiefs of Clan Gillean recovered their ancestral home. The present chief of the Clan Maclean, The Lord Maclean of Duart, KT, GCVO, KBE, is Lord Lieutenant of Argyll and Chief Steward of Hampton Court Palace.

Open to the public, every day, May to September 10.30am–6pm. Refreshments available.

Dudhope Castle

Dundee, Angus, Tayside.
Off A85.

This massive many-towered castle, built in the 16th century, was formerly the seat of the Scrymgeours, hereditary constables of Dundee.

Not open to the public.

Duffus Castle

Duffus, near Hopeman, Moray, Grampian.
5 miles north-west of Elgin off B9012.

Standing in 8 acres of land and surrounded by a water-filled moat is a fine ruined Norman mound. Duffus Castle was built in the 14th century but was preceded by a motte and bailey castle on the same site. When this artificial mound was built it would have been crested by a strong palisade and crowned with a wooden tower which formed the lord's residence. Attached to this motte was the bailey, also enclosed by a palisaded bank and ditch and containing wooden buildings such as the hall, chapel, and stable. The bailey was raised above the surrounding plain for defence reasons but was still dominated by the motte which could always be held separately should the bailey fall.

Where the main gate led into the bailey is now a great gap in the curtain wall, but inside and to the left is a small oven built of clay and stone, now preserved under a glass roof. In front the impressive 14th-century stone tower rises from the summit of the old Norman motte which, as already mentioned, is separated from the bailey by a wide ditch. Following the cobbled causeway, visitors will see signs of domestic buildings set against the curtain wall, and on the south and west sides, joist holes in the curtain show that there has been a range of timber buildings. The masonry of the hall is of a later type than that of the keep and suggests that the hall was probably rebuilt after the destruction of 1452. During the 17th century a stair led up the back wall to the upper floors and battlements. At the west end of the hall are two sunken cellars and beyond them a detached building set in the slope of the motte.

The keep was in its time a very fine structure with its ashlar plinth beautifully finished. It contained three storeys, including the hall, and must have been a formidable building with its timber floors spanning 36 feet.

The castle was the original seat of the de Moravias who later became the Murrays, and it was Freskin de Moravia, Lord of Duffus, who first owned Duffus Castle. About 1280 one of his three daughters, Helen, married Sir Reginald Le Chen, bringing the castle as part of her inheritance. Sir Reginald remained a true Plantagenet supporter even at the time of the revolt against the English domination which broke out in Moray, and in 1305 he received a grant from Edward I of 200 oaks to build his 'Manor of Dufhouse'. Soon after 1350 the last Cheyne, the Lord of Duffus, died leaving an heiress, Mary, who brought the barony to her husband Nicholas, son of the fourth Earl of Sutherland. The castle remained in the hands of the Sutherlands of Duffus until 1705 when it was sold to Sir Archibald Dunbar, ancestor of the present owner, Sir Edward Dunbar.

The castle is now in the care of Historic Buildings and Monuments, Scottish Development Department.

Open to the public, every day, any reasonable hour.

Dunaverty Castle
Southend, Argyll, Strathclyde.
10 miles south of Campbeltown off A83 Mull of Kintyre road.

The ruins of Dunaverty Castle, an early stronghold of the Lords of the Isles, stand spectacularly on a pyramid of rock with a sheer drop to the sea. In 1493 it was captured by James IV, and again in 1647 by Leslie, who massacred the garrison. All that remains are two mouldering old walls on the rock.

Open to the public all year round.

Dumbarton Castle
Dumbarton, Strathclyde.
½-mile south of Dumbarton East Station on the north shore of the Firth of Clyde.

The shipbuilding town of Dumbarton is overlooked by a large mass of basalt rock, 254 feet high. This rock probably has a longer history of fortification than most other similar sites in Britain, as excavations have shown the remains of fortification by the Ancient Britons or Picts against probable incursions of other Picts or Northumbrian raiders from the south.

Dumbarton, or Dun Breatann, means 'the fortress of the Britons', and in the Dark Ages it was also called Alcluith or Ailcluaithe, 'Clyde Rock'. It is first mentioned in historical records dated A.D. 440–60, and later documents refer to the political history of Strathclyde and to its stronghold of Alcluith as well as to the kings who stayed there. In A.D. 756 Alcluith was besieged by Picts and Northumbrians who together forced the Britons to surrender. In 780, and again in 870, the Rock was besieged by Irish raiders who, on the second occasion, reduced the garrison by hunger and thirst after 4 months of fighting. The next mention of Strathclyde is made in the 10th century, and in 1018 Malcolm II set his grandson—Macbeth's predecessor—on the throne of Strathclyde. Duncan governed Dumbarton until 1034 when he succeeded his grandfather as king.

During the Middle Ages Dumbarton changed from a political centre to a stronghold and port of entry in the west of the united Scotland. It grew in importance and, like Edinburgh and Stirling, became a royal castle. Edward I was very concerned to keep Dumbarton under his rule and to do this he appointed 'trustworthy governors', including

Sir John Menteith, who captured Wallace in 1305. In 1333, young King David and his consort Joan safely lodged at the castle before sailing on to France after the Scottish defeat at Halidon Hill.

Partly because of its strength but mainly because of its secluded position. Walter de Danyelstone, an unprincipled churchman, took possession of the castle in the 14th century and used it to bargain successfully for the bishopric of St Andrews. In 1443 the castle was seized by Patrick Galbraith but the deputy governor, Sir Robert Sempill, forced him out and retook the castle. The undeterred Galbraith returned the next day with more men, killed Sempill and moved back into Dumbarton. In 1489, James IV made two attempts to take the castle. The first attack was defeated when the garrison burnt most of the burgh, but during the second attack the castle surrendered. Soon after this episode Dumbarton became a shipbuilding and outfitting base for James IV's new navy and the king sailed from here on his expeditions to pacify the West.

James IV died on Flodden Field and in the disturbed times which followed, the castle was held for the Queen Mother by Lord Erskine. In 1514 the Earl of Lennox seized the castle, and until 1540, when James V took it over, Dumbarton changed hands several times. Mary Stuart succeeded to the throne in 1542 when Dumbarton was held by Mathew, Earl of Lennox—the father of Darnley, the Queen's future consort. But Lennox changed sides to support the English, and seized money and supplies which were being taken to Dumbarton by a French fleet; these he handed over to his new ally, Henry VIII. In 1544 and 1545, while Hertford invaded Scotland, Lennox negotiated with Henry VIII in England, and the Regent Arran captured the castle to make sure of Dumbarton's allegiance to the Scots.

After the disastrous Battle of Pinkie in 1548 the infant Queen Mary was housed at Dumbarton for some months before being taken to France. While she was abroad the castle changed hands between French and English, but it was regained for her from 1562 after her return to Scotland. From then on the castle remained in the hands of her supporters until 1571, when it was surprised and taken by one Captain Thomas Crawford of Jordanhill. Lord Fleming, the governor who had previously held the castle through a vicious siege in 1570, escaped to sea, but the Archbishop of St Andrews, John Hamilton, one of Mary's principal supporters, was captured and executed.

This was the end of the most important period in the castle's history. It rose to fame in the reign of Mary, primarily as a stronghold and port of communication for Scotland, and in the following half-century acted as a prison for some notable men, including the Earl of Morton in 1581 and Patrick Stewart, third Earl of Orkney in 1614. During the first 'Bishops' War' of 1639 the castle re-emerged as a stronghold, and in March of the same year the Covenanters captured the unsuspecting governor at church and forced him to surrender the keys. Dumbarton was returned to the Royalists by the Treaty of Berwick in June 1639 but changed hands again twice in the next two years. The castle was at this stage in a rather dilapidated state after its eventful career, and when Cromwell took control of Scotland, Dumbarton was surrendered to Major-General Lambert without resistance, probably because it had little or no defences left. In 1654 a Royalist force made a successful surprise attack on the Protectorate's garrison. After the Restoration, the castle was in such poor condition that improvements were begun in 1675 and carried on until the middle of the 18th century. Further renovations were made to develop the castle for coastal defence during the 1790s. By 1865, Dumbarton was so obsolete as a credible fort that it was abandoned. However, during both World Wars the army took it over once again.

The Dark Ages of Alcluith are represented by two gravestones with debased interlace ornament dating from the 10th or 11th centuries. They were found when the garden terraces in the Nether Bailey were excavated and from their position it seems likely that St. Patrick's Chapel lay here. The gravestones are now kept in the guardhouse. Presumably, Alcluith, which was a city and not merely a fort, would have been a complex of drystone ramparts and walls at different heights, fencing the rock slopes. In the level areas between the hilltops would have been civil and ecclesiastical buildings of the 'capital' of Strathclyde. On one of the summits a fortress would have been built in a secure defensive position in case the outer walls were penetrated. In medieval times the buildings were developed between the summits on the level ground and only in modern times, from 1488, were the rest of the buildings added. In the late 16th century batteries were erected on the north and east curtains, and in 1617 the Wallace Tower was added to strengthen the North Entry. During the 17th century a few minor repairs were made but the castle slowly decayed, until 1675, when plans were made for the improvements which occurred during the following ?0 years.

More repairs took place during the reign of George II, and in the following decade the western batteries were rebuilt and the old south defences replaced by King George's Battery and the Governor's House. The most interesting structures of Dumbarton Castle are the fortifications of the 17th and 18th centuries, which illustrate a painful struggle by military engineers to adapt a problem site to contemporary defensive needs. The old North Entry remained as weak as ever until 1795 when it was blocked in its present form; at about the same time several of the batteries were modified for coastal defence. Apart from the demolition of some of the buildings put up in the interior of the walls around 1795, the castle remains the same today.

Open to the public, April to September, weekdays 10am–7pm, Sundays 2–7pm; October to March, weekdays 10am–4pm, Sundays 2–4pm.

Dunbar Castle
Dunbar, East Lothian, Lothian.

The castle, which sits perched on a red rock above the fishing harbour of Dunbar, was always reckoned to be a Border fortress. It is now in ruins, but even so there are enough remains left to fire the imagination of enthusiasts. In 1339, Black Agnes, the Countess of March and Dunbar, defied the Earl of Salisbury and held the castle against him for over 6 weeks until supplies were brought in by sea. Mary, Queen of Scots stayed here with Darnley in 1566 after the murder of Rizzio. Two years later she was brought here once more by Bothwell after Darnley's murder – a few days before she surrendered to her rebellious nobles. The tragic queen returned a third time to gather her forces for a disastrous battle on Carberry Hill, after which Regent Moray ordered the castle to be dismantled. Today only crumbling red sandstone walls remain as a reminder of what had been one of Scotland's most formidable strongholds.

Just south-east of the town of Dunbar, off the Great North Road, is a stone marking the site of Cromwell's Battle of Dunbar in 1650.

Open to the public all year round.

Dunbeath Castle
Dunbeath, Caithness, Highland.
Off A9 at Dunbeath.

Dominating the sprawling village of Dunbeath is the white mass of Dunbeath Castle, spectacularly poised on the edge of a cliff. The original keep dates from at least 1428 but the present buildings were added in 1633, with more enlargements taking place on the seaward side in the 19th century. Montrose attacked the castle for 3 days before gaining entry but it was recaptured by General Leslie after Carbisdale.

Not open to the public.

Dundarg Castle
New Aberdour, Aberdeen, Grampian.
3 miles west of Rosehearty on B9031.

On a headland called Troup between Pennan and Rosehearty in Aberdour Bay stand the remains of the red-stone Dundarg Castle, which have now been excavated. The earliest evidence of fortification at this spot was an Iron Age fort built in the 4th century. The site was occupied as a fort continually, but the first recorded evidence is of the Comyn Earls of Buchan building a strong stone castle here in the 13th century. They chose the same site and used much of the material of the prehistoric structures.

The castle was destroyed by King Robert the Bruce in 1308 in his campaign known as 'The Harrying of the Buchan'. It rose again in this period and was again destroyed. It was rebuilt for a third time, this time by French engineers in the 16th century as a place of defence during the war between England and Scotland when the English were trying to coerce the Scots into making Mary, Queen of Scots a bride for Edward VI. At this time an inner gatehouse was built and the outer walls were provided with gun-loops for the use of cannon. After this, no major events are recorded and the castle today is a ruin.

Not open to the public.

Dundonald Castle
Dundonald, Cunninghame, Strathclyde.
Off A759, 5 miles south-west of Kilmarnock.

Now a ruin on an impressive hilltop site, Dundonald was built around 1350 by King Robert II, the first Stuart king, who later died there in 1390. His son Robert III was as fond of the castle as his father before him, and he too died here in 1406. Robert II was, in fact, not the original owner, but he reconstructed an older keep-gatehouse which stood on this site, which had two half-round towers projecting to the front of the gatehouse and a long entrance passage through its centre at ground level. Robert built over the original masonry and used much of the old stone, radically changing the basic plan and turning the old gatehouse into a model tower house by closing the central entrance between the two round towers and redesigning the accommodation. At the same time he added two lofty barrel vaults to the main building.

The interior of Dundonald, because of its reconstructions, was slightly different from other 14th-century castles, with a small elevated entrance opening directly into the private apartments instead of the usual thoroughfare into an open yard. The main entrance was replaced in the outer wall. The main body of the castle was refitted and then contained a lower vault which was divided into two storeys by a timber floor, and an upper vault with the great and unusually grand hall. This was enriched with ribs jutting from heavily moulded corbels in the side walls and dividing the vault into two great bays. This vaulting is of particular interest in that it is purely decorative and not structural at all.

Not open to the public.

Dunglass Castle
Dunglass, Dumbarton, Strathclyde.
3 miles west of Dumbarton on A82.

To the west of Bowling in the Kilpatrick Hills is the ruin of Dunglass Castle, the seat of the Colquhoun family from the 15th century to the 17th century. Dunglass means 'The Grey Fort', and this castle, jutting out into the Clyde at a most strategic point, was probably originally a dun or fort of the Britons of Strathclyde. The Romans too are thought to have had a station here.

Dunglass was the stronghold of the Barony of Colquhoun, and in military importance it was second only to Dumbarton Castle. It was used as an outpost of Dumbarton, and was originally built around 1380. Sir John Colquhoun, Chamberlain of Scotland, lived here during the reigns of James II and III, and after his death in 1478 his widow, Lady Elizabeth Dunbar, Countess of Murray, stayed on at the castle. In 1484 the Lords of the Council decreed that she should 'uphold the said lands, place, tenements and orchards yearly, in as good a state of repair as when she received them', presumably because she had been neglecting the place.

James IV attacked Dumbarton Castle during the first year of his reign and while trying to oust the Captain, the Earl of Lennox, sent for a heavy gun, named Duchal, to be based at Dunglass. Before the gun arrived, the Earl of Argyll, who was directing operations, was driven out of the town of Dunglass when the houses were fired, leaving the way clear for Lennox and his rebels to escape to the north where they were later surprised and defeated at Aberfoyle.

In the 16th century Sir Humphrey Colquhoun of Luss built the turreted mansion inside the walls of the old castle but did not spend much time here for not long after he was slain in his own castle of Bannachra. The story is told that having been beaten in a skirmish with the MacFarlanes of Arrochar he fled to Bannachra, but was followed by his enemies who surrounded the house and bribed one of the servants to point out his master, whereupon a skilled bowman killed the knight with an arrow.

The Colquhouns kept Dunglass until about the

beginning of the 18th century. In 1738 it belonged to the Edmonstones of Dentreath and from then on it deteriorated into its ruined state. In 1783 the Commissioners for Supply for the County of Dumbarton ordered stones to be taken from the castle to repair the nearby quay. This vandalism continued until 1812 when Mr Buchan of Auchentorlie bought the castle and added yet another wing to the 16th-century mansion.

Dunglass was a courtyard type of castle of which the main feature was a strong surrounding wall pierced by arrow-slits. Against this wall permanent and temporary buildings were erected, and although little of these remain there are signs of stone seats and windows to be found. Along the top of the south wall are still several corbels which supported a platform from which the defenders shot arrows or poured boiling pitch on the enemy below. The door in the south wall was the sea-gate, which was used as the main approach at this time when roads were almost non-existent; this was defended by a platform above and a gun-loop at the side. Inside the door a stair which led to the rooms above the gate rises sharply to the left. At the landing place by the sea-gate the Colquhouns moored their galleys, ownership of which was made compulsory by an act of James I for all lords having land near the sea. The ruins of Dunglass are situated within the confines of an industrial complex and, whilst there is a right of way, visitors must comply with Petroleum Spirit Regulations and check in at the gatehouse, turning in matches and lighters.

Not far away at Bowling are the remains of the Antonine Wall, built from turf and clay, which ran from Bo'ness in the east to Bowling in the west. This incredible defensive structure was built by the Romans around A.D. 143 to span the narrowest part of Scotland from coast to coast and act as a frontier line between the Forth and Clyde.

Open to be viewed from the outside only when accompanied by a security guard. It is advisable to telephone the Esso Bowling Terminal beforehand.

Dunnottar Castle
Stonehaven, Kincardine and Deeside, Grampian. Off A92, 2 miles south of Stonehaven.

The spectacular ruined fortress of Dunnottar covers an area of nearly 3 acres. The great tower or keep was built in 1392 by Sir William Keith, Great Marischal of Scotland, but an older fortress must have stood on the same site previously, for records mention that it was taken from the English by William Wallace in 1296.

Dunnottar was again besieged and taken by the English in 1336 but shortly afterwards it was retaken and destroyed by the Scottish Regent, Sir Andrew de Moray. By the end of the 14th century Dunnottar had come into the hands of William Keith and building works continued under his successors including the fifth Earl, George, who also founded Marischal College in Aberdeen.

Among the many subsequent additions to the fortress the most significant was the massive gatehouse of 1575. Earlier in the 16th century a new block had been built east of the keep. The west wing was also added shortly after 1581 and two other wings linking up with a 16th-century chapel were built early in the 17th century.

In 1639 the seventh Earl Marischal declared for the Covenant and took part with Montrose in the capture of Aberdeen. The story of Dunnottar's part in the Civil War is tragic. Montrose, who had been an ally of the Earl Marischal, tried but failed to win him over to the Royalist cause in 1645 and when Montrose realised he had been rebuffed he attacked the castle. The Earl Marischal had 'to stand on his own battlements and see the fires of war devouring his broad acres'.

Nevertheless, Montrose failed to dislodge the fierce Presbyterian earl, and Dunnottar remained Protestant property. King Charles II later signed the Solemn League and Covenant, and in 1650 he was entertained at Dunnottar by the Earl Marischal on his way south. In 1651 English troops besieged the castle under General Overton for 8 long months, until May, 1652. The governor, Sir George Ogilvy of Barras, surrendered eventually to Colonel Morgan; but the prize that the English had hoped to gain from this victory—the State papers of Scotland and the Scottish regalia—eluded them, as these had been smuggled out during the siege by Anne Lindsay, a kinswoman of Ogilvy's wife.

One of the darkest moments in Dunnottar's history was in 1685, during the rebellion of Monmouth and Argyll. One hundred and twenty-two men and forty-five women—Covenanting prisoners—were herded into the 'Whigs Vault' dungeon at Dunnottar, where many of them died.

Dunnottar was used by both sides in the struggle for power, and in Viscount Dundee's campaign, 14 years later, seventeen suspected Jacobites from Aberdeen—including George Liddel, a professor of mathematics—were imprisoned for over a year at Dunnottar. Finally, in 1715, the cannons from Dunnottar were used by the Jacobite army. After this rising the castle and all the possessions of the tenth Earl Marischal were forfeited, and in 1718 the castle was dismantled. In 1925 Viscountess Cowdray organised repairs and excavations to the ruins and these, including the eerie Whig's Vault and the finely restored drawing room are open to the public.

Open all year to the public, weekdays 9am–6pm, Sundays 2–6pm, closed on Fridays from November to April.

Dunollie Castle

Oban, Argyll, Strathclyde.
On A816 on northern outskirts of Oban.

The ruined Dunollie Castle crowns a promontory to the north of the town and is surrounded on three sides by the sea. It is the ancient stronghold of the MacDougalls, the Lords of Lorn, barons so powerful that they once owned a third of Scotland. Their descendant, MacDougall of MacDougall, Chief of the Clan MacDougall, is still in possession of the castle and some surrounding lands, though on a slightly smaller scale. There are no authentic records of the founding of Dunollie but the oldest part of the castle, the north curtain wall, was built in about 1150 by Somerled, the father of the first MacDougall. Nowadays only the keep of the castle remains, while fragments of other buildings, overgrown with ivy, can just be made out.

In 1647 the castle was besieged, and again in 1715 when the chief was fighting for the Jacobites it was besieged and this time forfeited, but was restored to the family in 1745 for their loyalty. Before all this, in Robert the Bruce's time, the then MacDougall married a daughter of the Red Comyn whom Bruce slew in St. Michael's Church, Dumfries. This and other deeds made the MacDougalls bitter enemies of Bruce and they resolved to thrash the uncrowned king in battle. Bruce and MacDougall met at Dalrigh near Tyndrum and in the ensuing fight Bruce narrowly escaped death. The feud continued when Bruce became king and he marched against the MacDougalls and practically annihilated the clan at a battle near the Bridge of Awe. After this defeat the MacDougalls retreated to Dunollie and lost all but a few of the lands around their ancestral home.

Not open to the public, as in a dangerous condition.

Dunoon Castle

Dunoon, Argyll, Strathclyde.
Opposite Dunoon Pier.

Until the 19th century, when tourism came to Dunoon, this tiny village lay clustered peacefully round its castle, which from the 11th century had been the seat of the High Stewards of Scotland. After the accession of the Stewarts to the Scottish throne Dunoon Castle became Crown property and was given to the Campbells of Lochow, ancestors of the Duke of Argyll, who were appointed hereditary keepers.

Mary, Queen of Scots visited Dunoon to see her favourite sister, Lady Jane Stewart, a natural daughter of James V and first wife of Archibald, Earl of Argyll. In 1646 the Campbells massacred the Lamonts at Dunoon after a raid by the Campbells on Lamont territories. They burnt Toward Castle and took several hundred prisoners, murdering most of them and taking the rest back to Dunoon, where thirty-six were hanged on one tree alone. Shortly afterwards the Earls of Argyll moved their seat to Inveraray, and Dunoon Castle was left abandoned to fall into ruins.

The Castle Gardens and Castle Hill where Dunoon Castle once stood are in a public area.

Dunrobin Castle

Golspie, Sutherland, Highland.
3 miles east of Golspie off A9.

Just north-east of Golspie, set in a magnificent park overlooking the sea, is Dunrobin Castle, seat of the Dukes of Sutherland.

The first structure dates back to 1275 but the earliest existing reference to the castle was in 1401. Later modifications were made to the original fortified keep in the mid-17th century by Earl John Glas, and between 1835 and 1850 by Sir Charles Barry, who enclosed the old castle on the north and east. These additions were destroyed by fire in 1915 but have since been restored by Sir Robert Lorimer, who also (in 1912) designed the library, drawing rooms and dining rooms. The principal rooms house Louis XV furniture, tapestries and paintings. The 19th-century gardens are styled after Versailles and include remarkable flower gardens bordering a 100-yard terrace.

Open to the public, 1 June to 15 September, Monday to Saturday 10.30am–5.30pm, Sundays 1–5.30pm.

Duns Castle

Duns, Berwickshire, Borders.
At the junction of A6112 and A6105.

About a mile north-west of the town is Duns Castle which incorporates part of a 14th-century tower traditionally thought to have been built in 1320 for Randolph, Earl of Moray.

Not open to the public.

Dunstaffnage Castle

Oban, Argyll, Strathclyde.
3 miles north of Oban on A816.

Dunstaffnage is without doubt one of the finest examples of strategic positioning in the Western Highlands, standing on a high promontory that is almost an island. The early Scots brought the famous Stone of Destiny—which forms the seat of the Coronation Seat in Westminster Abbey—from

Ireland to Dunstaffnage Castle, its first resting place in mainland Scotland. In the 9th century the stone was moved to Scone near Perth, and it was here that the kings of Scotland were crowned for many years, until in 1296 Edward I came to the English throne and took the stone, along with the ancient records of Scotland, to London. In 1603 James VI of Scotland, son of Mary, Queen of Scots, succeeded to the united thrones of the two kingdoms as James VI and I.

Originally a MacDougall castle, Dunstaffnage was taken by Robert the Bruce when he took his revenge on the MacDougall clan in the Pass of Brander in 1308. Bruce made Dunstaffnage a Royal Castle and put it in the care of the Campbells, whose chief was the Duke of Argyll. Dunstaffnage Castle was greatly enlarged in the 15th century on the orders of Alexander II, for his attack against the Norse Hebrides.

Dunstaffnage is mentioned once again in the records of 1746 when the famous heroine Flora MacDonald, who helped Prince Charles Edward Stuart escape to Skye, was held captive here. Dunstaffnage has not been used as a residence since 1810, when a great fire ruined it.

The 13th-century castle was roughly quadrangular with walls 10 feet thick and round towers. The gatehouse tower was built in the 16th century and was the family's home until burnt out in 1810, when they moved into Dunstaffnage House, the factor's home. This too was burnt out in 1940, and Angus Campbell, Captain of Dunstaffnage, moved to a small cottage on the estate where, until his death in 1958, he lived with some of the family treasures and fine paintings he had managed to rescue.

The castle is now in the care of Historic Buildings and Monuments, Scottish Development Department.

Open to the public, every day, summer 9.30am–7pm, Sundays 2–7pm; winter 9.30am–4pm, Sundays 2–4pm; closed Thursday pm and Friday in winter. Refreshments available.

Duntreath Castle
Strathblane, Stirling, Central.
2 miles north-west of Blanefield off A89.

The 15th-century castle is one of the most complete and extensive constructions of its kind in Scotland. It was built on a quadrangular plan with an entrance through the gatehouse on the west side, which was added by Sir James Edmonstone in the 16th century. Duntreath was given by James I in about 1434 to Sir William Edmonstone of Culloden, and it remained in the hands of his family until 1740 when it was abandoned. The ruined castle

Duntreath Castle (detail)

was later restored as the family seat in 1857 by Sir Archibald Edmonstone and is still in private occupation. It still contains medieval stocks and dungeons.

Not open to the public.

Duntrune Castle
Kilmartin, by Lochgilphead, Argyll, Strathclyde.
4 miles north of Kilmartin off A816.

Across the bay from the end of the Crinan Canal stands Duntrune Castle, possibly the oldest inhabited fortress in Scotland, dating back to the late 12th or early 13th century. It is basically an L-shaped tower building with additions made to it in the 16th century. The castle was a Campbell stronghold until 1792 when it was purchased by a neighbour, Neill Malcolm of Poltalloch, whose descendant, Robin Malcolm, lives there today.

Open to the public by appointment only.

Dunure Castle
Dunure, Kyle and Carrick, Strathclyde.
Off A719 at Dunure.

The fragmentary ruins of this former tower house crown a promontory above the sea. It was a Kennedy stronghold and in 1570 was the scene of the roasting of Allan Stewart, Commendator of Crossraguel, by the fourth Earl of Cassillis and 'King' of Carrick, Gilbert Kennedy. This incident kindled the feud between Bargany and Cassillis which eventually led to the Cassillis branch of the family being outlawed for a time.

On view all year round, from the outside.

Dunvegan Castle

Dunvegan Castle

Dunvegan, Isle of Skye, Highland.
24 miles from Sligachan on A863.

To the north of the village and surrounded on three sides by the sea is the Castle of Dunvegan, the home of the chiefs of the Clan Macleod since 1200. The castle was once accessible only by boat, but now the moat has been bridged and the castle opened to the public. Parts of it are reputed to date from the 9th century but the massive four-square tower shows signs of additional building from the 15th to 19th centuries.

Dunvegan may not be the oldest Scottish castle still standing today but it claims to be the oldest inhabited castle in Scotland today (see Duntrune Castle). The interior, which has over the centuries been greatly modernised, contrasts dramatically with the outward signs of powerful defence. It has walls 10 feet thick and a 15th-century dungeon, and houses many treasures including relics of Bonnie Prince Charlie, manuscripts of Sir Walter Scott and Dr Johnson, Rory Mor's two-handed sword and the 'fairy flag' thought to have been captured from the Saracens during a Crusade. The legend tells that once the flag is waved it will bring relief to the chief or any of his clan, ensuring a Macleod victory. If spread on his marriage bed it will endow the chief with children, or if unfurled at Dunvegan will charm the herring in the loch. The gift was made by the fairies on condition that it was used only in emergencies; twice it was flown in battle, and twice the Macleods won.

Dunvegan Castle is still the centre of the Macleod clan, who come here from all over the world.

Open to the public, Monday to Saturday, April to October 10.30am–5pm. Refreshments available.

Dupplin Castle

Forteviot, Perth and Kinross, Tayside.
Off A9 on B934, 5 miles south-west of Perth.

The castle stands in a wooded park and is the seat of Lord Forteviot whose father, Sir John Dewar, bought the estate in 1911 from the Earl of Kinnoull. In 1925, Sir John demolished the old houses round the castle and built a model village on the site. Dupplin Castle was built over the period 1828 to 1832 to take the place of an earlier tower house destroyed by fire.

Not open to the public.

Earlstoun Castle
Lochinvar, Stewartry, Dumfries and Galloway.
Off A713, 2 miles north of St John's Town of Dalry.

A typical late tower house built in the second half of the 17th century by the Clan Gordon. Its construction is thought to have taken place during the unsettled period following Cromwell's occupation. From this castle, four leading Covenanters started a train of events that led to the much lamented (in legend) Battle of Rullion Green. Nearby is Lochinvar, with ruins of a small castle on an islet which are said to have inspired the famous poem *The Young Lochinvar.*

Not open to the public.

Edinample Castle
Lochearnhead, Stirling and Central.
On A84, 15 miles north of Callander.

Just to the south-east of the village of Lochearnhead, at the head of Loch Earn, stands the white-washed castle of Edinample. This castle can be seen from across the Loch with the detail of the high Z-plan fortalice easily visible. It was built in 1630 by Sir Duncan Campbell of Glenorchy on the site of an older fortification of MacGregor origin—in fact the Campbells are said to have stolen the land from the MacGregors. Sir Duncan Campbell was a prolific builder and is thought to have built at least seven castles during his lifetime, including Edinample. One of the most fearsome aspects of this castle is the bottle dungeon, a round pit with access only through a narrow neck-like opening through which prisoners were dropped or lowered on a rope.

Not open to the public.

Edinburgh Castle
Edinburgh, Lothian.

In the centre of Scotland stands the premier Castle of Scotland, perched on a basalt rock that juts up 443 feet above sea-level. Not only has Edinburgh Castle been a fortress since the 7th century but a palace too, and a place of refuge for sovereigns during their minority as well as a prison for their enemies. It has in fact been described as 'the last post of defence for lost causes'.

The natural formation of this rock site must have marked it out as a possible spot for defence and retreat in time of trouble. It possessed springs of water, had slopes to the west suitable for grazing the community's cattle and stood high and clear of the surrounding marsh and forest land. The crest of the rock was more than likely a fort as far back as the Iron Age, but all traces of this early occupation have gone. Not until the 11th century is there any reliable information on the castle, when history records that Malcolm III, Canmore, married Margaret, sister of Edgar Atheling, King-elect of England, and that the king and queen made the Castle their royal residence. It is almost impossible to imagine the fortress as it was then, but the buildings are thought to have been on the highest part of the rock, surrounded by a wooden stockade reached by a flight of stairs. Only the chapel, which Queen Margaret had built for herself in the late 11th century, remains from this period. This remarkable woman is said to have decorated the palace, particularly her chamber, with luxuries unknown in Scotland at the time. There she lived and worked with her ladies until her death in 1093, after she had heard that her husband and their eldest son Edward had died during an ill-fated raid on England. Donald Blane, the king's younger brother and heir apparent besieged the castle

Edinburgh Castle

when the queen died, but he was unsuccessful; and under the cover of the mist the queen's body was taken to her Abbey at Dunfermline where she is buried.

David I, Queen Margaret's youngest son became Scotland's next king and during his reign founded many abbeys, including Holyrood in 1128. Forty-six years later in 1174, the castle was occupied by the English after William the Lion had been defeated by Henry II at Alnwick and forced to hand over this and three other Scottish fortresses as security for his ransom. Edinburgh remained in the hands of the English until the marriage of William to Ermadis de Beaumont, when it was restored to the Scots.

The castle was used once again for the marriage of Alexander III to Margaret, daughter of Henry III. The two young children were eventually taken to Wark where Alexander was persuaded to put nobles who sided with England into power. This sad king spent his last years at Edinburgh, and after his death—followed shortly by that of his only descendant, Margaret of Norway—Scotland was plunged into the troubles of the succession.

The castle was at that time an important focus on loyalty for the Scottish nation, as it housed the national documents of Scotland and served also as the treasury guarding the jewels of the Scottish kings. But in 1291–92 Edward I of England ordered the records and treasure to be removed into his safekeeping until another king was found. The treasure was taken from Edinburgh Castle and as suspected by the Scottish, many pieces eventually found their way to the royal wardrobe at Westminster. Edward still claimed that he would only look after the valuables until a successor had been found for the Crown of Scotland but this was obviously no more than an excuse, for when John de Baliol became king they were never restored to the castle.

Edinburgh Castle became a treasury and record house once again after the Wars of Independence. It was here that the 'black kist' of James III, which was said to hold 'fabulous wealth', was thought to be stored in David's Tower. No-one ever knew the truth of this tale, for Edinburgh was plundered again in 1650 by Cromwell, who took the Scottish records to Stirling Castle and then on to London, and no mention was made of the black kist. Some of the records were later restored in 1657 but the remainder were lost at sea on their way to Leith after the Restoration. Not long after, the records were transferred to the vaults below Parliament House and then to Register House.

The story of the Honours of Scotland is a prouder one. They were guarded so zealously by Kirkcaldy of Grange that a Parliament of the Queen's adversaries could not get hold of them and had to make do with counterfeits of gilded copper. They survived the siege which ended in 1573 and were used for the coronations of James

VI and Charles I. Edward I visited Edinburgh in 1291 and received homage from some of the Scots. When John de Baliol became king, Edward gathered his forces and, in 1296, advanced upon Scotland and besieged the castle, which surrendered after eight days. It remained an English garrison post until 1313, when a surprise attack by Sir Thomas Randolph, Earl of Moray and nephew of Robert the Bruce, recaptured the fortress. By the king's command the building and fortifications were totally destroyed except for St Margaret's Chapel.

The castle was once again occupied by the English during David II's minority and during this time the garrison restored part of the ruins. In 1341 William of Douglas and a group of friends, disguised as merchants carrying corn and wine to the troops, dropped their loads in front of the open gates which could not then be closed. They attacked the garrison and captured the fortress. David II returned from captivity in England after the Battle of Neville's Cross and began to rebuild the castle. In 1367 he added King David's Tower, which took 10 years to build. This was a large L-shaped keep at the south-east corner of the Castle Rock, and a fragment still survives incorporated in the Half Moon Battery of 1574. King David died here in 1371, and Robert II became king. It was he who granted the burgesses of Edinburgh the right to build houses within the castle walls for better protection in times of war.

Earl John, who is known as Robert III, was Scotland's next king. He lived at Edinburgh Castle with his Queen Annabella and the court and during his reign signed the Treaty of Alliance with France against England.

Not only was Edinburgh Castle a royal residence but it was frequently used as a refuge for the minorities of the ill-fated house of Stewart. James II was one of these, but he did not stay long, for his mother Queen Joanna smuggled him out to a ship at Leith and then to Stirling. Not long after the young king was returned to Edinburgh Castle, when the murder of the young Earl of Douglas and the Earl's brother took place on Castlehill. They were dragged out of the presence of James II and butchered during a royal banquet, known as 'the Black Dinner', where some say a bull's head was offered. After this murder the castle was besieged by the Douglases, and surrendered after nine months. The damages caused by this siege were then repaired until it was 'new better than befoir'. In 1497 David's Tower was the prison of Alexander, Duke of Albany, because of the king's suspicion about his frequent intrigues with England as well as the Duke's popularity in Scotland. The Duke escaped to a ship at Newhaven and sailed for France. Not long after, James III suffered a little of his own medicine, for he too was imprisoned in the same tower for 2 months. During this time he tried to make friends with a fellow captive, the Earl of Douglas, but the Earl refused to have anything to do with the king. However, Albany returned for political reasons and rescued James and, in gratitude, the king granted the burgesses high offices within the burgh in 1482.

By the time of James IV, son of the previous James, the castle was no longer a royal residence, yet the king stayed here often enough, attending mass and watching his master-gunner James Borthwick casting cannon. James loved tournaments and often took part in the ones he organised at Edinburgh. They made a pleasant interlude in the grim history of the fortress, as do other stories about the little natural daughter of the king, the Lady Margaret, who also lived there. Eventually, the warlike plans of France brought these pleasant times to an end and the castle prepared for war. The king was defeated, and after his death the captain of the castle wrote to the Queen Dowager in 1514 about a design for fortifications to the castle. He also repaired the walls near the well house and built a bakehouse and brewhouse.

In the spring of 1517 young James V was brought to Castle Rock, and led a neglected life there. Some additions were made before his reign, for the Great Hall was built in 1483 and the royal apartments in the Crown Square were added by the king's architect, Sir James Hamilton of Finnart, but on the whole James V took very little interest in the castle.

The king's first wife, Madeleine de Valois, lived mainly at Holyroodhouse, but her successor, Mary of Lorraine, often stayed at the castle. As a widow from 1542 she lived only to rule Scotland and to ensure the succession of her daughter Mary, Queen of Scots. Mary was then living in France to maintain the French alliance. But after all her struggles her opponents won, and Mary of Lorraine 'ended her life most christianly' in 1560.

Queen Mary visited the castle for the first time in 1561, riding from Holyroodhouse, and in the following year she returned again with her husband after the murder of Rizzio. Here her son, Prince James, was born in 1566, and salutes were fired from the castle. Between the time of her son's birth and the queen's next visit to the castle came the murder of Darnley and her abduction by Bothwell. In 1567, the day before Bothwell's divorce was announced, they rode to the castle and she stayed there until her marriage in the hall of Holyrood a few days later. Edinburgh Castle from then on belonged to James, Earl of Moray, until he appointed Sir William Kirkcaldy of Grange in his place. It is likely that this man turned traitor, for the Confederate Lords asked for help from Queen Elizabeth and bombarded the castle night and day. The garrison eventually surrendered and the principal officers were executed.

Regent Morton started to rebuild, and over David's Tower rose the Half Moon Battery. From this time the castle ceased to be more than a fortress occasionally visited by the king. James VI spent large sums of money on its upkeep in 1584, and the accounts for 1615 show that considerable building had taken place. (Charles I visited Edinburgh in 1633 and spent three nights before his coronation. Charles II made an equally brief stay in 1650. After this no king entered the castle until George IV in the 19th century.)

In 1639, Alexander Leslie took the castle and provisioned and garrisoned it to fight against the king. Four months later it was restored to the king but by 1640 the country was at war again and Leslie retook the castle once more.

In October 1648, Oliver Cromwell met the Marquis of Argyll in Edinburgh as a friend, but the next time he came it was as an enemy. Between the two visits Scotland, as a nation, had changed. The Scots resented the execution of Charles I and had proclaimed Charles II at the Market Cross of Edinburgh. This was construed by England as an act of war and Cromwell invaded Scotland. He took Edinburgh Castle in 1650 after damaging most of the eastern block of buildings and from then on, until the Restoration, the castle remained under an English garrison.

After the Restoration of Charles II Argyll was clapped into prison at Edinburgh Castle before his execution in 1661. For some years war had passed the castle by: although Charles II did not return to Scotland he paid considerable attention to the fortification of the castle, strengthening the eastern approaches, repairing towers and adding a fourth storey. Edinburgh Castle was not yet at peace, for the 'Glorious Revolution' which set William III on the throne of England created a war in Scotland and the castle stood its last long siege, held by the Duke of Gordon. Even though King James II bade him leave the castle, Gordon fought on until famine and disease broke out within the walls and he capitulated. This was the last of Edinburgh Castle's great sieges, all remarkable for one thing, that the fortress was never taken by open assault. It was surprised, bombarded into surrender, starved out and perhaps betrayed, but never actually captured.

During the Jacobite risings the castle was attacked more than once but never taken, and when Prince Charles Edward and his Highlanders rode into the city in 1745, Edinburgh Castle chose to give in gracefully to him rather than fight. The subsequent history is that of a garrison and a prison. From the outbreak of war with France in 1756 until the end of the Napoleonic Wars, there was a stream of French prisoners here. It is said that they were treated extremely well and on one occasion thanked General Dundas for his attention and good treatment.

Architecturally, Edinburgh Castle has seen many alterations, especially in the 17th century. Then, the King's Lodging and Great Hall, built in the 15th and 16th century, were modified. The palace buildings inside the castle precincts form three sides of a square with the impressive Scottish National War Memorial filling the fourth side. At the west end of the Palace Yard is the United Services Museum and on the south side is the Great Hall, former Parliament meeting place and banqueting hall. This contains a collection of weapons and armour, while the Scottish regalia—crown, sceptre and sword of state—are kept in the stone vaulted Crown Room. The castle esplanade is used each autumn for a 3-week military tattoo and has been the garrison's drilling ground for centuries. Outside the castle, on Castlehill, is the Outlook Tower and nearby Cannonball House, which has a cannonball embedded in a gable. This was said to have been fired at a couple of clansmen during the 1745 rising. Opposite these, a well marks the spot where more than three hundred women were burnt to death for witchcraft between 1479 and 1722.

The castle is now in the care of Historic Buildings and Monuments, Scottish Development Department.

Open to the public, every day, Summer 9.30am–5.05pm, Sundays 11am–5.05pm; Winter 9.30am–4.30pm, Sundays 12.30–3.35pm.

Edzell Castle
Edzell, Angus, Tayside.
6 miles north of Brechin off B996 and west of Edzell.

The ruined castle of Edzell occupies an important strategic position at the crossroads between the Cairnamouth Pass road and the road which leads up from Glenesk to the Forest of Birse Mounth, Fir Mounth and Mounth Keen passes. The castle faces west and was originally reached by an avenue from the parish church. Today, visitors approach the back of the castle coming along the road from the village. The site was chosen more for sun and shelter than defence, for on the north side the castle is protected by high ground. This Norman castle was the seat of the family of Stirling of Glenesk, who gave it to the Crawford Lindsays in 1357. The new owners abandoned the castle in the 16th century and moved to a more sheltered spot a mile north. This later castle, a fine tower house, dates from the early part of the 16th century and had a quadrangular courtyard mansion added about 1580. The Lord of Edzell, Sir David Lindsay, was a prolific builder and in 1604 he also added a summer house and bath house. He died in 1610, leaving his family in extraordinary debt, and his descendants remained at Edzell until 1715 when the estates had to be sold to pay off debts to the Earl of Panmure.

Edzell Castle (detail)

The castle itself has always been a fairly peaceful place. In 1562 Queen Mary held a Privy Council here on her way north to fight the Gordons and in 1589, James VI visited the castle. David Lindsay of Edzell was a staunch Covenanter, and so Glenesk was severely harried by Montrose's men. The castle does not seem to have been damaged at this time. During the Royalist rising in 1653 John Lindsay of Edzell was taken prisoner from his castle but was rescued the next day by the Roundheads. The natives of Glenesk, led by their laird, resisted the Presbyterian Settlement of 1690 and upheld Episcopacy, holding services in the great hall of Edzell when the parish church was denied them by a decree put out by the Lords of Justiciary. Lord Panmure forfeited the lands he had just bought when he joined the 1715 rising, and Edzell Castle went to a York Building Company whose agents began to tear it apart. In 1746 a detachment of Argyll Highlanders occupied the castle and badly damaged it, but its final ruin took place in 1764 when the roof and floors were sold on behalf of the creditors of the then bankrupt York Building Company. In the same year the Panmure estates were bought back by William Maule, Earl of Panmure of Forth and on his death in 1782 his nephew, the eighth Earl of Dalhousie, ancestor of the present owner, succeeded him. Between 1932 and 1935 the Edzell ruins were placed in the care of the predecessors of Historic Buildings and Monuments, Scottish Development Department, who have repaired and reconstituted the buildings.

Edzell Castle was never completed. On the north side the buildings extend only half way along the courtyard and on the left or south side foundations remain of four rooms which may never have been completed. The tower house, built on the L-plan, contains a staircase in its short wing. This lofty mass of building is balanced at the opposite end of the façade by the tall gable of the great hall. Midway between the two is the arched portal and above the portal is a group of four empty panels which once contained heraldic designs. The vaulted west range contained cellars and a kitchen. On the north side, the vaults have gone but at the far end of the buildings are signs of a second kitchen. Above this range was the great hall with separate drawing room and a parlour on the west wall. The main stair was situated in the angle between the two basic ranges, and remains show signs of a fine neo-classical entrance.

The tower house, with its two dark vaulted cellars and small dark prison, contained the handsome great hall with a minstrel's gallery. On its two upper floors, which are no longer accessible, were more private rooms. The most notable feature of Edzell Castle is the walled garden laid out by Lord Edzell in 1604 on the south side of the old tower house. Here Lord Edzell and his master mason indulged their imaginations; the walls were capped and banded and then enriched even more. Above, the wall is finished with a heavy coping in which a series of semi-circular niches were set to display busts. One recalls that Lord Edzell died in 'extraordinary debt'.

The castle is now in the care of Historic Buildings and Monuments, Scottish Development Department.

Open to the public, every day, April to September 9.30am–7pm, Sundays 2–7pm; October to March, 9.30am–7pm, Sundays 2–4pm.

Eilean Donan Castle

Dornie, Kyle, Ross and Cromarty, Highland.
Beside A87 on the outskirts of Dornie on the road to Kyle.

At the meeting of the three lochs, Duich, Alsh and Long, stands possibly the most picturesque and certainly one of the most photographed of all Scottish castles, Eilean Donan.

The existing castle was built in 1220 by Alexander II, to keep out the Danes, on the site, it is thought, of an earlier fortification. The castle lies offshore on a rocky islet now connected to the mainland by a causeway, and it was the ancient seat of the Macrae family, the hereditary Constables of the MacKenzies of Kintail who became the Earls of Seaforth. The castle was built as a typical tower house in the standard pattern, with a courtyard and the other usual features such as corbelled angle turrets, crow-stepped gables and a staircase turret. The present structure is very largely the product of reconstruction in 1932, which faithfully followed the original patterns.

In 1539 Donald Gorm, an aspirant to the Lordship of the Isles, was killed while attempting to reduce the MacKenzie power by capturing Eilean Donan. The next important event in the history of the castle was its almost total destruction in 1719 when it was garrisoned by mercenary Spanish troops fighting for the Jacobite cause. The English man o'war *H.M.S. Worcester* was responsible for its

Eilan Donan Castle

ruin, when it lay offshore and reduced the castle by bombardment. Eilean Donan remained in ruins until 1932 when extensive reconstruction was undertaken by Colonel MacRae, a direct descendant of the last Constable of the castle, at a cost of £230,000.

Open to the public, every day, Easter to September, 10am–12.30pm, 2–5.45pm.

Elcho Castle
Rhynd, Perth and Kinross, Tayside.
3 miles south-east of Perth on the south bank of the River Tay, off A912.

This fine 16th-century fortified mansion, built in whinstone rubble with freestone facings and quoins, stands as a somewhat mournful ruin beside the Tay on Moncrieffe Hill. It belonged to the Wemyss family for centuries, and Elcho or another castle on the same site was a favourite hideout of William Wallace. These and other facts of its early history are somewhat hazy, as early written records do not survive. It seems that as well as being built as a fortification with the normal defences the castle was intended to provide above-normal residential facilities, including wooden panelling and fireplaces.

Of the original outer curtain wall all that remains is a circular tower some 70 yards south-west of the main building. The castle is one of the few showing the change from the medieval fortress to the later idea of a mansion, but the main central keep is typical of all tower houses, containing the vaulted great hall with private apartments above it. Interesting features in Elcho Castle include the iron-grated windows and gun-loops, showing once again the mixture of residential and military architecture. The entrance to the castle was through a main doorway in the south-west face of the tower which also contained the main staircase. This tower is placed so as to give protection to the south and west faces. The other two faces were protected by smaller towers which no longer exist.

The Wemyss family first obtained a charter to the lands in 1468, and Sir John Wemyss was created first Earl of Wemyss in 1683 at the coronation of Charles I. The earldom was lost to the Wemyss family when Lord Elcho took Prince Charles Edward's side in the '45 rising and forfeited his tenure after Culloden. The title and the castle passed to his younger brother, who adopted his wife's maiden name of Charteris. Elcho was also the scene of a violent event which occurred later than most in Scotland: in 1773, during a great grain famine, a mob from Perth attacked the castle which was being used by the local landowner to hoard grain.

Open to the public, every day, Summer 9.30am–7pm, Sundays 2–7pm; Winter 9.30am–4pm, Sundays 2–4pm.

Ellon Castle
Ellon, Aberdeen, Grampian.
North of the junction of A92 and A948 at Ellon village.

The town of Ellon was the ancient capital of the Buchan; among its present, mainly 19th and 20th century features, only the castle, church and central square remain from the Middle Ages. The original castle was a timbered motte dating from the 13th century, situated to guard the crossing of the River Ythan where the present-day bridge stands. The mound on which this structure was built no longer exists, and the ruin of Ellon Castle stands on a nearby river terrace. This ruined castle dates from the 15th century, but the only part still visible from this period is the basement vault. The lower section of the tower above this, with triple gun-loops, was built in the 16th century. The round tower and walls of the middle structure are shown as the 'fortalice of Ardgith'.

On its acquisition by Baillie James Gordon in 1706 the present landscaped gardens at Ellon Castle were added in the form of a long terrace 200 yards long by 15 feet wide, surrounded by a massive stone retaining wall 18 feet high. These are in turn surrounded by vast lawns and paths around which stand huge yew trees and hedges.

Baillie Gordon's sons were murdered by their tutor and the property passed to the Earl of Aberdeen in 1752. He installed his mistress, Penelope Dering, a young girl from Pett in Sussex. In 1782 he commissioned the famous architect John Baxter to add two large modern wings. The castle eventually passed to the son of this union, who let the structure fall into ruin and then built a new house nearby. During the building of the modern house part of the castle was demolished with explosives to clear the way for the new house, which ironically was pulled down in 1929. The present Ellon Castle was originally the stables and servants' quarters of the original castle's modern wings, built in 1782.

Not open to the public.

Falkland Castle
West Port, Falkland, Fife.
On A912.

Falkland Castle was an older building on the site of the present Falkland Royal Palace, built in 1501, and little or no trace now remains of the original. The palace is, however, one of the loveliest in Scotland and is thought to have been started by James II and further decorated by James V in preparation for his first marriage to Magdalene, daughter of Francois I of France. James V later died at the palace shortly after the birth of his daughter Mary, Queen of Scots.

A National Trust for Scotland Property.

Open to the public, every day, April to September (weekends in October), 10am–6pm, Sundays 2–6pm.

Farnell Castle
Farnell, Angus, Tayside.
Off the A934 at Farnell near Brechin.

Farnell Castle was built in the 12th century as the palace of the Bishops of Brechin; Edward I of England, 'Hammer of the Scots', stayed here for a night in 1296. During the Reformation in 1566 the Bishops of Brechin were forced to leave and the castle was acquired by the fifth Earl of Argyll, whose half brother, the sixth Earl, granted the barony and lands to his kinswoman Katherine Campbell, Countess of Crawford in 1569. She passed them to her son James, fifth Lord Ogilvie of Airlie in 1578; in 1591, having been driven from his home in Forter Castle, Glenish by Argyll's men, he took his family to Farnell. From then until 1623 Farnell remained the principal home of the Ogilvies until it was sold to David, Master of Carnegie. On his death 10 years later the castle passed to his father David, Lord Carnegie of South Esk, and it has formed part of the South Esk estates ever since.

The original 12th-century building, known as the 'Black Cottage', is now thought to form the kitchen in the west wing. In the 13th century this was extended and a hall built above. Later, probably during the 14th century, one of the bishops built the east wing for his private use. This was made up of three storeys with ecclesiastical crow-steps on the gables, and a roofed balcony on the top floor. The round stair tower is thought to have been added by the Countess of Crawford in the 16th century but little is known of this period of the castle's history.

Farnell was completely restored in 1966 and is now a private residence.

Open to the public by appointment only.

Finella's Castle
Fettercairn, Kincardine and Deeside, Grampian.
2 miles north-east of Fettercairn off A94.

On the left bank of the Devilly Burn is a fragmentary relic known as Green Castle which has been identified as Finella's Castle, the place where King Kenneth III was murdered in A.D. 994.

According to the *Chronicle of Kings*, Kenneth was put to death by his own men, encouraged by the treacherous Finella, daughter of Connacher,

Earl of Angus, whose son he had killed. But the chroniclers Fordoun and Hollinshead tell a different tale. According to them, Finella feigned reconciliation with the king after the death of her son and received the monarch with lavish hospitality. She had a tower covered with copper and fitted with rich furnishings built inside her castle, but concealed behind the luxurious trappings were loaded crossbows. In the centre of the main room was a bronze image of the king holding a golden apple, which, if taken out of his hand, released a hail of arrows from the hidden crossbows on the unsuspecting victim. After dinner, the king was invited to admire the image and accept the apple—which he did, and died. Finella was said to have fled across the Hills of Garvrock and met her end in the Den of Finella at St Cyrus. The second tale is undeniably romantic but most unlikely.

Open to the public all year round.

Finlarig Castle
Killin, Perth and Kinross, Tayside.
Off A827, 3 miles from Killin.

The shattered ruins of Finlarig Castle, built in 1621–29 by the notorious Campbell laird 'Black Duncan of the Cowl', stand on heavily wooded ground near the village of Killin. Many dark deeds are said to have been done here, and not far away is a rare example of a gruesome 'heading pit', containing a block and sunken cavity for the head. According to a local legend the gentry were executed in the pit and the common people hanged on a neighbouring oak tree. Of the castle, signs of two vaults survive, with gun-loops and shot-holes.

Open to the public all year round.

Floors Castle
Kelso, Roxburgh, Borders.
3 miles north-west of Kelso on A6089.

On the western outskirts of Kelso is the magnificent 18th-century Floors Castle, probably designed in 1718 by Vanbrugh for the first Duke of Roxburghe but remodelled in 1838–49 by Playfair. It shows Tudor influence in the façade, which is surmounted by capped turrets. The grounds of the castle are enclosed in a formidable wall partly built by French prisoners from the Napoleonic Wars and set with ornate gates. A holly tree in these grounds is said to mark the spot where James II was killed when a cannon blew up during the siege of Roxburghe in 1460.

Open to the public, Easter Sunday and Monday, and from 3 May to 30 September; (May, June and September, Sunday to Thursday), (July and August, Sunday to Friday), 10.30am–5.30pm. Refreshments available.

Foulis Castle

Evanton, Ross and Cromarty, Highland.
2½ miles south-west of Evanton off A9.

Built early in the 12th century, the original castle was the ancient seat of the Clan Munro, who at that time leased the lands on the agreement that they 'furnished a snowball if required to do so, at midsummer'! They were an aggressive family who were represented at many battles, including Bannockburn and Pinkie. Robert Munro, known as the 'Black Baron', served under the great Gustavus Adolphus of Sweden with 700 of his men. He died at Ulm in 1633.

The Munro family motto is 'Castle Foulis in flames' and the original building was in fact destroyed by fire in the mid-18th century. The present comparatively modern building, built in 1754–72, is not an orthodox sort of mansion for its time as the then Chief of the Munros had spent considerable time in Holland and included many Dutch features in his castle.

Open to the public by appointment only.

Fraserburgh Castle

Fraserburgh, Aberdeen, Grampian.
At the northern end of A92 from Aberdeen.

The castle, which has been converted into a lighthouse, is in the centre of Fraserburgh on Kinnaird Head. It was built by the grandson of Alexander Fraser, the seventh laird of Philorth, who initiated the 'hill of Watch' and founded the village round the harbour.

Fraserburgh Castle was built in 1569 but only the central rectangular tower, built in 1570, remains today. Four floors of the original building still stand but the fifth was removed in 1789 to make way for the lighthouse's lantern chambers. Although the castle has been altered almost out of recognition from the original building, the Wine Tower at the foot of the rock is virtually unchanged. It was not, as its name implies, built as a wine store but was probably a watch tower erected against the possibilities of sea attack.

The castle is owned by the Lighthouse Board of Edinburgh.

Open to the public all year round until one hour before sunset.

Fyvie Castle

Fyvie, Banff and Buchan, Grampian.
At Fyvie village off B9005.

The impressive five towered, fortified 15th-century Fyvie Castle, standing in wooded parkland, was once described by Sir Herbert Maxwell as the

'crowning glory of Scottish baronial architecture'. Its magnificent south front, 150 feet long, with a full sized angle-turreted tower house at each end, has an immense gatehouse tower projecting from its centre. This magnificent façade has often been likened to that of a French chateau but there is no evidence of French influence in historical records. Traditionally the oldest part of the building, the Preston Tower, was built about 1400 by Sir Harvey Preston, who captured the English knight, Ralph Percy at the Battle of Otterburn in 1388. He was rewarded for his courage with the lands of Fyvie, and when he died in 1433 the castle passed to Alexander Meldrum, who was married to one of Preston's daughters. The other, Mariota, was the ancestress of Lord Leith. Fyvie remained as the family seat until 1596, when the Meldrums sold the barony of Fyvie to Alexander Seton, Lord Dunfermline. He became Lord High Chancellor of Scotland, although recent discoveries have proved that the lower part of this building was there much before the 16th century. It was Lord Dunfermline who renovated the castle and uncovered windows and gun-loops which had been hidden for over 300 years and at the same time built a magnificent wheel stair.

Legend tells of Agnes Smith, the daughter of a local miller, who fell in love with the laird of Fyvie's trumpeter, Andrew Lammie. The lovers were parted by her parents and the trumpeter sent to Edinburgh, but perhaps there is some truth in the tale, for on the house-top of Fyvie stands a crude sandstone figure of Andrew forever blowing his trumpet in the direction of the mill.

A National Trust for Scotland Property.

Open to the public, every day, May to September, 11am–6pm. Refreshments available.

Garth Castle

Keltneyburn, near Aberfeldy, Perth and Kinross, Tayside.
Off A827 near Keltneyburn.

North of the inn at Coshieville, where in the 18th century cattle-drovers met on their way from the north and north-west, is the recently restored but very small Garth Castle. Its first known occupant was Alexander, Lord Badenoch, great-grandson of Robert the Bruce. He was better known as 'the Wolf of Badenoch' and it is believed that he actually built the castle in 1370. 'The Wolf' was a notorious character who had a multitude of bastards but no legitimate heirs. On his death the castle and lands passed to his second bastard son, James, who was married to Janet Mengies of Fothergill. It passed by direct succession in the male line until 1577 when John Stewart, fourth lord of Fothergill and Garth, died without male heirs. His sister Marie took over the castle and it continued to be occupied by Stewarts until about 1750, when they moved to the present Garth House at Drumcharry about 1½ miles away. After 1750 the castle gradually became a ruin, but it was beautifully restored by Mr David Fry in the early 1960s and bought by the present owners in 1984.

Open to guests by appointment only.

Gight Castle
Methlick, Aberdeen, Grampian.
Off B9005 on a side road near A981 at Methlick.

The shattered ruins of Gight Castle stand on high ground surrounded by picturesque woods. Its history is associated with the wild Gordons and it was George, the second Gordon laird of Gight, who built the castle around 1560. Gight Castle was the largest of four castles built by the same architect and including Craig, Delgatie and Towie-Barclay. It was L-shaped and measured 68 feet by 53 feet along its two outer walls. The main doorway leads to a ribbed groin vaulted vestibule, which has shields bearing coats of arms at the intersections of the ribs, and symbols of the Passion on the central boss. In fact, all four castles show signs of intense Catholic piety at a time when the Reformation had swept Scotland. On the first floor, two stairs go up to the spacious great hall which is now an ivy-covered ruin.

The Gordons were a turbulent clan whose history was continually 'crowded with murder and death'. The first Gordon laird of Gight died at Flodden and one of his sons at the Battle of Pinkie.

A son-in-law was murdered as were three of his grandsons, including the third laird. Another grandson drowned, a third fell fighting in Holland and a fourth in Flanders. One grand-daughter's husband was murdered by her own brother, and so the story goes on from generation to generation until the unlucky thirteenth of the title, Catherine Gordon. She married 'Mad Jack' Byron, who gambled Gight away long before the birth of their son George, later Lord Byron.

Not open to the public, as in a dangerous condition.

Glamis Castle
Glamis, by Forfar, Angus, Tayside.
5 miles west of Forfar on A94.

The present Glamis Castle belongs to a period when strength and impregnability had long ceased to be the main objective of the tower house builder. Consequently, the traditional stark lines of the basic castle have here been decorated with an incredible amount of architectural decoration.

The present castle, which dates predominantly from the last quarter of the 17th century, contains fragments of a much earlier building thought to have been the 14th century original. In fact experts agree that is has been the Lyon family home since that time. King Robert II granted the lands of Glamis to the Lyon family (the Earls of Strathmore) in 1372, but whatever the exact date of the original the present castle was rebuilt in the 17th century by Patrick Lyon, first Earl of Strathmore and Kinghorne, in French chateau style. Shakespeare gave

Glamis Castle

Macbeth the title of 'Thane of Glamis' although Macbeth's castle in the play was at Inverness. In 1715 the Old Pretender, the only son of James II of England, stayed for a short while at the castle. It later became the childhood home of Queen Elizabeth, the Queen Mother; and Princess Margaret was born here in 1930. There are fine furnishings, paintings and armour on view in the castle and in the beautiful grounds is a sundial with 84 dials.

Open to the public, Sunday to Friday, May to September, 1–5pm. Refreshments available.

Glenapp Castle
Ballantrae, Kyle and Carrick, Strathclyde.
1 mile south of Ballantrae off A77.

The castle, set in grounds including a walled garden with lily ponds, was the home of Lord Inchcape. It contains a fine collection of paintings. It is now a private residence.

Not open to the public.

Glenbuchat Castle
Glenbuchat, Strathdon, Aberdeen, Grampian.
2 miles north of Strathdon off A97.

About 5 miles from Kildrummy is a fine example of Scottish military architecture, the ruin of Glenbuchat Castle. It was built on the Z-plan in 1590, with square towers at the north-east and south-west angles of the central block and was liberally provided with gun-loops. Its builders—John Gordon Younger of Cairnburrow—and his second wife Helen Carnegie are still remembered today, for their names and the date are carved over the entrace with the motto 'nothing on earth remains but fame'. Architecturally the most important feature of the castle is that the stairs, instead of being supported by corbels are carried by arches —a characteristic more often found in France than Scotland. This is possibly explained by the fact that Sir Robert Carnegie, Helen's father, was ambassador to the Court of Henri II. The last Gordon laird of Glenbuchat was a colourful character who in his youth studied with Simon Fraser, Lord Lovat, a lively rogue. 'Old Glenbuchat', as he was known, is said to have given George II nightmares, and he played an active part in both Jacobite risings. In 1715 he had some success against the Hanoverian troops and was imprisoned for a time at Edinburgh for his outspoken habits; but he continued to dabble in intrigue until he joined Prince Charles Edward in 1745 and became one of his principal advisers. After the Jacobite collapse he hid in the hills and eventually, at the age of 70, managed to escape to Norway by boat and then to Sweden by sled. He died in poverty in France in 1750.

The castle ruins are now in the care of Historic Buildings and Monuments, Scottish Development Department.

Open to the public at any reasonable hour.

Glendevon Castle
Glendevon, Perth and Kinross, Tayside.
6 miles south of Gleneagles on A823.

Standing high on a terrace on the east side of the valley is the tall whitewashed tower house of Glendevon Castle. It is an early 15th-century fortalice, said to have belonged to the Douglas who was stabbed by King James II at Stirling in 1452. By the 16th century the castle belonged to the Crawfords, but after 1766 the keep passed into the Rutherfords' hands.

It was built on the Z-plan and was originally a hunting seat for the laird. The present structure has been turned into a restaurant, bar and shop.

Open to the patrons of the restaurant, bar and shop.

Grandtully Castle
Grandtully, Perth and Kinross, Tayside.
On A827, 4 miles north of Aberfeldy.

This tall and shapely tower house lies to the west of the village in a fine wooded estate in the sheltered valley of Strath Tay. It was built in the 16th century around a much older nucleus. The original castle, built probably about 1414, is said to have stood a mile to the east of the present structure. It is the seat of the Stuart-Fotheringham family who have been here since the late 14th century, descending from Alexander, fourth High Steward of Scotland.

The main block, which incorporates a square keep and entrance with its guardrooms and prison pit below, are part of an earlier building, but the upper parts of the structure including the turrets and dormer windows were added in 1626 by Sir William Stuart, Sheriff of Perth and his wife Agnes Moncrieff. Further restoration took place in 1893, and the castle as it now stands is privately owned.

Grandtully was much in demand as a headquarters, because of its excellent strategic position it was used by Montrose, General MacKay, Argyll, Mar and Prince Charles Edward. One of MacKay's officers is said to have been shot dead in one of the angle-turrets and his blood to have permanently stained the floor. More recently, the famous Admiral Earl Beatty was tenant here; and another shooting tenant, the Maharajah Duleep Singh, distinguished himself one August 12th by shooting 220 brace of grouse in one day.

The surrounding park contains some magnificent elm trees and just beyond the castle is the road to the Church of St Mary, known to date back at least to 1533.

Not open to the public.

Guthrie Castle
Guthrie, by Forfar, Angus, Tayside.
7 miles east of Forfar off A932 to Friockheim.

Guthrie Castle stands west of the village and was built in 1468 by Sir David Guthrie, Comptroller of the Exchequer; it has been inhabited by the Guthrie family until recently. Originally a massive square tower, 60 feet high with walls 10 feet thick, the tower was repaired and enlarged in 1848 but it is still basically the same shape and style. The castle contains some good examples of 15th-century wall paintings and in the grounds is a fine walled garden, a 'wild' garden and a spring garden. The castle is a private residence.

Not open to the public.

Hailes Castle
East Linton, East Lothian, Lothian.
Off A1 on the banks of the River Tyne, 5 miles east of Haddington.

On the south bank of the River Tyne are the beautiful ruins of Hailes Castle, described in old charters as 'the place and fortalice of Hailes'. It was built in the 13th century by the Earl of Dunbar and March before the War of Independence and represents not so much a castle as a fortified manor house. At the end of the 14th century the Hepburns enlarged the castle by adding a great square tower and huge curtain walls. The family were destined to leave their mark on history: one of them, James, fourth Earl of Bothwell, abducted and married Mary, Queen of Scots in 1567. Among other members of the Hepburn family who played a part in the history of their country were Hepburn of Hailes and his son Patrick who, in 1388, together saved the banner of Douglas from falling into the hands of the English at Otterburn.

Another, Patrick Hepburn, who died in 1482, was created Lord Hailes, and he was succeeded by his son, also Patrick, who in 1488 was belted Earl of Bothwell for services rendered to the Crown. One member of this illustrious family was Bishop Moray of Brechin, while John Hepburn, Prior of St Andrews, founded St Leonard's College in the University of St Andrews in 1512 and some years later enclosed the cathedral and Priory in a fine precinct wall with towers.

Hailes Castle was never of strategic importance and itself played no prominent part in history. It was attacked in 1400 by the Earls of March and 'Hotspur' Percy, who after burning the village of Hailes and making two unsuccessful attacks on the castle were put to flight by the Master of Douglas. In 1443 it was besieged and captured by Archibald Dunbar. In 1507 all was quiet again and building operations were in progress for King James IV's visit. In 1532, the castle was burnt and in 1650 it was partially dismantled by Cromwell, but the remains were sold by the Setons in about 1700 to David Dalrymple, better known as Lord Hailes. In 1926 the then-owner, the Earl of Balfour, transferred the castle into the care of the Government.

The ruined castle shows signs of 13th-century masonry in the eastern section, with 14th and 15th century additions in the western part. The tower, which was at the north-west angle of the original castle, contains a vaulted pit prison with only an air shaft—prisoners were lowered into this dungeon through a hatch in the roof. The upper part of the tower contained living rooms but at a later date the interior was made into a dovecot. The hall and other apartments seem to have been at the east end of the castle where there are remains of a massive outside wall. Of the 14th-century work, only the west tower and lower part of the wall remain. The tower has a vaulted basement with living rooms over it and pit prison in its north wall more horrible than the one in the older tower. The 15th-century work contains a chapel and basement bakehouse, and the final work of the 18th century includes the completion of the west tower and the roofing of the chapel so that it could be used as a granary.

Open to the public, April to September, weekdays 10am–7pm, Sundays 2–7pm; October to March, weekdays 10am–4pm, Sundays 2–4pm.

Harthill Castle
Oyne, Aberdeen, Grampian.
1 mile south-east of Oyne off A979.

Harthill Castle, dating from 1601, was the home of the Leiths, an unruly clan. One particular laird, John, was known as 'the violent laird'; he was constantly in conflict with authority and was imprisoned on numerous occasions in Edinburgh and Aberdeen. During one imprisonment in the Aberdeen Tolbooth, he set fire to the prison and released all the prisoners. The Leiths were also known for their feuds with the neighbouring clan, Abercrombie of Westhall Castle. The castle is a Z-plan tower house with a barmkin, the gateway to which still stands.

Open to the public by written appointment only.

Hermitage Castle

Hermitage Castle
Hawick, Roxburgh, Borders.
12 miles south of Hawick on A7 or B6399 roads.

The castle was built on a bluff overlooking a strip
of level ground on the north bank of Hermitage
Water. On either side, two small streams run
down to the main river and their gullies have been
joined at some early date by artificial ditches and
banks to make a moat round the castle. Behind the
castle are moors and high pasture and in front,
'Liddesdale, England's western way into Scotland'.

A castle was built to watch over this way as far
back as the 13th century and some fragments of
the structure near the centre of the present
building no remarkable part in history, and was so
neglected that by the end of the 18th century it was
a complete ruin. However, the Duke of Buccleuch
repaired the remains in 1820 and in 1930 it was
placed in the care of the Government.

As for the architectural style of Hermitage Castle,
it seems that the primary building probably formed
an oblong block with narrow open court in the
middle. The main entrance was in the south wall
and the spiral stair in the north. On top and
around the original English structure, which appears to have come to grief in the border wars of
Richard II, a powerful rectangular keep or tower
house in the style then popular in Scotland was
added. However, definition between the two
periods is a little vague as during the later alterations
and repairs much of the original work was obscured. The exterior of the castle is a grim, bleak
rubble-built pile in which the brown sandstone
walls are broken by few openings. Inside, in the
little 14th-century courtyard of the manor house,
the walls are really quite different, built in beautiful

large squared red free-stone ashlar, with round
arched doors leading off to the various ranges
which have been drastically changed from the
original by modern restoration. By now the castle
comprised a central tower with an oblong central
court enclosed by a cross wing and screen walls.
At each of the four corners of the main keep were
small square towers again connected with walls.

According to legend the original owner, the
wicked Lord Soulis, who was noted for his excesses,
met a terrible end wrapped in lead and boiled to
death in a cauldron by the local people: and the
castle, 'unable to support the load of iniquity
which had long been accumulating within its
walls', is supposed to have partly sunk beneath the
ground.

Open to the public, April to September, weekdays
10am–7pm, Sundays 2–7pm; October to March,
weekdays 9.30am–4pm, Sundays 2–4pm.

Hoddom Castle
Lockerbie, Annandale and Eskdale, Dumfries and
Galloway.
Off A74, 1½ miles south-west of Ecclefechan.

Hoddom Castle stands overlooking the River Annan
and is approached by an avenue lined with beech
trees mentioned by Thomas Carlyle as the 'kindly
beech rows'. The castle dates from the 16th
century and was a massive example of the tower
house style. Today it is in a state of ruin, and not
safe for unsupervised visitors. The castle was the
seat of the Johnstones, and in its original state was
well known as a border keep. There are plans to
restore Hoddom Castle to its former appearance.

Not open to the public.

Hume Castle
Greenlaw, Berwickshire, Borders.
Off A697, 10 miles north of Kelso.

Hume Castle is in a commanding position at a height of some 600 feet above sea level and has a history dating back to the 12th century. The castle was rebuilt at the end of the 18th century on the old foundations, in the present 'imitation antique' form. The walls stand high round a large courtyard about 130 feet square, in the form of a simple curtain wall on which battlements once stood. Hume Castle is the ancient seat of the Home family and has had a stormy history, taking part in most of the wars affecting the border area. For instance, it was captured in 1547 by the invading English under Lord Somerset. Two years later it was retaken by the young Lord Home and 20 years later it was again captured by the English, this time under the Earl of Sussex. In 1650 it surrendered to Cromwell under the threat of artillery bombardment.

Open by appointment only—keys with the caretaker.

Huntingtower Castle
Perth, Perth and Kinross, Tayside.
3 miles north-east of Perth on A85 on the River Almond.

A highly impressive mixture of two medieval tower houses joined by a gangway at parapet level. Later, in the 17th century, a lower work was built to link the two towers internally, but a story is told of how a daughter of Ruthvens once leapt from one parapet to another to escape discovery in her lover's chamber. 'The fair woman chose not to repeat the leap and the next night eloped and was married'. After this extraordinary exploit the space between the towers was named 'The Maiden's Leap'.

Until 1600 it was known as Ruthven Castle, and belonged to a family who came to Perthshire from East Lothian towards the end of the 12th century. The Ruthvens became well known in Scottish history for Sir William Ruthven was held hostage by the English for the ransom of King James I of Scotland, and three generations later, in 1489, the first Lord Ruthven was created a Lord of Parliament. His son was slain beside his king, James IV, at Flodden in 1513. William, the second Lord Ruthven, was Provost of Perth, an Extraordinary Lord of Session and Keeper of the Privy Seal. He married Janet, eldest daughter and co-heiress of Patrick, Lord Halyburton of Dirleton in East Lothian, and by this alliance Dirleton Castle and its lands became Ruthven property.

Patrick, third Lord Ruthven, was educated at St Andrews and was one of the leading nobles to support the Reformers in Queen Mary's reign. As one of Darnley's supporters he took part in the murder of the Queen's favourite Rizzio at Holyrood in 1566. His son William was also implicated in the affair but both fled to England after the event and Patrick died there. His son returned to Scotland after receiving a Royal pardon. William, now fourth Lord Ruthven, was at Loch Leven Castle when Queen Mary signed her resignation of the Crown.

He voted against the Queen's divorce and was present at the infant James' coronation in 1567. In

Huntingtower Castle

1571 he was Treasurer of Scotland and in 1581 the king made him Earl of Gowrie.

In 1582 the castle was the scene of the 'Raid of Ruthven'. James VI, then 16, accepted an invitation from the Earl of Gowrie to his hunting seat and while there was forcibly persuaded by a gathering of nobles—including Gowrie—who demanded dismissal of the royal favourites, the Duke of Lennox and Earl of Arran, so that they, instead, might use the king. For a time the king was forced to comply with them but eventually he escaped; although he at first forgave his captors, in 1585 he was persuaded to change his mind and ordered the Earl of Gowrie banished. The Earl only got as far as Dundee when he was apprehended, and was finally beheaded at Stirling on 4th May 1585.

The estates and honours of William, the first Earl, were restored in 1586 to his son James, who died at the age of 14 and was succeeded in 1588 by his brother John, the third and last Earl of Gowrie; educated at Padua University, he was suspected of practising necromancy and witchcraft. He was killed in 1600, with his brother Alexander, at his Perth town house, for an alleged attempt on the life of the king, and the bodies were carried to Edinburgh as an example to the populace. Here the Lords and Parliament pronounced 'Sentence and Doom' and annexed the title and estates to the Crown. The two Ruthven brothers' bodies were hanged, drawn and quartered at the public Cross of Edinburgh and the heads and quarters hung in the burghs of Edinburgh, Perth, Dundee and Stirling. The 'Act of Sentence and Doom' also abolished the surname of Ruthven and changed the name of the estates to Huntingtower, which remained Crown property until 1643 when it passed to William Murray, who was created Earl Dysart and Lord Huntingtower by Charles I. By 1663 the castle had been bought by James, second Earl of Tullibardine, Lord Murray, Gask and Balquhidder. He died without heirs and the lands passed by marriage to the Atholl family, but in 1760, on the death of the Dowager Duchess of Atholl, the castle was occupied by a colony of calico printers.

The castle is now in the care of Historic Buildings and Monuments, Scottish Development Department and contains some very fine painted wooden ceilings of *c* 1540. These are ornamented with a knotwork pattern drawn in black on a white ground and are thought to be the earliest Scottish tempera painted ceilings now in existence. Viewed from any point, Huntingtower Castle is a picturesque sight, and the broken line of the walling and corbelled parapets give a good idea of a typical 16th-century Scottish fortified house.

Open to the public, every day, Summer 9.30am–7pm, Sundays 2–7pm; Winter 9.30am–4pm, Sundays 2–4pm.

Huntly Castle
Huntly, Aberdeen, Grampian.
On A96, in the town of Huntly, approximately 40 miles north-west of Aberdeen, on the main road to Elgin.

The ruined green mound of the Norman motte of Huntly Castle, sometimes called Strathbogie, rises high above the nearby rock-strewn gorge of the River Deveron. It has a memorable history, being the scene of some of the most famous events in Scotland's past, as well as being for a time the headquarters of the Roman Catholic faith in Scotland.

Huntly Castle came into being in the 11th century when the Scottish kings were imposing Norman civilisation and institutions on their mainly Celtic subjects. There was no Norman conquest of Scotland, as in England by William the Conqueror, but the Scottish kings invited the Norman barons to settle north of the Tweed by giving them lands to be held in feudal tenure from the Crown. The Scots or Celts opposed the 'Normanising' policy and for more than a century and a half (until Moravia was tamed by Alexander II) every Scottish king had to face constant revolts among his subjects beyond the Spey. Strathbogie was situated on one of the routes northward which the kings had to keep open to make sure that the royal garrisons could be reached. The actual site of this castle, in the angle formed by the confluence of the Bogie and Deveron rivers, is tactically strong.

The first Norman baron to settle here was Duncan, Earl of Fife, sometime in the latter part of the 12th century. He built the first castle and took the title of 'de Strathbolgyn'. Huntly Castle at this time consisted of a conical, flat-topped motte surrounded by a deep wide ditch topped by a strong palisade. The interior buildings were of earthwork and timber, as stone keeps were far too costly. The wooden buildings have of course disappeared long since but the earthworks still remain. In 1307, King Robert the Bruce was brought to the Peel of Strathbogie—as the castle was then called—to recover after he fell sick at Inverurie. His enemies soon followed him and on Christmas Eve 1307 he dragged himself out of bed and defeated them at the Battle of Barra. David de Strathbolgyn turned against the Scottish king shortly before Bannockburn, and as a punishment his lands were taken by Bruce and granted to Sir Adam Gordon of Huntly in Berwickshire. The Gordons finally settled here in 1376, and in 1408 Sir John Gordon was succeeded by his sister Elizabeth, who married Sir Alexander Seton. Their son, also Alexander, was made Earl Huntly between 1445 and 1449.

No-one is certain when the Gordons replaced the earthwork castle with a more substantial stone fortress, but probably late in the 14th or early in the 15th century, a strong stone tower house was built on the north side of the Norman bailey. (This was later demolished in 1394.) Lord Huntly took King James II's side in the struggle between the royal house of Stewart and the baronial Douglases. On his way south to join his master he was intercepted by the Earl of Crawford and the Battle of Brechin ensued. Although he won, Huntly received bad news from home and decided to return rather than carry on with the campaign. In his absence, the Earl of Moray had burnt the early wooden Norman castle of Strathbogie. Huntly chased the invaders and broke their power before returning to begin building a new stone castle at Strathbogie. This later castle was still unfinished when the first Earl of Huntly died here in 1470, and it was completed by his son.

This new oblong castle, with its round tower at the south-west corner, was a grand place and was often visited by royalty and people of distinction. In January of 1496 Perkin Warbeck—the Pretender to Henry VII's throne—married the beautiful Lady Catherine Gordon in the king's presence at the castle. In 1506 Alexander, the third Earl, received a charter confirming his lands and an order that in future the castle name be changed from Strathbogie to Huntly. George, the fourth Earl of Huntly, disliked the gloomy 15th-century palace that his grandfather left and between 1551 and 1554 practically rebuilt it from the ground floor upwards. But Huntly Castle was again changed in the 17th century by the first Marquess after James VI had destroyed much of the building in 1594. (In 1597, the Earl had made his peace with the king, and two years later was created the first Marquess of Huntly.)

The second Marquess joined the king in the Civil War and sealed his devotion on the scaffold. His castle suffered sorely, and in 1640 it was occupied by the Covenanting army who mutilated much of the interior. In 1644 Montrose held the castle against General Leslie, but was starved into surrender. After the Civil War the castle was no longer occupied by the Huntly family, and by the 18th century it was fast becoming a ruin, although it was used once more by Government troops in 1746 during the Jacobite rising.

Finally, the widow of the third Duke of Gordon remarried and built her jointure house out of the ruins of the old castle across the river Deveron. What was left became a common quarry and dumping ground until 1923, when the ruins were handed over to the predecessors of Historic Buildings and Monuments, Scottish Development Department and the entire castle area cleared and where possible repaired. Alongside these ruins, there still remains the grand earthworks of the first Norman Lord of Strathbogie's Castle. The great Renaissance palace built from 1597–1602 by the first Marquess of Huntly remains, albeit roofless and tenantless, but with a stately row of first floor windows, a grand doorway with armorial bearings and splendid carved fireplaces. But probably the most memorable piece of architecture at Huntly can be found above the entry on the round tower of the palace. This has been called 'the most splendid heraldic doorway in the British Isles' and certainly comprises the most elaborate heraldic adornments to be seen in Scotland.

Open to the public, April to September, weekdays 9.30am–7pm, Sundays 2–7pm; October to March, weekdays 9.30am–4pm, Sundays 2–4pm.

Inchdrewer Castle
Banff, Banff and Buchan, Grampian.
Off A97, 3 miles south of Banff.

The 16th-century ruined castle of Inchdrewer was restored by the Richmond Herald, Mr Robin Mirrlees to its present state of round stair tower, battlemented top and angle turrets. It is the ancestral home of the Ogilvies of Banff but has not been occupied since January 1713, when the third Lord of Banff was murdered in his bedchamber above the great hall and the castle burnt down. The 'bad' Lord Banff returned unexpectedly from Edinburgh where he had been for many months arranging his son's wedding. Only the housekeeper, Elizabeth Porter, was at home, and after a hasty meal he retired to his chamber. In the night the castle burst into flames and only the housekeeper escaped to tell the tale of how she had heard a cry of 'murder'. Apparently she had tried to get into the laird's room but failed as the door was locked; according to her the two men inside (traditionally, named Stewart and Milne) refused to open up. Presumably the men murdered the laird and later burnt the castle to conceal the evidence.

Not open to the public.

Innischonell Castle
Kilchurn, Loch Awe, Argyll, Strathclyde.
On an island on Loch Awe off A85.

This is one of the several ruined castles found on the various islands in Loch Awe. Innischonell was once a royal castle under the Clan Campbell. It was built in the 16th century as a tower house and was at one stage captured by the MacArthurs.

Open all year round.

Inveraray Castle

Inveraray Castle
Inveraray, Argyll, Strathclyde.
On A83 at Inveraray.

A beautiful white-walled castle in a Royal Burgh and a hereditary seat and headquarters for centuries of the most consistently powerful, if by no means popular clan in Scotland, the Clan Campbell, Dukes of Argyll. It is built of blue-green schist and the cones of its slated angle towers are stained a deeper green by the weather, giving the castle a strange colour combination which endows it with a mysterious air of unreality.

The present castle was one of the earliest examples of the Gothic revival. It was replanned in 1743 by Roger Morris and completed in 1770. The old castle, which dated from about 1550, stood 80 yards from the present front door, was finally demolished in 1773, the new one having been built in 1760 and scarcely lived in by the third or fourth Dukes. It was the fifth Duke who, as Marquess of Lorne and heir to the Dukedom, commissioned Robert Mylne to undertake the magnificent interior decoration; thus it now shows signs not only of neo-Gothic style but also of neo-Scottish baronial architecture in its square turreted shape with massive battlements and tower rising from its heart, totally unexpected and exotic to visitors approaching from the town and catching a glimpse of the pretty gothic windows through the wooded park.

The interior of Inveraray Castle contains a wealth of 18th-century splendour and architectural curiosi-

ties, with great hall, armoury and state rooms open to view. In addition to the many historic relics the castle contains portraits by Gainsborough, Ramsay and Raeburn, fine furniture and plate and early Scottish armaments.

Open to the public, last Saturday in March to second Sunday in October, April/May/June/ September 10am–1pm and 2–6pm, Sundays 1–6pm, closed Friday; July/August 10am–6pm, Sundays 1–6pm. Refreshments available.

Inverlochy Castle
Inverlochy, Inverness, Highland.
Off A82, 2 miles north of Fort William.

On the banks of the Loch stands the old Inverlochy Castle, castle of the Comyns, a simple square 13th-century courtyard contained by four high curtain walls. The enclosure has two entrances topped with plain pointed arches, below which hung a heavy two-leaved door held by a draw bar and protected by a portcullis. Outside the curtain wall, a wide ditch and outer bank surrounded three sides and protected the castle while on the fourth side was a water gate on to the Loch. The eventful history of the castle dates from the War of Independence, reaching its climax three centuries later during Montrose's campaigns. Inverlochy was the scene of the Campbells' defeat by Montrose in 1645. Nearby, the modern Inverlochy Castle is now turned into part of a cattle ranching scheme started in the 1950s on the Canadian ideal. The old castle is now a hotel.

Not open to the public.

Inverness Castle
Inverness, Highland.
At Inverness at the junction of A82 and A862.

In this 'capital' of the Highlands, easily accessible from the sea and also a junction of the main routes from the south across the mountains and from the east along the Moray Firth, stands the present and relatively modern Castle of Inverness. Carved stones, burial cairns and hilltop fort remain to prove that the site was inhabited long before written historical records; in A.D. 565, Inverness was known to be the capital of the Pictish kingdom. By the 12th century a chartered burgh had been established here in the shelter of a royal castle.

To avenge his father King Duncan, murdered by MacBeath in his castle at Inverness in 1039, Malcolm III of Canmore razed the castle of MacBeath and built another nearby in 1057, on a spot known as Castle Hill. This stronghold was taken by troops of Edward I of England in 1303, and recaptured by Robert the Bruce in 1310. James I of Scotland held Parliament for all the northern chiefs and barons in the castle in 1427, and in 1455 the Lord of the Isles captured both the town and the castle. In 1508, the Earl of Huntly was made Governor.

The Queen Regent, Mary of Guise, visited the town in 1555 and was imprisoned in the castle by the Earl of Caithness for protecting robbers. In fact the castle was not well known for its hospitality, for when Mary, Queen of Scots, visited Inverness in 1562 she was refused admission to the castle and forced to spend the night at a house in Bridge Street. In 1607 the castle was repaired and strengthened but in 1645 it was besieged by Montrose. It was captured by Jacobites in 1715 but recaptured some days later by government and Hanoverian supporters. In 1718 it was repaired again and enlarged, and at the same time the name was changed to Fort George; but the new building did not last long, and in 1746 Prince Charles Edward and his Highlanders blew it up. The present building was put up in two parts in 1834 and 1846 and is used as the Sheriff Court House and administrative office.

Not open to the public.

Jedburgh Castle
Jedburgh, Roxburgh, Borders.
Turn off A68 at Jedburgh.

Jedburgh Castle, built in the 12th century, was occupied on many occasions by the English: it was one of the first five fortresses ceded to England under the Treaty of Falaise in 1174 to provide security for the ransom of William the Lion. It eventually became a royal residence. Malcolm IV died there in 1195 and Alexander III was married to Jolande, daughter of the Count of Dreux in Jedburgh Abbey in 1285. The castle was finally demolished in 1409 by order of the Scottish Parliament, who found the periodic occupations by the English distinctly embarrassing.

In its place there is now an interesting Georgian building of 1832, still known as the castle but in fact housing the county jail. It was built to the specification of John Howard, the prison reformer, but in 1880, when five new prisons were opened in Scotland, Jedburgh was closed and its inmates moved to Edinburgh. It is now on view to interested visitors.

Open to the public, every day, Easter to September 10am–12 noon, 1–5pm, Sundays 2–5pm. Refreshments available.

Kelburn Castle
Fairlie, Cunninghame, Strathclyde.
On A78 between Largs and Fairlie.

Although early records are lacking, there is little doubt that the family of de Boyville (later Boyle) came to England with William the Conqueror in 1066. They settled in various parts of the country including Wales and Cumberland, and the Welsh branch later went to Cork where they eventually became Earls of Cork and Shannon.

Another branch of the de Boyvilles settled in Scotland. Hugo de Morville was one of the powerful Norman barons invited by David I in 1124 to help found a new power structure in Scotland. The Boyles, who were related to the de Morvilles by marriage, eventually received the lands of Kelburn in 1140 and have been there ever since. It is likely that the original stone keep of the castle was built about 1200. In 1581 John Boyle of Kelburn added to it, making his castle about twice as big again, with a fine tower at the south-west corner to balance the old tower in the north-east. In 1694 David Boyle, who was created Lord Boyle and Earl of Glasgow in 1699 and 1703, ordered the building of the new house which is attached to the castle and is a fine example of a Scottish mansion of the time of William and Mary. In 1870 the sixth Earl added the Victorian wing, and the present house is still inhabited by the Earl of Glasgow, a descendant of the de Boyville family.

Open to the public only by written request. The gardens and estate are open daily from Easter to mid-October as Kelburn Country Centre. Refreshments available.

Kellie Castle

Kellie Castle
Pittenweem, Fife.
3 miles north-west of Pittenweem off A921.

A very fine example of early Scottish domestic architecture, Kellie Castle was built at three different periods: around 1360, when the north tower was built; the 16th century when the east tower was added; and the 17th century when the two towers were joined by the main block with the addition of the south tower. Owned by the Oliphants for 200 years before being sold in 1613 to the Earl of Mar and Kellie, the castle was virtually abandoned in the early 19th century, until it was taken over and restored by Professor James Lorimer, father of Sir Robert Lorimer the architect. His son, grandson of James, bought the castle in 1948 and he in turn sold it to the National Trust for Scotland in 1970.

Outside Kellie Castle is a fine walled garden with lawns and a mass of old roses, whilst inside are some fine plaster ceilings done in the 17th century. The withdrawing room is entirely decorated with landscapes painted directly on to the panels in a style much liked by Charles II.

A National Trust for Scotland property.

Open to the public, April to October, Easter. April and October weekends only, May to September daily, 2–6pm. Refreshments available.

Kemp Castle
Turin Hill, Angus, Tayside.
3½ miles north-east of Forfar off A94.

At the summit of Turin Hill is all that remains of the Iron Age fort known as Kemp or Camp Castle, which is believed to be one of the oldest stone forts in Scotland. It was originally a large oval enclosure measuring 900 feet by 400 feet with two ramparts. Later a smaller area within the earlier enclosure was surrounded by a stone wall. The fort was abandoned later in the Iron Age, and a circular dun, about 90 feet in diameter with a wall 12 feet thick was built.

Not open to the public.

Kilchurn Castle
Dalmally, Argyll, Strathclyde.
On A85 at the north-east end of Loch Awe, some 4 miles west of Dalmally.

On a peninsula near the top of the loch is one of the grandest baronial ruins in Scotland, now surrounded by marsh. The castle dates from 1440 and was built by Sir Colin Campbell of Glenorchy, first Earl of Breadalbane, whose arms with those of his wife are over the gateway. The Campbells, who were anti-Jacobite in the 18th century, offered the castle to house Hanoverian troops in 1746, but apart from that the only other excitement in the history of the castle was in 1879 when the gale which caused the Tay Bridge disaster blew down one of the tower tops.

Not open to the public.

Kildrummy Castle
Kildrummy, Aberdeen, Grampian.
Off A97 overlooking the valley of the Upper Don.

This 'noblest of the northern castles' is now an imposing ruin on the summit of the ridge above the north side of the main road to Strathdon, guarded on two sides by a ravine. The old red sandstone basin of Kildrummy has for many centuries been a centre of human habitation and local archaeological excavations have produced stone axes and arrowheads from the Bronze and Iron Ages. In fact there are signs of numerous hut circles from the Iron Ages to be found on the slopes of the Don.

It was the Normans of the 12th century who built the first manor with its castle about a mile northeast of the present building. Here a timbered earthwork castle was carved out, and alongside was built the parish church. By the 15th century the little motte and bailey stronghold lay abandoned. Meanwhile a newer 13th-century stone castle was built to a design of St Gilbert, the last of the Scottish saints, on the pattern of the mighty Chateau de Coucy near Laon. At this stage the castle consisted of an enormous semi-circular curtain wall defended by five projecting round towers, the largest of which was known as the Snow Tower. At some time during the 13th century the plans were altered to include a chapel, and it was not until the end of the century that the castle was finished. By this time, Scotland was under the rule of Edward I and Kildrummy, under the Earl of Mar, became heavily involved in the struggle to put Bruce on the throne. In 1305, after his defeat at Methven, Robert sent his queen and her ladies to the castle for safety while he fled to the Western Highlands. In 1306 the castle was besieged by Prince Edward of Caernarvon (afterwards Edward II), and Sir Nigel Bruce, the Scottish king's youngest brother, was eventually forced to surrender it. Luckily the queen had escaped northward before the siege, but she was later caught at Tain. Now the burnt-out castle was partially dismantled, according to the records; but by 1333 it had been restored again and a new gatehouse with two massive drum towers added. Apart from the famous fight for the castle in 1335 between Dame Christian, Bruce's sister, and the Earl of Atholl, Kildrummy led a fairly peaceful existence for the next 30 years.

David II stayed here often, and in 1367 he captured the castle from Thomas, Earl of Mar, after a quarrel. In 1404 Sir Malcolm Douglas, the husband of Isabella Douglas, Countess of Mar, was murdered by a gang of assassins hired by Alexander Stewart, a son of the notorious 'Wolf of Badenoch'. Two years later Stewart himself arrived at the castle and forced the poor woman to marry and provide him with the Earldom of Mar. He became a brilliant international figure of his time, and even spent a little of his wealth on renovating the castle. In 1435 he died and the castle and earldom were annexed by James I, and granted by the crown in turn to various people. Ultimately James IV bestowed Kildrummy on Alexander, first Lord of Elphinstone, in 1507, and his famiy remained in possession until 1626 when they were forced to hand over the castle to the legitimate heirs, the Erskines, Earls of Mar.

In the 17th-century civil wars, Kildrummy Castle was garrisoned by Royalists and in 1654 was captured by Cromwell when part of the castle was burnt. It was later set on fire again in 1690 by the troops of Viscount Dundee, rather than allow it to fall into the hands of William of Orange. Thereafter it was made partly habitable and formed the headquarters for the Earl of Mar when he organised the final details for the 1715 rising. After the rising collapsed Kildrummy Castle was dismantled, and became the local quarry until 1898, when Colonel James Ogston organised repairs and excavation work on the site. In 1951, the Colonel's niece placed the castle in the care of the predecessors of Historic Buildings and Monuments, Scottish Development Department.

The old castle is remarkably symmetrical and uniform in layout, except for the chapel and elaborate Edwardian gatehouse, which spoilt the basic simplicity of the design. As already mentioned, the castle is based on the French Chateau de Coucy. It stands with its back to a steep ravine and on two sides the ground slopes away to a second ravine. On the open sections the castle is protected by a wide, deep, dry ditch which was probably built first as a defensive enclosure for the workmen and materials. The modern mansion, built in 1900, faces the old ruin across the northern ravine which is spanned by a bridge. Below the castle is a medieval quarry which has been enlarged to provide stone for the modern building and is now converted into a superb rock garden. The old castle is one of the best surviving examples of a 13th-century stone castle in Scotland, and the only one of its period that still contains a complete range of domestic buildings including hall, kitchen, solar and chapel, Kildrummy is still in good condition mainly because it was dismantled not by victorious Scots—who would have torn it apart—but by a tired invading English army who were ordered to get the work done and return to

England as quickly as possible. All they did was to throw down one side of the building and leave the rest.

Open to the public daily 9.30am–7.30pm.

Killochan Castle
Dailly, Kyle and Carrick, Strathclyde.
Off A77, 3 miles north-east of Girvan.

Killochan Castle is an impressive 16th-century stronghold which was added to in the 18th century and has since been modernised and made structurally sound. It was the ancient seat of the Cathcarts, later the Earls of Cathcart who lived here up to the last war. In the tower is an enormous funnel-shaped west window which has only recently been discovered. It is said to be unique and was designed to light up the main banqueting hall during the last meal of the day.

Not open to the public.

Kilravock Castle
Croy, Inverness, Highland.
12 miles east of Inverness, off B9091 near the A96.

Kilravock dates back to 1209 when there was a dwelling on the site of the present castle. This was built in 1460 as the seat of the Chief of the Clan Rose. The original tower keep was enlarged by the tenth Baron who built on the main part of the castle in 1553. Later a grand staircase was added on the north side giving an 18th-century façade. On the fourth floor of the keep there is a room where Mary, Queen of Scots, slept in 1562. This is now a museum where correspondence between Mary and the tenth Baron is on display. On the day before the Battle of Culloden, Bonnie Prince Charlie dined at Kilravock and some of the Prince's personal possessions are also to be seen, such as his punchbowl and the boots he wore at Culloden.

Open at all times to residents and to the public only on Wednesday for guided tours at 11am, 2, 3, and 4pm. Refreshments available. The gardens are open daily except Sunday.

Kincardine Castle
Kincardine, Kincardine and Deeside, Grampian.
Off A94 at Fettercairn.

Once this was a highly important royal castle, but now there is no sign of the original buildings, just a name on the Ordnance Sheet and a field marked 'King's Park where once a monarch ruled and one was murdered'. The royal castle was built in the reign of William the Lion, and there in 1296 John

de Baliol resigned the Scottish crown in favour of Edward I of England. The castle was finally demolished in 1646.

Not open to the public.

Kinclaven Castle
Kinclaven, Perth and Kinross, Tayside.
7 miles north-west of Luncarty.

The ruins of the 13th-century castle of Kinclaven stand on a piece of land overlooking a wide bend in the River Tay at its junction with the Isla. The ruined 13th-century castle is a magnificent example of the courtyard type of defensive structure cornered by projecting towers and enclosed by strong walls. The castle was a royal residence in the reign of Alexander II (1214–1249); in 1297 Wallace came to Perth, and having forced the castle to surrender, burnt it down.

The ruins are only of interest to archaeologists.

Not open to the public.

Kindrochit Castle
Braemar, Kincardine and Deeside, Grampian.
Off A93 at Braemar.

When Robert II granted a licence to 'our dear brother Malcolm de Drummond' to build a fortalice there, the site had already been a hunting seat and residence of King Robert I of Scotland. In addition to being a sort of 14th-century Balmoral it had a more warlike purpose, being strategically sited in order to defend the ancient mountain passes of the Cairnwell and Tolmouth which connected the southern parts of the kingdom to the wilder north.

As it grew more important, one end of the palace was torn down and in 1390 a massive stone tower, the fifth largest in Scotland, was built by Sir Malcolm Drummond, the Constable of the castle. In 1402 he was ambushed and murdered, but the castle still stood, until suddenly and mysteriously at the beginning of the 16th century it became derelict and uninhabited and by 1618 had fallen into ruin. There is a tale told in connection with the mystery: apparently the 'galar Mor' or 'terrible plague' broke out in the castle and the people of Braemar barricaded the gates and refused to let anyone out of the building. Great cannons were dragged over the Cairnwell from Atholl and turned on the castle, and Kindrochit is said to have 'crashed in ruin amid the shrieks of those trapped within its walls'. The undisturbed degeneration of the site was aided by the legend that in 1746 a Hanoverian soldier was lowered into one of the vaults in search of treasure, but quickly scrambled out when he found a ghostly company seated round a table heaped with skulls.

In 1925, under D. W. Douglas Simpson, excavation work was begun, and though nothing alarming appeared the famous silver gilt Kindrochit Brooch was unearthed and the walls of the main part of the castle were traced. The building is now scheduled as an Ancient Monument by Historic Buildings and Monuments, Scottish Development Department.

Open to the public at all times.

Kinlochaline Castle
Oban, Lochaber, Highland.
Near Ardtornish at a private road off A884.

At the head of Loch Aline is the small but sturdy castle of Kinlochaline, perched on the top of a rocky bluff where the Black Water joins the sea loch. The building dates from the 15th century, possibly earlier. It was improved in the 16th century and again partially restored in 1890. Built on an oblong plan, it measured 43 feet by 34 feet with 10 feet thick walls rising four storeys to a parapet and walk. At the first floor level an entrance, originally reached by a removable stair, and later changed for the present stone stair, opens into a guard room, a main Hall with its arched fireplace and a stairway which leads down to two vaulted cellars. The main turnpike stair which rises from the south-east angle of the building leads to the parapet, but on its way, up at second floor level, branches off to a narrow passage only 4 feet high, which in turn leads down another flight of stairs to the south-west corner of the building. Experts have failed to establish why this was built into the structure.

The building is locally known as Butter Castle and there is a legend attached to the name, for the locals believe that its builder, the Lady Dubchall, paid the masons in butter.

The castle was originally the seat of the chiefs of the Clan Aonghais or MacInnes who were vassals of the Lords of the Isles and hereditary bowmen to the MacKinnons of Skye. John of the Isles is said to have declared, in gratitude for services rendered 'My blessing upon you, Chief of Kinlochaline—while the MacDonald is in power, MacInnes shall be in favour'. Nevertheless, the same MacInnes was treacherously murdered with his five sons at Ardtornish nearby and the lands given to Maclean of Duart by Donald of the Isles in 1390, when presumably the Macleans built the present castle. Kinlochaline was attacked and burnt by Montrose's army in 1644, and again by Cromwell's troops.

Open to the public at all reasonable times—keys on request from Castle Cottage on the foreshore. Visitors are only welcome on foot and are asked to leave their cars in the park where the Ardtornish private road branches off A884.

Kinnaird Castle
Brechin, Angus, Tayside.
4 miles south-east of Brechin off A933.

Now the seat of the Earls of Southesk, the present building replaced older ones which had been occupied since the early 15th century. In 1790, Playfair organised extensive alterations and it was later transformed once more by Bryce (1854–1860) on the lines of a 16th-century French chateau. The castle is situated in a large and well-wooded deerpark.

Open to the public by written appointment, made well in advance.

Kisimul Castle
Isle of Barra, Inverness, Highland.
On a small island in the loch at Castlebay, off A888.

At high water the castle seems to rise straight from the sea. It was started about 1030 and ever since then has been a stronghold of the chiefs of the Clan MacNeil of Barra, private chiefs, one of whose ancestors was said to have refused Noah's hospitality as the 'MacNeil has a boat of his own'. After the decline in the fortunes of the Highlands and Islands which took place at the end of the 18th and beginning of the 19th century, the chiefs left their ancient castle and went to America. The castle was left in ruins for centuries, but in 1938 the 45th clan chief, an American architect, bought the castle and began to restore it. In 1960 the castle restorer and Chief, Robert Lister MacNeil, held a gathering at Kisimul Castle at which he welcomed back MacNeils from all over the world. On his death in 1970 his son, Ian Roderick, a distinguished Professor of Law at Cornell University, became 46th Chief of the MacNeils of Barra and still maintains an interest in the castle.

The story is told that one of the first MacNeil Chiefs, a rather eccentric man, ordered an old piper to blow night and morning on the battlements before announcing aloud on the winds that the MacNeil of Barra had eaten and that other princes and lesser men might now take their meals.

Open to the public, Wednesdays and Saturdays, May to September, 2–5pm.

Knock Castle
Ballater, Kincardine and Deeside, Grampian.
Between A937 and A93 beyond Ballater golf course.

On a hilltop commanding the strategic meeting place of the tributaries of the Muick and Gairn, stands this grim old ruin—a plain rectangular keep-tower built in 1600. There is a horrifying tale attached to this castle. Apparently, when the Gordon laird was feuding with his neighbour Alexander Forbes of Strathgirnock over boundary rights, his seven sons set out to cut peats in the fields and unwittingly cut them on Forbes's land. The infuriated Forbes beheaded the seven sons, tying the severed heads one by one to the tops of the spades and leaving the grisly implements stuck in the ground. A servant from Knock found them and fled back to the castle; he blurted out the news to the laird, who had been standing at the head of the stairs, whereupon he fell over the banisters to his own death.

Not open to the public.

Knockderry Castle
Kilcreggan, Dumbarton, Strathclyde.
2 miles north of Kilcreggan or 7 miles south of Garelochead off A814.

On the east side of Loch Long stands the castle built about 1850 on top of the dungeons of an older building which features in Scott's novel *Heart of Midlothian*. It is now a hotel.

Not open to the public.

Lauriston Castle
Edinburgh, Midlothian, Lothian.
3 miles west of the city off A93.

Lauriston Castle was built around 1590 by Sir Archibald Napier, father of John Napier, the inventor of logarithms. The previous castle on the site had been sacked and burnt by the Earl of Hertford in 1544. From 1590–1827 the castle was merely a square tower, which now forms the south-west corner of the building. In 1827–72 the major part of the rest of the building was added and in 1872–73 a library was built.

The most famous of Lauriston's owners was undoubtedly John Law, the financier and Comptroller General of the Finances of France, and virtual Prime Minister of France in 1720. Before his time Sir Alexander Napier, first owner and builder of the castle, and his son Alexander, were most colourful figures. Others owners included William Law, a wealthy banker who bought the castle as a retreat for his old age; Thomas Allan who added the dining room, drawing room and bathrooms, and his successor William Ramsay who owned the neighbouring Barnton estates. The last owner, William Reid, will probably be best remembered for the fact that he refurnished and renovated the castle as it is today—a museum of late Victorian and Edwardian taste.

Open to the public all year round; April to October, daily 11am–1pm, 2–5pm; November to March, Saturdays and Sundays 2–4pm.

Lauriston Castle

Leslie Castle
Leslie, Aberdeen, Grampian.
10 miles south of Huntly off A97.

There has been a castle on this site since as far back as 1067. The castle has, in effect been built three times. The second time was in 1661 by William Forbes and the last in 1986 by the present owners. It is the original seat of the Leslie clan and is now once again in the possession of the Leslies. The building is one of the last examples of the L-plan tower house built in the north-east of Scotland.

Not open to the public.

Lickleyhead Castle
Auchleven, Insch, Aberdeen, Grampian.
On the outskirts of Auchleven off A992.

On the banks of the Gadie near the village of Auchleven is the home of Mrs Arbuthnot Leslie, whose family has restored and furnished this fine old Scottish tower house over the years. This particularly lovely castle gives a great impression of height and has a long soaring roundel stair tower which corbels out at only a few feet above the ground. Above the entrance of this tower are the initials of the first Forbes laird and the date 1629. However, internal evidence points to an earlier date and it is known that the Leslies had a fortified house on this site in 1450. This was sold by them in 1499 and the site and castle has since been owned by several Aberdeenshire families before returning to the Leslies, through marriage, in the early 1920s.

Open to the public by appointment only.

Loch Doon Castle
Dalmellington, Cumnock and Doon, Strathclyde.
2 miles south of Dalmellington off A713 on the Loch Doon road.

This 14th-century castle stood originally on an island but was rebuilt on the loch side when the water level of the loch was raised by a hydro-electric scheme a few years ago. The walls of this massive building, once known as Castle Balliol, vary from 7 to 9 feet in thickness and stand about 26 feet high.

Open at all times.

Lochinch Castle
Lochinch, Merrick, Dumfries and Galloway.
Off A77 near Dunragit.

A 19th-century building in Scottish baronial style, completed in 1867, and now the home of the Earl of Stair. It was built to replace the nearby ruins of Castle Kennedy, erected in the reign of James IV (1473–1513). This was burnt down in 1716 and was originally the seat of the Kennedy family, passing to the Stairs in the 17th century.

Lochinch Castle is famous for its magnificent landscaped gardens containing rare shrubs and laid out by the second Earl of Stair from the inspiration of Versailles. The gardens were neglected for many years until the mid 19th century when original plans were discovered and they were then restored to their original beauty.

Gardens open to the public April to September, daily.

Loch Leven Castle
Loch Leven, Perth and Kinross, Tayside.
On an island on Loch Leven, off M90 at Kinross.

The rugged ruins of this 15th-century fortress sit on an island which was originally much smaller but has grown to a size of 8 acres since the surface of the loch was lowered in the 19th century. There was a castle on this site before the 15th century; it is recorded that the site was held in 1335 by Allan de Vipont against an English force acting for Edward Balliol. By the end of the 14th century it belonged to the family of Douglas of Lochleven; and here in 1567 Mary, Queen of Scots, was imprisoned until 1568, when William Douglas helped her escape.

The courtyard wall encloses the greater part of the original island and this is entered from the north through an arched gateway. Inside the yard, the ruined buildings include what was apparently a stable and round 16th-century tower as well as three other unidentified buildings. There are also signs of the wheel stair in the main tower and a solar or room above the hall which occupies the whole of the second floor.

Open in summer, weekdays 10am–6pm, Sundays 2–6pm. Ferry service, weather permitting, from June.

Lochmaben Castle
Lochmaben, Annandale and Eskdale, Dumfries and Galloway.
9 miles east of Dumfries off A709.

A stone castle has existed on this site since 1330; it was in the hands of the English almost continuously between 1290 and 1385, enabling Annandale to be governed almost entirely as an English shire. At one time it was the great castle of the Bruces, Lords of Annandale, where some say the hero king was born and where he spent much of his youth.

In those days it was a huge and powerful stronghold covering as much as 15 acres and with four moats to defend it. It stood intact into the 17th century, when it was left to fall into ruins.

Open all year round.

Lochnaw Castle
Leswalt, by Stranraer, Wigtown, Dumfries and Galloway.
4 miles north-west of Stranraer off A718 on B7043.

Set in terraced lawns by the edge of its own loch and surrounded by natural woodlands is the ancient home of the Agnew family, hereditary sheriffs of Galloway for 300 years. This is an extremely picturesque castle originally built in 1426 in an area famous for its rhododendrons. Lochnaw is now run as a guest house.

Open to the public, all year, Monday to Saturday 10am–5pm; closed on Sundays (except for residents). Refreshments available.

Loch Ranza Castle
Isle of Arran, Bute, Cunninghame, Strathclyde.
On a promontory jutting into the bay at the northern end of the Isle of Arran on A841.

The picturesque ruin of Loch Ranza Castle with its two square towers was built in the 13th and 14th centuries and enlarged in the 16th century.

Robert the Bruce is said to have landed here on his return in 1306 from Rathlin Island in Ireland, at the start of his campaign for Scottish independence. It is also believed that this is the castle Sir Walter Scott had in mind for his novel *Lord of the Isles* but there is no trace of the nunnery referred to in the story.

Open at all reasonable times.

Loudoun Castle
Galston, Cunninghame, Strathclyde.
5 miles east of Kilmarnock on A71.

In the upper Irvine valley, above the former coal-mining town of Galston, stands the largely ruined castle of Loudoun. The castle was the seat of the Campbell Earldom of Loudoun and hence that of the former hereditary sheriffs of Ayrshire. Records point to Loudoun as having been one of the most imposing castles in the west of Scotland, but there is little sign of this strength left today as the building was largely destroyed by fire in 1941. Part of the old castle grounds now form the local golf course.

Not open to the public.

Maclellan's Castle
Kirkcudbright, Stewartry, Dumfries and Galloway.
On A755 at Kirkcudbright.

Sir Thomas Maclellan built his castle in the 16th century on the site of a ruined monastery given to him in 1569. He was also granted the lands and fortress of Castledukes in 1577, and it is thought that he used much of the stone from this site for building his castle. Although Maclellan's Castle was not planned for defence, as fortification was no longer necessary at this time, it is a notable example of late 16th-century domestic architecture. Above the entrance doorway are heraldic carved panels bearing arms and initials. Inside, the ground floor contains vaulted cellars and a kitchen in the north wing with its fireplace and sink still in evidence. From the entrance, the main staircase leads to the great hall with its adjoining rooms. Additional stairs starting from the first floor gave separate access to the second floor rooms and continued up to the third floor, which is now mainly ruined. There is a tradition that some of the rooms were never used and the structure is said to have been roofless since 1752, but no evidence has been found on these reports. Not far from the castle on its eastern side is the site of the Old Greyfriars kirk, containing a quaint monument erected in memory of Sir Thomas Maclellan and his wife. The tomb was placed there by his son Robert, later first Lord Kirkcudbright, as his father, who had been Provost of Kirkcudbright, was granted the special privilege of burial within the kirk.

Robert Maclellan, who succeeded his father in 1597, spent little time at the castle. His son Thomas was a great soldier, fighting in the Wars of the Covenant and commanding a regiment raised at Galloway at his own expense, and he too was but rarely to be found at the castle. In fact, the expense of these adventures drained the family fortunes and the estates never recovered. In the 18th century Maclellan's Castle, which had stood empty for some time, passed to Sir Robert Maxwell of Orchardton and in 1782 the walls were sold to the Earl of Selkirk. In 1912 the castle was put into the care of the predecessors of Historic Buildings and Monuments, Scottish Development Department, by Sir Charles Hope-Dunbar.

Open to the public, every day, April to September, Monday to Saturday 9.30am–7pm, Sundays 2–7pm; October to March, Saturdays 9.30am–4pm, Sundays 2–4pm.

Mains Castle
East Kilbride, Lanark, Strathclyde.
10 miles south-east of Glasgow on A726.

A little to the north of the old village is the 15th-century Mains Castle keep. It is near the site of the

12th-century castle motte which once belonged to the Red Comyn until his murder at Dumfries when it was ceded to the Crown. It was later given by Marjory Bruce to the grandson of John Lindsay but the reason for the gift is 'hidden'. The site is of interest in that there are in a ¼-mile radius, an 8th-century crannog, the 12th-century motte and the 'new' castle, dating from the 15th century. Archeological evidence shows that all three were inhabited in the 15th century. The 'new' castle has been well restored from its previous ruined state.

Open to the public by written appointment only.

Maybole Castle
Maybole, Kyle and Carrick, Strathclyde.
On A77, 10 miles south of Ayr.

One of a group of twenty-eight baronial mansions which once stood within the parish, Maybole Castle dominates the main street. It was the capital of the Kennedys under their Chief the Marquis of Ailsa, and is still used by the family as the office of the Cassillis and Culzean estates. It was built about 1560 by the Earl of Cassillis, head of the powerful Lowland family, and was their town house for many years. An ancient legend tells that the castle was the prison of a countess of Cassillis who had eloped with Johnny Faa, King of the Gypsies, but her husband, John Kennedy, sixth Earl of Cassillis, arrived home in time to catch his wayward lady and hang Johnny Faa and his band. The countess was said to have been imprisoned for life; but surviving letters dispute the legend and show that John and his wife lived very happily together for over 20 years.

Not open to the public.

Meggernie Castle
Glen Lyon, Perth and Kinross, Tayside.
West of Aberfeldy off A827.

A fine late 16th-century whitewashed fortalice, set amidst old trees. Now the seat of a wealthy southern proprietor, it was built by 'Mad Colin'— Colin Campbell in about 1580. Amongst other exploits, he abducted the Countess of Erroll and held her here. Another sad lady is said to haunt Meggernie, the wife of a later Menzies laird who murdered her in a fit of jealousy and dismembered her corpse. It is the upper half which is said to materialise. In the early 18th century, James Menzies, then the owner, introduced larches to Scotland. He imported them from Austria where he had seen them growing during his banishment from Scotland for having taken part in the Jacobite rising of 1715.

Not open to the public.

Megginch Castle
Errol, Perth and Kinross, Tayside.
10 miles east of Perth off A85.

Some 10 miles east of Perth is the 15th-century castle of Megginch, built on a 50-foot rise. According to legend there was a monastery here, and the yew hedge round the monks garden grew so profusely that it now stands over 70 feet high.

The castle was built in 1460 on an L-plan, including a circular staircase tower. It was strongly fortified with gun-loops and arrow-slits in the turrets, and in its time withstood countless attacks from bands of Royalists, Protestants and Highlanders. In 1575 a new wing was added to the long north front of the castle by Peter Hay, a brother of Edmund Hay, Provincial of the French Jesuits and friend of Mary, Queen of Scots. At the same time he laid out the top section of the kitchen gardens and the rose walk to the north of the castle where the white Jacobite rose, the white rose of York and the red rose of Lancaster still bloom together. In 1644 the castle was bought by John Drummond, whose descendants still live there.

Robert Drummond, who made six voyages to China and captained the first copper-bottomed ship of the East India Fleet to Bombay in 1783, died in 1815. During his lifetime he built the Gothic Arch at the bottom of the Beech Walk which his uncle Adam Drummond, fourth laird of Megginch had planted during the '45 rebellion 'so that out of this war and time of troubles for Scotland, something of enduring beauty shall continue to grow'. The Drummonds have been keen gardeners and botanists for generations. Adam imported the Banksian Rose from China in 1796 and the double red Camellia. Colin Drummond brought the golden Alstroemerias from Canada in 1770, and his son Adam, later an Admiral, laid out the bottom kitchen garden in 1820. In 1840 the Admiral's eldest son John Murray Drummond laid out the intricate beds and topiary of the flower garden, and his daughter-in-law Cherry was said to 'scatter seeds wherever she went' which accounts for the abundance of flowers growing in the woods nearby and the huge patch of pink violets by the West Lodge.

The gardens are open to the public, Wednesdays, April to October 2–6pm.

Menstrie Castle
Menstrie, Clackmannan, Central.
In Menstrie on A91.

This 16th-century fortified house contrasts dramatically with the modern buildings surrounding it. It was the ancient home of the chiefs of the West Country clan Alister who came east in the 15th century with that Earl of Argyll who became Chancellor of Scotland and lived at Castle Camp-bell. The MacAlister clan changed its name to Alexander, and in 1567 Sir William Alexander was born here, a poet, statesman and coloniser who became first Earl of Stirling and founder of 'New Scotland'. It was he who advised James VI to found the order of the Baronets of Nova Scotia, who instead of inheriting their knighthoods and lands bought them for hard cash, thereby financing this new territory.

Menstrie Castle was scheduled to be demolished until public outcry stopped the project. It is now a showpiece of the county containing a museum with commemoration rooms displaying the coats-of-arms of all the 'bought' baronetcies.

Open to the public, May to September, Mondays 2.30–4.30pm, Wednesdays 9.30am–12 noon, Thursdays 6–8pm.

Methven Castle
Methven, Perth and Kinross, Tayside.
3 miles out of Perth on A85.

This mid 17th-century building is a handsome fortalice splendidly situated on a long, low ridge east of the village of Methven. Most of the main section was built by Ludovick, second Duke of Lennox, a distant cousin and favourite of James IV,

on the site of a battle fought in 1306 when Robert the Bruce was defeated by the English. It was built around an earlier work and consists of a tall five-storeyed block with round towers. James IV settled Methven on his wife, Margaret Tudor, sister of Henry VIII, who later married Henry Stewart and made him Lord Methven. She died here in 1540.

Open to the public by appointment only.

Midmar Castle
Echt, Aberdeen, Grampian.
On B9119, 3 miles west of Echt.

This stronghold of the Gordons, thought to have been built by George Bell who was buried nearby in 1575, was the first of a series of tower houses which can only be described as artistic master-pieces. It was designed to a Z-plan with a central block flanked by square and round towers at diagonally opposite corners. The main building is ornamented with crow-stepped gables and large rectangular turrets resting on elaborate tiers of key-pattern corbelling. The square tower has circular corbelled turrets and the round tower is finished with an open battlemented parapet, while dominating the whole building is the staircase turret capped by a graceful S-shaped roof. Around the castle is an old walled garden and beyond this a dell of sycamores surrounded by the slopes of

Midmar Castle

the Hill of Fare from where, off the road, one can catch a glimpse of this castle sometimes referred to as a 'veritable symphony in stone'.

Not open to the public.

Mingary Castle
Ardnamurchan, Lochaber, Highland.
Near Kilchoan on the Ardnamurchan coast, off A861.

This early 13th-century ruined curtain wall castle was the fortalice of its ancient lords the MacIans of Ardnamurchan, part of the great clan Donald, who played a major part in the eventful history of the Lordship of the Isles and who were outlawed in the early 17th century. From then on they gradually disappeared from the area. James IV visited Mingary Castle and held court here in 1495 when he received the submission of the island chiefs. The castle was later captured by Montrose in 1644 and used as a prison for Covenanters.

Entry to be avoided as the castle is in a dangerous condition.

Morton Castle
Thornhill, Nithsdale, Dumfries and Galloway.
2½ miles north of Thornhill off A76.

Standing on a steep promontory above the loch near the old Roman road is the ruined 13th-century Morton Castle. According to tradition the site was the seat of Dunegal, Lord of Nithsdale, and the great 12th-century cross now standing on the lawn at Friar's Close stood originally in front of the castle until Riddell, a friend of Burns, took it away in 1788. This information fits in with what is known of the kingdom of Dunegal which included Nithsdale and much of Clydesdale and dated back to around 1120. Dunegal's grandson was first Sheriff of Nithsdale in the early 13th century and his son may have built the present castle about 1250.

It is a very unusual type of building for early Scotland, consisting mainly of residential apartments with fine windows and an ornate gatehouse and with hardly any defences at all. The castle was occupied until 1715.

Open to the public all year round.

Muchall's Castle
Stonehaven, Kincardine and Deeside, Grampian.
Just off A92 to Aberdeen.

A very charming L-plan house overlooking the sea on a picturesque coast of red cliffs and gullies set in otherwise rather bare countryside. It was built

between 1619 and 1627 by Alexander Burnett of Leys, the Burnett laird who completed Crathes Castle in 1596. Muchalls was his second home but it was his son Thomas, later created a baronet of Nova Scotia in 1626, who finished the building.

The centre of the castle contains a courtyard with a well and around the buildings is a curtain wall set with triple gun-loops on each side of the turreted gateway. Inside this is the great hall, with its remarkable ceiling of delicate white pargeted plaster work done by Italian workmen. The designs include six coats of arms, medallions of the heads of biblical and classical heroes, and three 'knops' with hooks for hanging lamps. Above the fireplace is another splendid piece of workmanship, a magnificent sculptured overmantel dated 1624 and bearing the Royal Arms of Scotland, which at that time, after the Union of 1603, contained the collar of the thistle inside the Garter, surmounted by the Scottish crest. Also on this floor are the withdrawing room and the laird's study with similar plaster ceilings to that already described.

Muchalls was occupied by Lord Robertson, Lord Justice General of Scotland towards the end of the 19th century, but is now the home of Mr and Mrs A. Simpson, who have filled it with antiques.

Open to the public, May to September, Sundays and Tuesdays 3–5pm.

Muness Castle
Unst, Shetland Isles.
Off A968

Built at the end of the 16th century, this is the most northerly of all castles in Britain, and except for the removal of its topmost storey, surprisingly complete after all these years. The oblong block of the castle, 73 feet by 26 feet, has two circular towers,

Muness Castle

built mainly in local rubble, attached to north and south corners of the building. In the south-west wall is the main entrance to the castle, the doorway of which comes from an old farmhouse at Lund and is therefore much older than the castle itself. Above the doorway is a panel with an inscription in Gothic lettering which states that the originator of the castle was one Lawrence the Bruce and the message goes on to beg his heirs and offspring 'to help and not hurt the structure always'. This is followed by '1598' in Roman lettering and the initials L.B. The structure of the castle takes the form of a normal tower house, four storeys tall, of which only three still exist.

Open to the public, every day.

Murthly Castle
Murthly, Perth and Kinross, Tayside.
9 miles north of Perth, off A924 at Caputh.

Set among woods on the south bank of the River Tay is the ancient property of Murthly Castle, said to have been a hunting seat of Scottish kings. Since 1615 it has been the seat of the Stewarts of Murthly or Grantully who descend from Sir John Stewart of Bonkyl.

Sir William Stewart of Grantully acquired the western range with its five-storey tower at the end of the 16th century and it was later added to in the 17th and 18th centuries. Finally in the 1830s Sir John Drummond Stewart decided to outdo the Duke of Atholl and build a huge new mansion to the design of Gillespie Graham, making certain that all the main apartments were just a little bit larger than the Duke's. He never completed his Tudor-type palace as he died prematurely in 1838. He was succeeded by his brother, Sir William Drummond Stewart, who was a great traveller, as well as being a compulsive builder and he brought home many treasures from his journeys including two unfortunate Red Indians who lived in a pagoda in the garden.

Open to the public by appointment only.

Neidpath Castle
Tweeddale, Borders.
1 mile west of Peebles on A72.

A large well preserved L-plan tower house. The earliest known lairds were Frasers, the last of whom was Sir Simon, who defeated the English three times, in the space of a day, on 24 February 1303. He was later captured by them and put to death. Through his daughter the castle passed to the Hays of Yester, who later became the Earls of Tweeddale. The greater part of the present build-

ings date from the 14th century but the main tower block was rebuilt by the second Earl of Tweeddale, during the reign of Charles II. This was after he had defended the castle against the Cromwellian army and had to surrender. In 1686 the castle was bought by the second Duke of Queensberry who bestowed it on his son William Douglas, later to become the first Earl of March. His grandson, the fourth Duke of Queensberry, gained notoriety by laying the surroundings of the castle to waste by destroying all the fine old trees.

His deed and name live on in a sonnet by Wordsworth where he is described as 'Degenerate Douglas'. In 1810 the Earl of Wemyss inherited the title Earl of March along with Neidpath Castle and property.

Open to the public, Easter to October, Monday to Saturday, 10am–1pm and 2–6pm, Sundays 2–6pm.

Newark Castle
Ettrick and Lauderdale, Borders.
8 miles west of Selkirk off A708.

Beyond the Buccleuch mansion of Bowhill on the right bank of the River Yarrow is Newark Castle, former principal stronghold of the great Ettrick Forest. This 15th-century ruin was originally built as a royal hunting seat, bearing the arms of James I on its west side, and from then on it was held successively by the Douglases and Scotts of Buccleuch. Here Sir Walter Scott based the scene in the *Lay of the Last Minstrel* where the minstrel sang to his sorrowing Duchess of Buccleuch and Monmouth after her royal husband's execution. Not far away at Philiphaugh is the scene of the battle between Montrose and the Covenanters in 1645, the last blow to Charles I's hopes of retaining Scotland.

Not open to the public.

Newark Castle
Inverclyde, Strathclyde.
4 miles east of Greenock on A8.

On the eastern side of Port Glasgow overlooking the River Clyde is the large turreted mansion built by the Maxwells in the 15th century. It is still almost complete and in good repair; the buildings forming three sides of a court, the arched passage in the west range and a portion in the north-eastern enclosure wall with its dovecot are all still standing. Newark Castle originally consisted of a simple keep built around 1484 and a gatehouse built a few years after. At the end of the 16th century the two detached portions were added by Patrick Maxwell. These contained a kitchen, wine cellar and bakehouse, with a splendid hall and two other rooms on the first floor and a long open apartment—which may have been the gallery or withdrawing room—on the second floor.

Open to the public, April to September, weekdays 9.30am–7pm, Sundays 2–7pm; October to March, weekdays 9.30am–4pm, Sundays 2–4pm.

Niddry Castle

by Winchburgh, West Lothian, Lothian.
1 mile west of Newbridge off A89.

Niddry Castle is an early 16th-century L-plan tower house. It is sited on a rocky outcrop above the Niddry Burn near Winchburgh. George, third Lord of Seton, began building the castle but never saw it completed as he was killed at the Battle of Flodden in 1513. The fifth Lord of Seton gave comfort to Mary, Queen of Scots, at Niddry after her escape from Loch Leven Castle in 1568. Around 1600 the castle was extended by adding more and spacious accommodation. In 1676 one John Hope acquired the castle but 50 years later the building was abandoned. Having lain in a ruinous state for many years the castle is now being extensively and faithfully restored.

Open to the public, May to September, 10am–5pm, Sundays by special appointment.

Noltland Castle

Kirkwall, Orkney.
On the northern coast of Westray overlooking its harbour at Pierowall.

The castle is protected to the west by a line of hills, to the north by the rocky coast and to the south by the small freshwater loch, Loch Burness. It was originally built around 1420 by Thomas de Tulloch and was later besieged by Sir William Sinclair of Warsetter. It subsequently fell into the hands of Gilbert Balfour, a younger son of Balfour of Mountquhannie in Fife. In 1546 he was implicated in the murder of Cardinal Beaton for which he did voluntary penance, rowing in a French galley. He obviously survived the ordeal and reappeared later as Master of Queen Mary's Household and husband of Margaret Bothwell, sister of Adam, Bishop of the Orkneys who granted him land on Westray.

Balfour was attracted by trouble, and on Bothwell's direction he played a prominent part in the murder of the queen's husband, Darnley. In fact Knox said that he actually 'laid hands on the king to kill him'. When Bothwell fell from grace, Balfour retreated to Orkney where he spent his time as Sheriff, quarrelling with his brother-in-law, the

Bishop. In 1571 he was found guilty of treason by Parliament and his estates forfeited. Even this punishment failed to subdue him; 2 months later, in October, he raised one hundred men of the Queen's party in Edinburgh and attempted to capture first Inchkeith and then Blackness Castle, which he held for his exiled monarch.

Noltland Castle in the meantime had been taken by the Queen's half-brother, Lord Robert Stewart, but the Privy Council ordered him to hand back the building to its legal owner—having presumably forgotten all about the forfeiture order of 1571. Gilbert Balfour's luck turned: he was not powerful enough to regain the castle and his schemes for putting Mary on the throne of Scotland failed, so he fled abroad and joined the Swedish army, in whose ranks he died in 1576.

Gilbert Balfour designed many of the additions to Noltland Castle and turned it into a hideout for himself, which is why the building is so heavily fortified. In 1592 the castle was captured by Earl Patrick Stewart from Sir Michael Balfour, and in 1650, officers of Montrose's army sought refuge here after their defeat at Carbisdale. They were soon captured by local Covenanting leaders and the castle is said to have been burnt. What is left of the building, which was originally Z-shaped, are no less than seventy-one gun-loops which pierced the outer walls and made Noltland look something like a 'man-of-war's hull'. The castle is externally a forbidding place, furnished with corbelled parapets and cylindrical turrets and topped with a high pitched roof. The main door to the castle is in the south-west tower, and inside, a guardroom or prison sits under a spiral staircase which leads to a vaulted guard chamber and via a wide passage into the great hall. From a landing a smaller and newer stair ascends to the upper storey, which at one time contained living rooms, and the great hall—a rather poorly lit and stern looking place. Across the upper end of this hall a thick diaphragm wall crossed the building and carried on up to its summit forming a massive gable. In this way the lord's private rooms were cut off from the hall and the hazard of fire was minimised.

Not open to the public.

Ormond Castle

Avoch, Black Isle, Ross and Cromarty, Highland.
1 mile south-west of Avoch on A832.

Immediately south of the small fishing village of Avoch on the south shore of Black Isle stand the ruins of Ormond Castle, set above the surrounding countryside on a mound. The position of this castle must have been of considerable importance in the past as it guarded the approach to Inverness up the Moray Firth. Very little is known of the actual dates and structure of the building but it is believed to have been the home of Andrew de Moray, who was at William Wallace's right hand at the Battle of Stirling Bridge in 1297. In 1979, a cairn was built by the people of the parish, to commemorate the raising of the standard for Wallace. This event is remembered by parades in July. The flag of St Andrew flies over the cairn throughout the year.

Open all year round.

Oxenfoord Castle
Pathhead, Midlothian, Lothian.
10 miles south-east of Edinburgh on A68.

Oxenfoord Castle stands 1 mile north of the village of Pathhead, situated in fine parklands. The existing castle was built in mansion style to a design of Robert Adam in the years 1780–85. This modern structure is on the site of an older castle of which no traces remain. The 'Adam' Castle was later added to by one William Burn. Oxenfoord Castle is now a girls' private boarding school.

Not open to the public. Visiting by written appointment only.

Penkill Castle
Girvan, Kyle and Carrick, Strathclyde.
2½ miles east of Girvan on B734 off A77.

Penkill Castle stands in the valley of the Girvan with four other castles nearby, all of which are occupied. The castle is an example of a typical 16th-century tower-keep, and it contains a series of fine mural paintings by William Bell Scott. It was a favourite haunt of the pre-Raphaelites, a creative group including Dante Gabriel Rossetti, who is said to have written many of his poems here.

Open to the public by written prior arrangement. Refreshments available.

Pitcaple Castle
Pitcaple, Inverurie, Aberdeen, Grampian.
3 miles from Inverurie on A96.

A high wall runs along the right-hand side of the A96 coming into the village of Pitcaple, partly screening the castle and its surrounds. The castle is a 15th-century Z-plan tower house built on lands which James II granted to David Leslie in 1457, and it is probable that construction began on the castle at this time. Mary, Queen of Scots, visited Pitcaple in 1562 and dined and danced under a famous thorn tree in the garden, which

was lovingly preserved until it died in 1856. The castle changed hands on numerous occasions during the civil wars and was at one time burnt out by the Covenanters. Evidence of this can still be found on the stonework of the lower floors.

One of the most interesting features found at the castle is a little escape shaft in the outside wall. After his capture, the Marquis of Montrose spent a night at Pitcaple in 1650 while on his way to Edinburgh to be executed. He arrived at nightfall bound and gagged and bearing a label around his neck 'James Graham, a traitor to his country'. The Lady of Pitcaple, who happened to be his cousin, put him in the room where the shaft began, hidden behind some furniture, and during the night she tried to persuade him to escape through the small opening. He is said to have replied, 'rather than be smothered in that hole, I'll take my chance at Edinburgh'. He was executed a short time later.

In the 19th century a wing designed by William Burn was added, giving an air of incongruity to the structure. However, as the castle was continuously occupied, the mixture of stark 15th-century military and 19th-century residential blends together in a way that does not seem too odd today. Pitcaple is privately owned by Mrs C. Burges-Lumsden, who has done much to maintain the castle in its present condition.

Open to the public, by written appointment only.

Pitsligo Castle
Pitsligo, Banff and Buchan, Grampian.
½ mile south-east of Rosehearty off A98.

The ruins of Pitsligo Castle date from 1424 when the massive keep was built housing three rooms, one on top of the other: a basement kitchen, a banqueting hall and the sleeping apartment for the whole family—with room for twenty-four beds—on the top floor. The castle was built by one Sir William Forbes, the founder of the famous family. It is probable that the castle fell into disrepair after the 1715 and 1745 risings, as the last Lord Portsligo was heavily involved in these and, as was the cause elsewhere, was probably made to forfeit his lands.

Open all year round.

Polnoon Castle
Eaglesham, Inverclyde, Strathclyde.
2 miles off A77 at Newton Mearns.

A little to the west of the village of Eaglesham stand the sparse ruins of the 14th-century Polnoon Castle, built by the Montgomerie family.

Open all year round.

Rait Castle
Nairn, Highland.
3 miles south of Nairn off A96.

The 15th-century Rait Castle stands complete to its wall-head, lacking only a roof and floors; it is well known for its large round tower. The interior consists of a long hall over an unvaulted basement, and above the hall are the usual residential quarters. The only points of interest in the local history relating to Rait Castle are the massacre of the Comyns in 1524 outside the castle at nearby Balbair; and the fact that the Duke of Cumberland is reputed to have stayed here while his army camped nearby before marching to defeat the Jacobites at Culloden in 1746.

Not open to the public.

Ravenscraig Castle
Kirkcaldy, Fife.
On A955 at Kirkcaldy.

This imposing ruin, founded by James II in 1460, is surrounded by a deep rock-cut ditch and is sited on a rocky promontory between Dysart and Kirkcaldy. It is said to have been the first castle in these islands designed for defence by firearms and was completed by James's queen, Mary of Gueldres. At a later stage it passed to the Sinclairs, Earls of Orkney, and it is now in the care of Historic Buildings and Monuments, Scottish Development Department.

Open to the public, every day, Monday to Saturday, Summer 9.30am–7pm, Winter 9.30am–4pm,
Sundays, Summer 2–7pm, Winter 2–4pm.

Roslin Castle
Roslin, Midlothian, Lothian.
Off A6094 at Roslin.

Situated on a steep promontory overhanging the North Esk River is the 14th-century Castle of Roslin, built by Sir William Sinclair and now in ruins. His grandson later started the keep, which was enlarged by the third Earl of Orkney but destroyed in 1544, only to be restored once more around 1580 and later abandoned. The huge fragments of rock which remain indicate a castle of terrific strength surrounded by a moat and only accessible by a drawbridge. Roslin Castle was the scene of a defeat for Edward I of England in his war with Robert the Bruce in 1302.

Not far from the castle is the well-known Rosslyn Chapel, renowned for its elaborately detailed carving and founded by the third Earl of Orkney in 1446. According to legend the Prentice Pillar, a pillar of entwined ribbands, was finished by an apprentice during his master's absence. The master mason, on his return, was so jealous of the boy's skill that he hit him with a mallet and killed him.

Not open to the public.

Rossend Castle
Burntisland, Fife.
Off A92 at Burntisland.

Rossend Castle was built in the 13th century as an ecclesiastical building and fortified in the 16th century. In the troubled 12th century it was the home of the Abbots of Dunfermline but later became a secular residence. Mary, Queen of Scots, is reputed to have stayed there, and it was here that her young French admirer Chastelard was finally arrested and executed. He died 'protesting not so much the innocence of his intentions as the impelling power of his love'. Cromwell stayed at Rossend in 1651 having captured it without doing much damage. It is said that he fired one shot from a cannon which hit the Provost's apartments, and the castle and town promptly surrendered.

Not open to the public.

Rosyth Castle
Rosyth, Fife.
On A92, 4 miles west of Aberdour.

Until recent years the Castle of Rosyth stood on a small island only accessible at low tide, but the land has slowly been reclaimed, bringing the site of the castle well inland. The castle remains date back to the 15th century when the tower was built, and to this was added a rectangular enclosure in the 16th and 17th centuries. The entrance is in the north range of the wall and above its gateway are two armorial panels set below a crown with the Royal Arms of Scotland and a date, 1561. It is difficult to envisage the remains of the rest of the buildings but obviously there was a turret stair in the main section of the building which rose from the first to the upper floors. The old tower, with walls 10 feet thick, is built of ashlar and has weathered well. It includes a staircase to the upper floors, daily living rooms and a hall which once had a barrel-vaulted ceiling.

According to historical records, the king granted the barony of Rosyth to Sir David Stewart in 1428 and Rosyth remained with this family until the end of the 17th century when the line died out for lack of male decendants.

Not open to the public.

Rothesay Castle
Rothesay, Isle of Bute, Strathclyde.

The first stone castle of Rothesay was an enormous shell keep built around 1098 and which is first recorded in 1230, when it was attacked by the Norsemen. It survived the attack, as a circular curtain with four massive round towers, and still stands today on the summit of a flat-topped mound surrounded by a water moat. The fortress was again attacked and captured in 1263 by King Haakon of Norway, but soon afterwards he was defeated at Largs and the castle was restored to Scottish hands.

In 1401 Robert III made Rothesay a royal burgh and his son became Duke of Rothesay, a title since borne by the eldest sons of the Scottish Kings and one of the titles of the present Prince of Wales. James IV and James V added considerably to the circular curtain wall and its towers by erecting the large oblong donjon, which combined the functions of a fortified gatehouse and royal residence for the king. Already, in 1498, the noble family of Bute had been made hereditary keepers of the castle, but in 1544 it was captured by the Earl of Lennox on behalf of the English and the Butes were thrown out.

During the 17th century, Rothesay became once again an important fortress in the civil conflicts and it was held first for King Charles and later for Cromwell. When the Roundheads withdrew in 1659 they are said to have partially destroyed the building and what remained was burnt down by Argyll's Highlanders during the 1685 rebellion. From then on, Rothesay lay in ruins until 1816–17, when it was repaired by the second Marquis of Bute, a member of the Crichton-Stuart branch of the Stewart family. The third Marquis also spent much time and money on further repairs and renovations in the later 19th century.

Rothesay is unusual in that the parapets have been built into later masonry, sealed up as it were, but still visible. This is possibly one of the only 13th-century castles which still shows these parapets and they illustrate that the loopholes were designed so that an archer could keep a look-out while reloading his crossbow in shelter. Also visible are the putlog-holes which were used to support a timber war-head in times of siege so that the garrison could get a better view of what was happening at the base of the curtain. The 13th-century north-western or Pigeon Tower is still in good order, but practically the whole of the eastern side of the donjon was rebuilt in the late 19th century.

Inside the donjon, through the long vaulted passage, are the porter's lodge and a guard room on the left and on the right a postern leading to the moat. In the floor of the entrance passage is a trap door which opens into a damp prison lit by a single loophole. Further along this same passage are the slots for a portcullis and through this section one reaches the courtyard. The first floor of the main building can be reached either by a narrow stair in the east wall or an external flight of steps from the courtyard. It contains the great hall with private apartments above and privies which were afterwards converted into rooms.

Down in the courtyard is the two-storeyed chapel of St Michael built in whinstone rubble and probably dating from the early 16th century. Behind the chapel an outside stair called the Bloody Stair leads to the summit of the curtain wall. Under the protection of Historic Buildings and Monuments, Scottish Development Department.

Open to the public, April to September, every day 9.30am–7pm, Sundays 2–7pm; October to March, Saturday to Thursday 9.30am–4pm, Sundays 2–4pm.

Rough Castle
Falkirk, Stirling, Central.
1 mile east of Bonnybridge off A80.

Some of the finest Roman remains in Scotland can be found at the great Rough Castle fort on the Antonine Wall. Here, in open country with extensive views over the bracken-clad slopes, is a magnificent stretch of the wall, the Military Way and its Roman fort. The fort covers an acre of ground and was originally excavated in 1903. However, because of the weather the fort slowly deteriorated and now it is once again being restored by Historic Buildings and Monuments, Scottish Development Department, who are also clearing the surrounding defence ditch.

A National Trust for Scotland property.

Open to the public, Summer, except Fridays; Winter, except Fridays and Sunday afternoons.

Saddell Castle
Saddell, Campbeltown, Argyll, Strathclyde.
10 miles north of Campbeltown on the west coast of the Mull of Kintyre.

Half way down the east coast of the Mull of Kintyre stand the remains of Saddell Castle, a large square battlemented tower house dating from 1508. Little is known of the history of Saddell and records do not show it to have played any major part in the history of Scotland. Neither is much known of the more interesting period of Kintyre's history prior to 1508. It is known, however, that there was a castle on the existing site before the present one. This was probably built in the mid 12th century by Somerled, Lord of the Isles, who was also responsible for the building of Saddell Abbey, the ruins of which stand near the castle.

The Mull of Kintyre was one of the gateways to Scotland through which the civilising Christian influence came from Ireland.

Not open to the public.

Sanquhar Castle
Sanquhar, Nithsdale, Dumfries and Galloway.
10 miles north of Carronbridge on A76.

The earliest records show a castle standing at Sanquhar in 1484; as the seat of the Crichton family, it protected the town when it became a royal burgh. The castle passed to the Duke of Queensberry in 1639. He also built Drumlanrig Castle, but having spent one night there on its completion returned to Sanquhar, which he preferred. Sanquhar was the place where the Covenanters proclaimed two major declarations against Charles II in 1680 and James II in 1685. The reason was that they feared a return of Catholicism to Scotland, and on both occasions they declared wars which were never fought. The castle structure is in typical tower-house style, the main parts of it dating from 15th, 16th and 17th centuries.

Not open to the public.

Scalloway Castle
Scalloway, Mainland, Shetland.
Off A970.

Orkney and Shetland were Scandinavian possessions and were made a part of the dowry of Margaret, daughter of Christian I, King of Norway and Denmark, on her marriage to James III of Scotland. By 1471, both islands were officially annexed to the Scottish crown. In 1564 Queen Mary granted the whole of the royal estates in both Orkney and Shetland to her half-brother, Robert Stewart, who later became Earl of Orkney in 1581. He and his successor, Earl Patrick, who held the estates until 1609, tragically misgoverned these islands.

It was Earl Patrick who built the castle in about 1600 as a headquarters for his representative and a residence for himself, although the Earl's Palace in Kirkwall was his principal home. He was obviously a cruel man, of whom many dark stories are told, including one to the effect that mortar for the castle was mixed with blood from the men he forced to work there. However, Earl Patrick paid for his misdeeds in 1615 when he was executed with his son for trying to gain power by force.

Scalloway Castle is thought to have been built with materials from an older castle in Loch Strom, a few miles north, and was sited so that the Earl

could keep a close control over the growing trade of the port of Scalloway. The castle is a manifestation of the strength and pride of this powerful baron but as his power slipped so the castle became less and less important. During Cromwell's occupation of Shetland his soldiers scratched inscriptions on the plaster, and by 1703 the castle was virtually a ruin. About a century later the Earl of Morton granted permission to Sir Andrew Mitchell to plunder the building and strip the ornaments to furnish his house at Sand. It was left to rot until 1908 when the Marquis of Zetland put the castle into the care of the Department of the Environment, who renewed much of the building. The castle is four storeys high, built of rubble and harled with freestone dressings, and apart from the roof and flooring of the upper storeys it is still almost entire. It consists of a solid oblong block with a square tower containing the stair, and is topped by corbelled turrets. The entrance doorway is in the east wall of the stair tower. The castle has had two doors opening on to the main stair, with a vaulted guardroom under the upper flight of steps. Further along the ground floor passage are two vaulted apartments, one a kitchen and the other a storehouse.

On the first floor is the stately hall from which a turret staircase leads up to the second floor which contains two well-lit chambers and a single room with a fireplace. Above this, the third floor consisted of three rooms each with a fireplace—the two end rooms leading to turret rooms in the north-west and south-east corners of the towers.

Not open to the public.

Seton Castle
Port Seton, East Lothian, Lothian.
1 mile east of Cockenzie off A198.

Seton Castle, built by Robert Adam in 1790, is a magnificent building erected on the site of the demolished Seton Palace. Here Mary, Queen of Scots, James VI and Charles I were entertained by the Seton family. Nearby is the Collegiate Church of Seton which dates from the late 14th century. It was never completed but includes a fine tomb with two recumbent figures—probably of George, third Lord Seton, slain at Flodden in 1513, and his lady.

Not open to the public.

Slains Castle
Cruden Bay, Banff and Buchan, Grampian.
Just off A975 north of Port Erroll.

On a granite headland above Port Erroll is the ancestral home of the Earls of Erroll for three and a quarter centuries—the 'new' or second Slains Castle. This spectacular ruin is comparatively modern, first built at the end of the 16th century to replace Old Castle Slains, and three times rebuilt before it was finally abandoned. The old castle had been blown up by King James VI after the Earls Rebellion in 1594 and the new castle was built by Francis, ninth Earl of Erroll when he returned to Scotland after 3 years' exile abroad. One of the many distinguished guests at the house was Dr Samuel Johnson who wrote, 'the walls of the tower seem only the continuation of a perpendicular rock, the foot of which is beaten by the waves . . . I would not for my amusement wish for a storm, but as storms whether wished for or not, will sometimes happen, I may say without violation of humanity that I would willingly look upon them from Slains Castle.'

Boswell and Johnson went to see the Bullers of Buchan together from Slains. This eerie rock is an island surrounded by a narrow pathway with sea all round deep enough for a 'Man-o'-War to ride in'; a cavern called 'the Pot', inside the rock, is only accessible by boat. It is still there today, just north of Cruden Bay on the main road to Peterhead.

When Slains Castle was rebuilt for the third time in 1836 it was given a couple of round towers; the same architect who designed the castle rebuilt Cruden Parish Church, which he supplied with an almost identical tower to those on the castle.

All that remains of the Old Castle Slains, some 4 miles south-west of the modern castle, is a tall shattered keep on the neck of the promontory. These lands were given by King Robert the Bruce to Sir Gilbert Hay in the early 14th century, and for three centuries Slains was the scene of great pageantry and splendour which included tilting tournaments. As mentioned above, Old Slains was demolished by King James in the 16th century when the ninth Earl, converted to Catholicism, took part in the drawing up of a secret agreement —known as the Treaty of the Spanish Blanks—with King Philip of Spain against England. The secret was found out and the Earl of Argyll commissioned to put down the revolt. During the Battle of Glenlivet the ninth Earl was wounded, and he fled into exile leaving King James to blow up the castle.

Not open to the public.

St Andrews Castle
St Andrews, North-East Fife, Fife.

St Andrews, steeped in history, seat of Scotland's first university, with its cathedral, colleges and handsome town wall and gates, contains a castle set on a rocky promontory overlooking the sea and cut off from the land by a deep moat. It was founded in 1200 by Bishop Roger and was intimately connected with the cathedral dignitaries. In the course of time it served the threefold purposes of episcopal palace, fortress and state prison.

During the Wars of Independence the castle was captured, dismantled and rebuilt by both the Scots and the English. In 1332 it fell into the hands of the Scottish barons and was held by them until 1336, when Sir Andrew Moray recovered and dismantled it once more for David II. According to historical documents the castle was then rebuilt by two English lords, de Beaumont and de Ferrers. For some reason it once more lay in ruins 50 years later when Walter Traill was made Bishop. He carried out considerable rebuilding.

It is thought that James III was born here in 1451; certainly his father, James II, stayed at the castle often. The next period of historical interest seems to have occurred in 1546, when Cardinal Beaton incurred Henry VIII's wrath by refusing to ratify the marriage proposed by Henry for his son Edward with the infant Mary, daughter of James V. Henry declared war on Scotland in 1543 and in 1546, while the Cardinal was still strengthening his fort, the garrison was quietly and effectively overcome and the Cardinal murdered. The Protestants held out for a year, with Henry's help, until the French joined in the fight; and then the castle fell, disgorging John Knox and others who had fled here for refuge before the siege began.

Cardinal Beaton's successor was Archbishop John Hamilton, and he again rebuilt the castle, adding his armorial device—a five pointed star, above the present entrance. From then on the castle changed hands peacefully. In 1587 it was transferred with other church property to the Crown; in 1606 it was granted by James VI to the Earl of Dunbar; in 1612 it reverted to the Archbishopric and by 1645 its importance had dwindled so much that the Town Council ordered part of the building to be used for repairs to the harbour walls. In 1911 the monument was eventually handed over to the predecessors of Historic Buildings and Monuments, Scottish Development Department.

The sea is now the castle's greatest enemy. It encroaches more and more rapidly, and in 1807 some of the seaward walls fell. Since then precautions have been taken to protect the building and there is every hope that it will be safe for a long time yet. The oldest part of the ruins date from the 13th century but most of the work is of a later date, including the rock-cut well and the bottle-shaped dungeon in the Sea Tower. This is hollowed out of the solid rock, 24 feet deep and 15 feet wide, with a small circular entrance. Very few of its inmates could have survived more than a few weeks in its dank and ghastly conditions. Also at this castle is a very rare example of medieval siege technique—a mine and counter-mine, tunnelled through the rock and dating from *c.* 1546. Apparently the Earl of Arran mined almost to the foot of the tower while trying to capture the castle, and at the same time the defenders were counter-mining from inside the castle. Although the work was eventually abandoned, these tunnels still exist and are now floodlit.

Open to the public, every day, April to September, Monday to Saturday 9.30am–7.30pm, Sundays 2–7.30pm; October to March, Monday to Saturday 9.30am–4.30pm, Sundays 2–4.30pm.

Stirling Castle
Stirling, Central.
On A9 at Stirling.

Built in what must be quite the most powerful and strategic position in Scotland is Stirling Castle. It has been called 'the Key to Scotland', and others say that whoever holds 'Stirling and its bridges splits Scotland in two'. It forms a slender link between north and south, Highlands and Lowlands, and in its time has been a refuge for kings, a prison for disobedient subjects and a storehouse for munitions. In keeping with its importance, the castle changed hands more than any other in Scotland; the Battle of Bannockburn, within sight of its walls, was one of Scotland's greatest victories over the English.

According to records, the castle was in evidence before the 11th century. In 1124 Alexander I died there and was succeeded by his brother David, who often stayed at Stirling and in 1147 founded the nearby Abbey of Cambuskenneth. After Alexander's death, the castle faded from historical prominence for a generation. It regained its importance in 1174 when William the Lion was forced to sign the Treaty of Falaise, agreeing to the chief Scottish castles, including Stirling, being garrisoned by English soldiers. From then on it is doubtful whether Stirling was occupied for very long periods until 1214, when King William, returning from an expedition into Moray, died at Stirling Castle.

During subsequent reigns the fortress was often visited by royalty and councils were held within its walls. However, this peaceful time was rudely interrupted by King Haakon of Norway who unsuccessfully attempted to invade Scotland from the west.

Stirling is particularly remembered for its part in the Wars of Independence, and as the castle dominated the passage to the north of Scotland it became the focus of military operations. Initially the English had no trouble taking the castle, for after Edward's triumphant capture of Berwick in 1296—which inspired such terror in the Scots— the garrison at Stirling ran away and left only the porter with the keys. Edward did not stay long here, but he stopped once more at Stirling on his way south. The next year, the Scots, under Wallace, beat the English at Stirling Bridge. Sir Marmaduke

Stirling Castle

de Twenge, keeper of the castle, was forced to retire before the victorious Scots; but only a year later, Edward took the castle again and is recorded as having repaired the damage done by Wallace.

When the Scots again attacked Stirling the Governor, John Simpson, appealed to Edward for support, but the English king's barons refused to leave their comfortable homes to fight in the bitter Scottish winter and the garrison was forced to surrender. Sir William Oliphant became Governor, and for some years Edward stayed away from Stirling.

In 1304 Edward began his great siege of Stirling Castle, then the last stronghold in the patriots' hands. He had spent the winter at Dunfermline making careful plans for the attack. For 3 months the garrison held out, and it finally surrendered only when forced by the lack of food. On 24th July Oliphant and his followers marched out of the castle, and were immediately sent off to various English prisons. Apparently Edward forbade his followers to enter the castle after the surrender until it had been struck by the 'War Wolf'—a very novel engine he had had specially made for the attack.

The castle remained in English hands for 10 more years, preventing communication between north and south. However, in 1313 Edward Bruce, brother of King Robert, blockaded the fortress and forced Sir Philip Mowbray, the English Governor, to agree to give up the castle unless he was relieved before 24th June 1314. Edward II sent a detachment of troops to assist the garrison but the Scots drove them back and finally won the castle after the Battle of Bannockburn. King Robert then destroyed the fortifications to prevent English garrisons from using them again, but after the Scots defeat at Halidon Hill, Stirling was in fact again garrisoned by the English under Sir Thomas de Rokeby, who repaired much of the building.

In 1337 Stirling Castle was besieged by Sir Andrew Moray but was relieved by Edward III and heavily provisioned in case of another attack, which came in 1342 when the Scots forced the castle to yield.

When the Stewarts came to the throne Stirling became a royal residence once more. In 1373 Robert II's son, Robert, Earl of Menteith and Fife and later the Duke of Albany, was made keeper, until 1424 when King James I returned from captivity in England. James was horrified at the power of his nobles and in trying to establish his own authority executed Lord Murdoch, two of Murdoch's sons and his father-in-law, the aged Earl of Lennox. This antagonised many powerful people and is thought to have been the reason why he was assassinated in 1437 by Sir Robert Graham, who was accordingly tortured to death at Stirling.

James II was taken to Stirling Castle by his mother after his coronation at Holyrood. Stirling's

Stirling Castle (detail)

governor, Alexander Livingstone of Callander, obtained custody of the child but was duped by Sir William Crichton, the Chancellor, who smuggled James out of the castle and back to his own haunt, Edinburgh Castle. In later years the king made Stirling a dower house for his queen, Mary of Gueldres, and at the time of his marriage great tournaments and feasts took place here. Three years later Stirling witnessed grimmer deeds. James II, believing that William, eighth Earl of Douglas, was plotting against him, invited the nobleman to Stirling with a letter of safe-conduct. The Earl arrived, and after dinner the king invited William to discuss the 'league of Douglas' which he had entered into with the Earl of Crawford. William refused to dissolve the league; and at this James II, who desperately feared this powerful combination, broke down, seized his dagger and struck the Earl. His courtiers completed the deed and the corpse was flung out of the window. James was later declared guiltless by Parliament, but after a few weeks the ninth Earl of Douglas, brother of the late Earl, attacked the city and castle, causing much damage.

In 1451 James III was born at Stirling Castle and on the death of James II succeeded to the throne of Scotland. He enjoyed literary society which in those days was to be found mainly among church-men and having founded the Chapel Royal of

Stirling he endowed it with the revenues of Colding-ham Priory in the Holmes and Hepburn country. These two embittered families joined together to start an insurrection, which spread like wildfire. James III handed over his son, the Duke of Rothesay to Shaw of Sandie and marched north; but Shaw gave the young heir to the rebels, and when King James returned to Stirling he was refused entrance. In 1488 he was defeated and later slain at Sauchieburn.

James IV visited Stirling often, mainly for the hunting there. He ordered many structural improvements to the building and erected the Chapel Royal. Although the king welcomed many distinguished guests to the castle he also made the mistake of including Perkin Warbeck, the imposter who claimed the throne of England. However, James IV obviously enjoyed himself surrounded by all this gaiety, until in 1513 Nicholas West, Henry VIII's envoy, persuaded him to abandon his league with France. In September 1513 he was killed on Flodden Field.

Stirling Castle then became the home of the widowed Queen Margaret and her infant son; she later married the Earl of Angus and gave up the regency, which was handed to the Duke of Albany, one of James III's younger brothers. He demanded custody of the royal children and when Queen Margaret refused, Albany rode to Stirling and installed a garrison of 140 men in the castle, took the princes and handed them over to the Earl Marischal and Lords Fleming and Borthwick.

James V spent much of his childhood at Stirling, and the castle was ceded by Queen Margaret to her son. He completed many of the Palace buildings and improved defences, and as king stayed here often with his second wife, Mary of Guise. The country prospered under his humane and courteous leadership; but in 1542 James V died, a week after the birth of his daughter Mary, and the Earl of Arran was appointed Governor of the Realm.

Mary remained at Linlithgow until July 1543 when Cardinal Beaton and a group of nobles took the child and her mother to Stirling Castle. On 9th September the young Queen was crowned, and for 4 years she stayed at Stirling with her mother. After the Battle of Pinkie the rock fortress seemed unsafe and Mary was moved to the island priory of Inchmahome in the Lake of Menteith, but she later returned to Stirling on her way to France. In 1561 Mary came back to Scotland once more and in 1565 she visited Stirling Castle again to see Henry Stewart, Lord Darnley, with whom she was very much in love, while he was ill and confined to bed in the castle for 2 months. In 1566 Stirling was again chosen to guard a royal infant—the 2-month-old Prince James was brought here and later in the year baptised at an elaborate and expensive ceremony, far more elaborate than his mother's plain coronation.

In 1567, a few days after Queen Mary's abdication from the throne, the 13-month-old Prince was crowned James VI at Stirling, where he was cared for by the Earl of Mar and Atholl, who was made Regent. This was confirmed and again after the civil war which followed. The Earl of Mar was Regent until he died in 1572 and was succeeded as Regent by the Earl of Morton. He made many powerful enemies and in March 1578 he was compelled to resign, but by the end of May he had regained his position and issued a proclamation declaring that the king was free. The nobles still resented Morton bitterly, and in 1578 Atholl and Argyll collected an army to march to Stirling to free the king. The king ordered them to disband immediately and a reconciliation banquet was held in Stirling Castle to show that the grievance no longer existed.

In 1579 Esme Stewart, Lord of Aubigny, arrived at the castle and dazzled the young king, who made him his confidant and soon afterwards Earl of Lennox. In 1581 Morton was condemned to death for his part in Darnley's murder, having been betrayed by Lennox and another of the king's favourites, James Stewart. But Lennox's triumph was short-lived, for in August the king was seized by his nobles, including the Earls of Mar and Gowrie, who took him to Stirling where they issued proclamations declaring the king a free agent. Nevertheless, James Stewart's hold on the king continued until 1585, when the castle was attacked by rebellious lords and Arran forced to flee. The king, Montrose and Crawford shut themselves in the castle and stayed there until they received the guarantee that no harm would come to them if they surrendered. This they did and the castle was restored to the Earl of Mar.

In 1594 Prince Frederick Henry, James VI's eldest son, was baptised at Stirling Castle at a cost of £100,000; he was the last Prince of Scotland to be brought up in Stirling, spending 9 years here. When James became King of England at the Union of the Crowns in 1603, the Palace of Stirling became far less important and was used mainly to house distinguished prisoners, including Presbyterian ministers as well as Huntly, the Roman Catholic Marquess. James promised his Scottish subjects that he would return every 3 years, but he only made two visits. During the last one, in 1617, he listened to a deputation from Edinburgh University discoursing in Greek and Latin—for him a most enjoyable evening.

Neither was Charles I a frequent visitor to Scotland, as he spent only 2 nights here in 1633, and his successor Charles II also paid a brief visit to the castle in 1650. Stirling Castle's importance grew again with the arrival of General Monk in 1651. He commanded Cromwell's men against the castle and forced it to surrender, after which he garrisoned it with Englishmen.

After the Restoration the castle reverted to the Earl of Mar and his heirs, but when George I came to the throne the castle was reclaimed by the Crown and entrusted to distinguished soldiers. (In 1923 King George V restored the office of keeper to the Earl of Mar and Kellie once more.) In the 1715 rising the castle was used by the English to prevent the Highland Jacobites from joining their friends in the south, and in 1746 the castle again held out against the Highlanders. So Stirling, which had ceased to be the seat of royalty, virtually ended its history with the rebellion of '45.

As to the actual structure of the castle, in Edward I's time it was reckoned to be the strongest castle in Scotland and was built mainly of wood. When the castle was occupied by the English a lot of building took place but all traces of the castle as it was at the time of the Battle of Bannockburn (1314) has since disappeared. What is left today dates only from the 15th century. It was probably James III who built the striking central turreted gatehouse, curtain walls and flanking towers which give the castle its commanding dignity. He also had the Great Hall built to hold his parliaments and state ceremonies. James IV too spent much money on the castle, building a new palace behind the previous building. On his death, his son continued and finished the work on the Royal Palace, a remarkable building including beautiful sculpture in early classic Renaissance style.

James VI is said to have pulled down a previous chapel built by James III before he built the present one in 1594. To explain the present structure in more detail it would be best to divide it into three sections: the courtyard dating from the 17th century and containing the outer defences; the ancient castle or citadel containing the principal buildings defended by rampart walls; and the Nether Bailey, a slightly lower area of ground than the citadel, enclosed by a rampart wall and steep bank.

The courtyard is entered by crossing a deep, wide fosse, formerly bridged. From the ditch rises a great curtain wall with arched entrance and gateway set with massive oak doors and, overhead, a keystone bearing the Crown and Cypher of Queen Anne. Inside this curtain wall and included in the ancient castle is the 'Foir Front' or façade defended by a fosse spanned by a drawbridge and ramp. Also included in this group of buildings is the gatehouse with a main entry and two flanking passages protected by doors and iron portcullises. Stairs lead up from the ground to the portcullis chamber, and the rooms above this were reached by a separate turnpike stair. The side passages led off to guardrooms on top of pit prisons. Further on through the passage there is the Parade or lower square with James V's Palace, the Great Hall and the Castle. This eastern section of the castle, dating from James III's reign, consists of a massive wall pierced with windows, and behind the wall are the vaulted kitchens containing two great fireplaces. At an earlier date an upper storey would have been built over the kitchen but this was removed before 1689. At the north end of the kitchens are storage vaults and an arched gateway, the entrance to the Nether Bailey and what was the road into the castle from Ballengeich.

The Great Hall built by James III underwent a ruthless structural change at one stage and partition walls and floors were put in to make soldiers' barracks. All that is left is a disfigured shell of a once magnificent building which had an oak roof, a dais for royalty flanked by two oriel windows, and a minstrels' or trumpet gallery. Under the hall were more storage vaults for wood and coal.

The palace built by King James V under the direction of the notorious Sir James Hamilton of Finnart, the King's Master of Works, has been changed very little since completion. It was designed in classic Renaissance style with a series of recessed ornamental panels. Between these are the windows of the royal apartments protected with wrought-iron grilles. The whole building is decorated with sculptures of one form or another, some pleasant, some grotesque, some complete and some mutilated. The rooms of the Palace are grouped round an open court called the 'Lion's Den' and on the first floor were the royal apartments with the top storey built to house members of the court.

James VI built the Chapel Royal in early classic Renaissance style and to this day the façade remains unaltered, except for the removal of the coats of arms and royal badges during Cromwell's time. Inside, the timber roof was painted in blue and decorated with flowers, while the walls contained panels of arms and badges.

At the west end of the chapel, a vaulted passage leads to the garden and over this passage is the room where King James II is reputed to have killed Douglas, but this cannot be so as the room was built long after this episode.

Around the castle are two very old gardens—the Nether Garden and the Douglas Garden—and underlying the castle rock to the west was at one time the King's Park enclosed by a high wall and containing the famous Knot-Garden built in 1627. Other buildings in the precincts of the castle and also in the keeping of the Crown include the 17th-century mansion known as Argyll Lodging and the ruin of a 16th-century town house called 'Mar's Wark', with one of the few complete remaining kirks in Scotland, the 'Haily Rude', close by.

Open to the public, every day, Summer 9.30am–6pm, Sundays 10.30am–5.30pm, Winter 9.30–5pm, Sundays 12.30–5pm. Refreshments available.

Stornoway Castle

Stornoway, Isle of Lewis, Ross and Cromarty, Highland.
On A866 at Stornoway.

High above the harbour at Stornoway stands the castle of the same name. The present structure dates from the 1840s and was built in the baronial style by Sir James Matheson. The castle stands at the centre of a wooded park and both grounds and castle were donated to the town by the late Lord Leverhulme, to be a technical college specialising in crafts and trades suitable for use on the Isle of Lewis—weaving, fishing and navigation.

The existing castle stands on the site of an older structure which was the seat of the famous Mac-Kenzies, Lords of Seaforth. This earlier castle was built to protect the island from first Norsemen and later the incursion of 'buccaneers' from the mainland, who were encouraged unofficially by the central Scottish government in an attempt to bring the Outer Hebrides under the Scottish Crown. These latter events took place in the 16th and 17th centuries but were not successful. The first time that Stornoway and Lewis came under the control of the mainland was during the subjugation of Scotland by Cromwell, and the old castle was destroyed by Cromwell's troops in the middle of the 17th century.

The site stood abandoned until the current castle was built.

Not open to the public.

Stranraer Castle

Stranraer, Wigtown, Dumfries and Galloway.
On A77 at Stranraer.

The castle stands in the centre of the town and was built towards the end of the 15th century to a tower house plan; from its parapet walk there is a magnificent view of Stranraer and its surroundings. The castle's main claim to fame is that it was the headquarters of Lord Graham of Claverhouse during his persecution of the Covenanters. As military commander and Sheriff of Galloway, it was his grim duty to bring the non-conformist south-west of Scotland into line. It is said that many Covenanters were imprisoned and died in the castle dungeons, which continued to serve as Stranraer's town jail into the 18th and 19th centuries. The castle still stands today, somewhat altered from its original form and very much neglected, in the back streets of the town.

Open to the public, May to September, every day, 10am–5pm.

Strome Castle

Strome Ferry, Ross and Cromarty, Highland.
Off A890 on the north shore of Loch Carron, 5 miles south-west of Lochcarron village.

Overlooking the north pier of the ferry are the ruins of Strome Castle, built in medieval times. It was one of the principal fortresses on the west coast of Scotland and a stronghold of the Mac-Donalds of Glengarry. The castle was destroyed in 1602 during a long siege by English soldiers, following numerous attempts to subdue it.

A National Trust for Scotland property.

Not open to the public.

Tantallon Castle

North Berwick, East Lothian, Lothian.
3 miles east of North Berwick on A198.

The extensive rose-red ruin of Tantallon Castle, commanding magnificent views over land and sea from the Lammermuirs to the Lomonds, stands on the rocky coast of the Firth of Forth opposite the Bass Rock. A castle has existed on this site since before 1300 under the name of 'Dentaloune', and by the early 14th century it was in the possession of the Earls of Fife. By 1374, William, first Earl of Douglas and Mar, was in residence at Tantallon, perhaps simply as a tenant of Isabell, Countess of Fife.

The first Earl Douglas had been married to Margaret, a sister of Thomas, Earl of Mar, but he later made his brother-in-law's widow, the Countess of Angus, his mistress and she joined him at Tantallon. This clever woman resigned her title in favour of her illegitimate son George Douglas (who became Earl of Angus) so that he would be accepted as a nobleman. This move was successful and he later married Mary, second daughter of King Robert II. George became the first Earl of Angus of the Douglas line; he was captured at the Battle of Hamilton by the English and died of the plague in 1403 while still a prisoner. William, his son, the second Earl, was one of the nobles who met King James I at Durham in 1424 and escorted him back to Scotland after his imprisonment in England. In 1425 he was a supporter of the king when Murdoch, Duke of Albany, his two sons and aged father-in-law, the Earl of Lennox, were executed by royal command.

James, who succeeded his father as third Earl, made Tantallon his headquarters, and in 1443 withdrew there with his ally Crichton to resist the royal forces. In January 1446 he was commanded in his absence to forfeit his lands for leading a rebellion against the Crown, but a few months later he died. James II granted the castle and lands to George, brother of the late Earl, in 1452, and in the 'Black Douglas' Rebellion of 1455, this 'Red Douglas' was again rewarded by the king with the Lordship of Douglas.

At the siege of Roxburgh in 1460 he was at the king's side when the king was killed and was himself wounded, but seven days later he was at

Kelso placing the crown on the boy king's head. He died in 1463 and his son Archibald succeeded him as fifth Earl. He was nicknamed 'Bell-the-Cat' by the Scots for his high-handed ways, and in 1491, having joined a treasonable contract with the king of England, he was ordered by James IV to ward himself in Tantallon. The Earl defied the royal order and instead prepared to defend the castle against attack. Three months later, in October, the king laid siege to Tantallon, gathering guns from Linlithgow and weapons from Leith. But 'Bell-the-Cat' must have patched up his quarrel with the king for at Christmas that year he was sent a 'black velvet gown lined with lamb's wool and with bukram to the tail of it' by James IV.

By 1492 he had become Chancellor of Scotland, but the friendship did not last long for he fell into disgrace and was warded again in Dumbarton Castle. At Flodden his two sons, George, Master of Angus, and Sir William of Glenbervie, were killed with their king.

The sixth Earl, Archibald, a widower and son of the Master of Angus who was killed at Flodden, succeeded 'Bell-the-Cat', his grandfather. In 1514 he married Queen Margaret, King James IV's widow, and the corrupt pair spent most of their time making treasonable plans with her brother King Henry VIII to take over Scotland and remove the two young princes. But in 1515 John, Duke of Albany, became regent and guardian of the royal children, and realising that Angus and the Queen Mother were involved in this plot against the rightful heirs of Scotland he seized Tantallon and proclaimed Angus a traitor. The next year the castle was returned to Angus until 1528 when Parliament again decided his treachery had gone too far and ordered him to forfeit the title and lands once more. In the meantime, in 1517, Angus was appointed one of the six regents to the child king, and after turning traitor again he was forced into exile by Albany in 1521. He must have had considerable powers of persuasion, for in 1525 he was made warden of the East and Middle Marches until King James found out about his suspicious alliances with England and banned him to 'north of the Spey'. Angus fled to Tantallon where he and his brother George and a kinsman, Sir Archibald Douglas of Kilspindie, entrenched themselves. An act of Parliament was passed ordering 'forfeiture of their lives, lands and goods' but the Earl managed to slip over the border where he waited on events. After this the king seized the castle, but during harvest time was forced to let his army disperse, and the Earl took the opportunity to provision the castle against another conflict. In October 1528, King James returned to besiege Tantallon but after 20 days the king gave up and Angus returned victorious. Patrick, Earl of Bothwell, tried again in January 1529 to take Tantallon, but without success, and eventually Angus asked

for a reconciliation between himself and the king, offering to be a loyal subject in the future as he had in the past! James agreed to accept the offer only if Tantallon Castle was part of the bargain but Angus refused to hand over his fortress; he continued to live there until May 1529 when he retired to England and the castle was surrendered to the king.

For 14 years Tantallon belonged to the Crown who ordered repairs and strengthened its defences. When the king died after the Battle of Solway Moss in November 1542, Angus returned to his estates but continued his alliance with England. By 1543 England and Scotland were at war and Angus sat at Tantallon while verbal battle raged between the two kings. His brother George was imprisoned in Blackness Castle for his part in the family's treasonable actions and Sir George's sons, David and James, had actually offered to surrender Tantallon to the invaders. But the English fleet arrived in time to rescue Angus and his guest, the English ambassador, Sadler. The English advanced as far as Stirling, burning Holyrood and harrying the countryside. At Melrose, Douglas tombs were desecrated and Angus was so outraged that he changed sides and joined the national cause. He was made Lieutenant of Southern Scotland, but in 1545 decided to change sides again and rejoin the English. Henry replied by offering 2,000 crowns for the devious Earl's head. Angus died at Tantallon in winter 1556–57, and was succeeded by his nephew David who died a few months later. When he died, the Queen handed over the castle to the care of the laird of Craigmillar and, in 1558, repairs were made to the building by the Crown. David's son, Archibald, became eighth Earl at the age of 2, and when he was 18 Angus was appointed Warden of the West Marches and a year later Lieutenant-General of the Realm. He seems to have inherited the family's treacherous blood, however, and after Morton's execution, sentence was passed on him demanding that he forfeit his lands and title. He fled for exile to England and was received at the court of Queen Elizabeth.

By 1582 Angus was allowed back, only to be exiled again for his opposition to Arran, and later recalled in 1585 and his estates restored. He died in August 1588 leaving no male heirs, and the Earldom reverted to William Douglas of Glenbervie. His son William, who became tenth Earl in 1591, was a Roman Catholic who for his faith was exiled in 1589. He embraced Protestantism and was restored to favour, but three years later he had a change of heart, reverted to Papacy and was ordered to ward himself in Glasgow. Later that year he was excommunicated and allowed to go into voluntary exile in France, where he died in 1611.

His son William became eleventh Earl, Marquis of Douglas. While he was attending the General

Assembly in 1639 Tantallon was taken over by Covenanters. This eventually resulted in General Monk attacking the castle in February 1651 and capturing it. The Earl of Angus returned, and in 1699 the castle and barony were purchased by Sir Hew Dalrymple, Lord President of the Court of Session, who abandoned the building and left it to decay.

The existing remains consist of the castle proper, an outer bailey and various defensive outworks on two sides—the steep cliffs above the sea protect the other two sides. This frontal curtain, wall flanked by round towers, includes a central gatehouse which recalls 14th-century French chateaux. It is thought to have been built by William, first Earl of Douglas, and was carefully planned to match the site. It consisted of the Mid Tower and the Douglas Tower with a wing to the north containing the Hall. The East Tower, which originally contained five storeys, is now a ruin, as is the Douglas Tower and Hall which at least shows signs of domestic quarters. What is left of this once magnificent castle is now in the care of Historic Buildings and Monuments, Scottish Development Department.

Open to the public, every day, Summer 9.30am–7pm, Sundays 2–7pm; Winter 9.30am–4pm, Sundays 2–4pm; closed in winter on Wednesdays and Thursdays am.

Threave Castle

Taymouth Castle
Kenmore, Perth and Kinross, Tayside.
On A827, 7 miles west of Aberfeldy.

The castle was formerly the seat of the Earls of Breadalbane—a branch of the Clan Campbell whose lands once stretched almost from the Atlantic to the North Sea. The present castle, built in 1801, replaced a much older structure known as Balloch Castle. It is built of blueish-grey stone from local quarries and stands amidst vast estates which at one time, under the Earls of Breadalbane, were the size of the three Lothian counties combined. The building today is used as a co-educational school for the children of Americans in Europe.

Not open to the public.

Terpsie Castle
Alford, Aberdeen, Grampian.
2½ miles north-west of Alford off A944.

This striking Z-plan castle is being extensively restored. The two towers, at diagonally opposite corners of the crow-stepped, gabled main block, are well supplied with shot holes, covering every face-wall and approach. The castle was built by one William Gordon, who was intruding on Forbes'

territory from the nearby Gordon lands around Huntly. His descendant, the fifth laird, Charles Gordon, fought at Culloden, and afterwards, while in hiding, was tempted to go back to Terpsie, where for a while he hid in a recess in the roof. He was discovered by English troops detailed to search for him but when they found him he was heavily disguised and the local minister claimed not to recognise him. The officer in charge of the troops, being suspicious, took him to a nearby farm where his children were held and they unwittingly gave him away. He was removed to Carlisle and executed.

Not open to the public while being restored.

Thirlestane Castle
Lauder, Ettrick and Lauderdale, Borders.
30 miles south of Edinburgh at Lauder on A68.

To the north-east of Lauder is Thirlestane Castle, built around 1590 for the first Baron Maitland of Thirlestane and incorporating a 14th-century fortress. The present imposing structure, built in red sandstone, was altered in the late 17th century by Sir William Bruce for the first and only Duke of Lauderdale. It is considered the most splendid example of castle decoration in Scotland and contains a fine collection of portraits as well as furniture and china.

Open to the public, Easter, May to September, Wednesday, Thursday and Sunday; July and August, Sunday to Friday; grounds 12–6pm, castle 2–5pm. Refreshments available.

Threave Castle
Threave, Stewartry, Dumfries and Galloway.
2 miles from Castle Douglas off A75.

On an island on the River Dee is the ruined Threave Castle, the early stronghold of the 'Black Douglases', the Earls of Nithsdale and Lords of Galloway. It was built during the 14th century by Archibald the Grim, Earl of Douglas, and consists of a four-storey tower enclosed by an outer wall dating from 1455, when it was captured by King James II. In 1640 the Covenanters dismantled the castle and finally it was used to house French prisoners during the Napoleonic Wars.

The history of Threave Castle was bound up with the Douglases, but when James II took the fortress, Threave became a royal castle under various keepers. From 1473 to 1526 it was cared for by the Lords Maxwell who were made hereditary keepers, but it was later dismantled. It is now under the protection of Historic Buildings and Monuments, Scottish Development Department.

In 1948 the estate was presented to the National Trust for Scotland. They have established the National Trust School of Practical Gardening and the gardens are now especially famous for the displays of daffodils.

Open to the public, daily except Thursdays, April to September.

Tilquihillie Castle
Strachan, Banchory, Kincardine and Deeside, Grampian.
2 miles south-west of Crathes off A957.

In the lower part of the Feugh valley not far from the village of Strachan is the Z-plan tower house of Tilquihillie Castle. It was built by the Douglases in 1576 and although entire was unoccupied for many years. The castle is now being restored for habitation by its present owners.

Not open to the public.

Tolquhon Castle
Tarves, Aberdeen, Grampian.
Off B999 between Udny and Tarves.

Tolquhon Castle was the principal manor house in the ancient Thange of Formarture, the country between the Rivers Don and Ythan. In the 14th century it belonged to the Prestons, lords of Craigmillar Castle near Edinburgh, but in 1420 it passed to the Forbes family through a Preston heiress, Marjorie, second daughter of Sir Henry Preston, who Sir John Forbes married.

The oldest part of the castle, the Preston's Tower, was probably built by Sir John Forbes, and it remained unaltered until 1584–9 when William Forbes, the seventh laird, employed Thomas Leiper, the architect, to build a large quadrangular mansion with an impressive gatehouse. William Forbes was apparently a very likeable and cultured man who founded a bede-house for paupers in Tarves, and also erected for himself and his lady a stately tomb at the parish kirk nearby. He collected a notable library and was much respected in local affairs, often helping his neighbours sort out their legal tangles. Though the family are often mentioned in local chronicles of the time, they were not of any historical importance at this stage.

However, the sixth laird fell at the Battle of Pinkie in 1547, and in 1589 James VI visited the newly enlarged castle. Alexander, the tenth laird, was colonel of a cavalry regiment under Charles II and saved the king's life on Worcester Field in 1651, for which he was knighted. By 1716 the estate had to be sold because of Alexander's previous rash speculations which had cost most of the family's money. William Forbes, the eleventh laird, refused to move until he was forcibly ejected in September 1718 by a party of Redcoats.

Tolquhon was ultimately bought by the Earl of Aberdeen and continued to be occupied until the mid 18th century, when it was left to decay. In 1929 the ruins were put into the care of the predecessors of Historic Buildings and Monuments, Scottish Development Department, by the Marquess of Aberdeen.

Tolquhon illustrates the enormous advance in comfort and civilisation in the homes of the Scottish lairds that took place between the 15th and 17th centuries. Avenues of magnificent old trees lead to an arched forecourt entrance flanked by ornate gun-loops. Inside is the main castle with its gatehouse in the centre flanked by drum towers with heavily grated windows and walls enriched with carving. To the left of the gatehouse rises Preston's Tower, crowned by a fragment of machicolated parapet. Through the gatehouse is an inner close whose surrounding buildings are much more refined than the rest of the castle— well planned, spacious and with generous windows. The Preston's Tower is a ruin, most of which, except for the vaulted basement, has toppled over, although part of the great hall on the first floor does still survive. The new house is still largely intact, with its kitchen, cellars and service stairs topped by a well-lit hall, off which is the laird's private room and above what was once a garret. Also in this section of the building are two good bedrooms off the main stair and a long galley opening on to a vaulted bedroom which is topped by yet another room.

Open to the public, April to September, weekdays 10am–7pm, Sundays 2–7pm; October to March, weekdays 10am–4pm, Sundays 2–4pm.

Torthorwald Castle
Nithsdale, Dumfries and Galloway.
4 miles north-east of Dumfries off A76.

Torthorwald Castle stands on a series of early medieval earthworks and was, from at least the mid-13th century, a stronghold of the Kirkpatricks. In 1418 William de Carleil married the heiress and from then onwards the castle remained mainly in Carlyle hands until 1715.

The present barrel-vaulted remains were built mainly by William, but in 1544 Lord Carlyle looted the castle, taking all its contents in a raid against his sister-in-law. Thirty years later, Michael Carlyle abducted the 6-year-old heiress, Elizabeth Carlyle, from the castle and for years traded her among rival branches of the family.

Not open to the public.

Towie Barclay Castle
Auchterless, Turriff, Aberdeen, Grampian.
At the point where A947 crosses the River Ythan on B992.

The castle was built in the late 16th century in the Gothic style, probably by the master mason who built Gight Castle nearby. It consists of a single, high, rib-vaulted chamber in two bays, decorated with yet more ridge, transverse and diagonal ribs. The most remarkable feature of all is without doubt the small oratory above the entrance to the hall. This oratory or chapel with its original stone altar and religious carvings make it the most complete late medieval chapel in a Scottish castle. Towie Barclay was once four storeys high, but in 1792 a nearby tenant farmer removed the turrets and battlements and took two storeys off the tower, truncating the remaining stump with slate. By a miracle the great hall survived and was, until fairly recently, used as the local Free Church Sunday School. In 1971 the restoration of Towie Barclay was started and this has won many top architectural awards and accolades.

The top two storeys have been reinstated and many previously obscured early features have been revealed such as gun-loops and arrow slits. The interior has been described as 'one of the noblest and most imaginative of all tower house interiors'. The great hall has recently, since restoration, been described as 'perhaps the richest room in Scotland'. The castle was the historic seat of the Barclay clan, the most famous member of which was the Russian Prince, Barclay de Tolly, immortalised in Tolstoy's *War and Peace*.

Open to the public by written appointment only.

Turnberry Castle
Turnberry, Kyle and Carrick, Strathclyde.
10 miles north of Girvan off A77.

On a promontory immediately to the south of Maidenhead Bay are the remains of Turnberry Castle, the childhood home of Robert the Bruce. It was here that Bruce and his little band landed when he came from Arran to Carrick and Galloway at the beginning of his final campaign of liberation.

Not open to the public.

Udny Castle
Udny, Ellon, Aberdeen, Grampian.
South of Pitmedden off B9000 or B999 roads.

The stout rectangular tower of the castle, five storeys high and crowned on one side with ornamental battlements, was built by three successive lairds and finally completed in the 17th century. The family of Udny of Udny first appear in records dated 1426 and from that date there have been fourteen Udny lairds bearing the name. The last of them, the late J. H. Udny of Udny, was succeeded by the eleventh Lord Belhaven and Stenton. In 1875 the old keep was restored and linked to a modern three-storeyed house. This modern building has since been demolished leaving the old keep intact.

Open to the public by written appointment only.

Urquhart Castle
Drumnadrochit, Inverness, Highland.
16 miles south-west of Inverness off A82.

Standing on a high sandstone promontory projecting into Loch Ness is Castle Urquhart; before the loch was raised 6 feet by the building of the Caledonian Canal, the castle was 50 feet above water level.

Loch Ness is at the centre of the Great Glen (Glenmore) which extends from Inverness to Oban, dividing the Central from the Northern Highlands. The Great Glen is one of the major faults in the geological structure of the British Isles, formed at least 300 million years ago and still not entirely stable to judge by the frequent earth tremors which shake Inverness and attest to movement along the line of the fracture. From prehistoric times, this great natural avenue has played a major part in Scotland's development, and in the 6th century it was the path for Columba from Iona and Molnug from Lismore—the two great saints of the west who travelled to the Pictish capital at Inverness, converting the people. During the 12th and 13th centuries, the Great Glen was used by the Celts as the province of Ergadia in the south-west and Moravia in the north-east as a line of communication and resistance against the feudalising and unifying policy which was being enforced by the 'Normanised' kings.

About 12 miles above Inverness is the fertile Glen Urquhart; with its sunny slopes and good natural drainage, the well-stocked loch nearby as a source of food, and the surrounding forests providing game and fuel, it was an obvious and ideal settlement for early man. It is now possible to find not only the ruins of the medieval castle but quantities of vitrified stone left from the Iron Age, at about the beginning of the Christian era. Experts suggest that the site had been occupied by a dry stone fort interlaced with timbers, and when these caught fire, either accidentally or encouraged by an enemy, the stone walls were fused into vitrified remains. From excavations around this area it seems that the old fort may still have been inhabited when St Columba visited the Glen in the 6th century; and there, according to records, he baptised an aged Pictish chief, Emchatu, his son Virolec and the whole household. It was in St Columba's time too that the Loch Ness Monster was first mentioned.

By the 16th and 17th centuries the outlets of Glenmore had been strongly garrisoned by royal castles or by castles whose owners held them as trusted vassals of the Crown. At the lower end were Inverlochy and Dunstaffnage, and at the upper outlet, Urquhart and Inverness Castles. Castle Urquhart was built mainly as an observation post, controlling the whole upper part of the Great Glen, with a view almost as far as Inverness to the north and Fort St Augustus to the south. Not far away, as in all early manorial settlements, is the farm of Borlum and the church, which began its existence as the lord's private chapel. A royal castle is said to have stood at Urquhart in the reign of William the Lion (1165–1214) although no records support the tale. But after the last rising in Moravia had been suppressed in 1229, the lordship of Urquhart was given to the very powerful Durward (de Lundin) family, hereditary keepers of the palaces of the Scottish kings. Their first recorded chief, Alan Durward, Lord Urquhart, was one of the leaders of the new Anglo-Norman aristocracy who had married a king's daughter; as well as owning vast estates in Angus, the Mearns and Mar, he also held Bolsover Castle in England. Alan Durward was for years the true power behind the throne of his brother-in-law, the young Alexander II. When he died in 1268 the estates passed to

another great Anglo-Norman family, the Comyns, Lords of Badenoch. It was not until 1296, when Edward I penetrated as far north as Elgin, that the Castle of Urquhart was next recorded. Sir William Fitzwarine was made its constable, and immediately the king returned to England the castle was besieged unsuccessfully by the nationalists under Sir Andrew de Moray. The next year another attack by the nationalists was successful, and Sir Alexander de Forbes took over as keeper. In 1303 Edward again marched north to Elgin and reduced Urquhart Castle, appointing Sir Alexander Comyn of Badenoch, a Scottish baron in the king's service, as his constable. In 1308 the castle was retaken by Bruce, who later granted it to Sir Thomas Randolph whom he made Earl of Moray. In 1333, during the second War of Independence, Castle Urquhart formed one of the five fortresses left in Scotland to fly the white St Andrew's Cross, and it was successfully held against the English by its constable, Sir Robert Lauder. In 1346 the barony and castle reverted to the Crown and in 1398 became the king's property by an act of Parliament, and it was then that repairs were started.

During the 14th and 15th centuries, Glen Urquhart was the centre of the struggle between the Lord of the Isles and the Scottish Crown. The Lord of the Isles claimed the Earldom of Ross of which the Great Glen was a part, and in the struggle that followed Glen Urquhart was seized in 1395 and given to his brother, Alexander of Keppoch. In 1411 the Earl of Mar beat back the Lord of the Isles with the victory at Harlaw; but when James I was murdered, in 1437, the Lord of the Isles again seized the castle and held it until the Treaty of Ardtornish was agreed and he was forced to hand over castle and lordship in 1476 to the Earl of Huntly, chief of the Gordon family. Glen Urquhart was reported to be a desolate waste, and in 1509 King James IV granted the lordship of Urquhart to John Grant of Freuchie— 'The Red Bard'—who was ordered to repair and improve the castle.

But the Macdonalds, Lords of the Isles, were still very far from content, and when James V died at Flodden in 1513 the new Lord of the Isles, Sir Donald Macdonald of Lochalsh, captured the castle. He stayed for 3 years and stripped the people and lands of all they owned. In 1545 the Macdonalds returned again with their allies the Camerons of Lochiel, besieged the castle and burned all the nearby buildings. They plundered the castle and stole all the local livestock. Nevertheless, sometime during all this turmoil in the course of the 16th and 17th centuries, the Grants managed to reconstruct the castle to give us the basis of the present stately ruins. The building has progressed over the years from an early Norman motte with its bailey to a stately gatehouse. There is no record of Cromwellian occupation of the castle but in 1676 the building was repaired once more, and in 1689 was garrisoned by Whig soldiers, who are said to have blown up some of the buildings when they evacuated the castle, to prevent anyone else from using them. In 1695 the Laird of Grant was paid a vast sum in compensation for damage done to his property, but the buildings were never repaired. By 1708 the structure was beginning to decay and in 1715 it was partially blown down in a storm, and from then on remained a roofless shell. The owners managed a few urgent repairs, but in 1912 the ruins were handed over to the Government, who have since repaired much of the damage.

Only the lower storeys of the gatehouse now remain, with portions of the circular wall of the south drum tower. The gatehouse, a rectangular block 51 feet broad with a barrel-vaulted entrance wide enough for carts or for three men abreast, was defended by a portcullis with an outward-opening gate behind it and then a second inward-opening one. On either side of the entrance are lodges containing signs of an oven, and to the north of the gatehouse is a building containing a prison.

Within the gatehouse on the right is the Upper Bailey, overhung by a rock on which stood the prehistoric fort and later the Norman motte. The only buildings left in the Upper Bailey are parts of the circular dovecot and a smithy with traces of a large chimney. In the Nether Bailey are many more signs of habitation, including kitchen, hall, parlour and lord's private room. Only the basements beneath these apartments now remain, but the outer wall here is still 9 feet thick and in places 20 feet high.

Not far from this is the keep, isolated by a deep stone-lined fosse. The keep, a fine tower, is almost the only surviving part of the castle to carry any architectural detail. It contains a hall with a stair leading to the three upper storeys and a wall walk, of which a small part still remains. The middle section of the curtain wall belonging to the earliest castle also survives.

Open to the public, every day, April to September, Monday to Saturday 9.30am–7pm, Sundays 2–7pm; October to March, Monday to Saturday 9.30am–4pm, Sundays 2–4pm.

Westhall Castle
Oyne, Aberdeen, Grampian.
A little to the north of Oyne off A96.

A little to the north of Oyne is the 16th-century Westhall Castle which is now owned by Lord Glentanan. This L-plan house with its barmkin or walled courtyard is remarkable for its fine label corbelling, and was built by the Abercrombies who were frequently at feud with the Leiths. Eventually, it passed to a branch of the Leith family.

Not open to the public.

Winton Castle
Pencaitland, Tranent, East Lothian, Lothian.
On A6093 in Pencaitland, 3 miles from A1.

One of the finest examples of Renaissance architecture in Scotland is to be found at Winton Castle which was built by George, eighth Lord Seton and third Earl of Winton. It was built between 1619–20 on the site of an older house and was probably designed by William Wallace, the King's Master Mason for Scotland. Winton Castle is particularly interesting because of its fine spiral stone-work chimneys and the plaster ceilings and fireplaces in the drawing and King Charles's room. Many of the plaster ornaments are identical to those in Pinkie and Moray House, and are probably the work of the same plasterers.

Open to parties by written appointment.

Yester Castle
Gifford, East Lothian, Lothian.
Off A6137, 2 miles south-east of Gifford.

The mid 13th-century Yester Castle stands on a promontory at the junction of Hopes Water and a stream. Little now remains above the ground except for a stretch of curtain wall. The original castle was triangular in plan, approached from the south where a wide ditch turned the promontory into an island. The ruined gatehouse seems to have had two flanking towers but the most remarkable feature of Yester is the underground chamber. Known as Goblin Hall, it is reached by a flight of steps and is about 37 feet long by 13 feet wide, with a high pointed vaulted roof and staircase leading down to a well and bolt-hole in a nearby gulley.

The castle is situated in the grounds of Yester House—a finely proportioned mansion by William Adam built in 1745. It is the seat of the Marquess of Tweeddale, but the lands of Yester and Hay families have been in possession of the Gifford and Hay families from at least the 12th century. It was an early Gifford, Sir Hugo, who was thought to be a wizard, who built the Goblin Hall in the 13th century.

Not open to the public.